THE
COMPLETE
BOOK OF
PHOTOGRAPHY

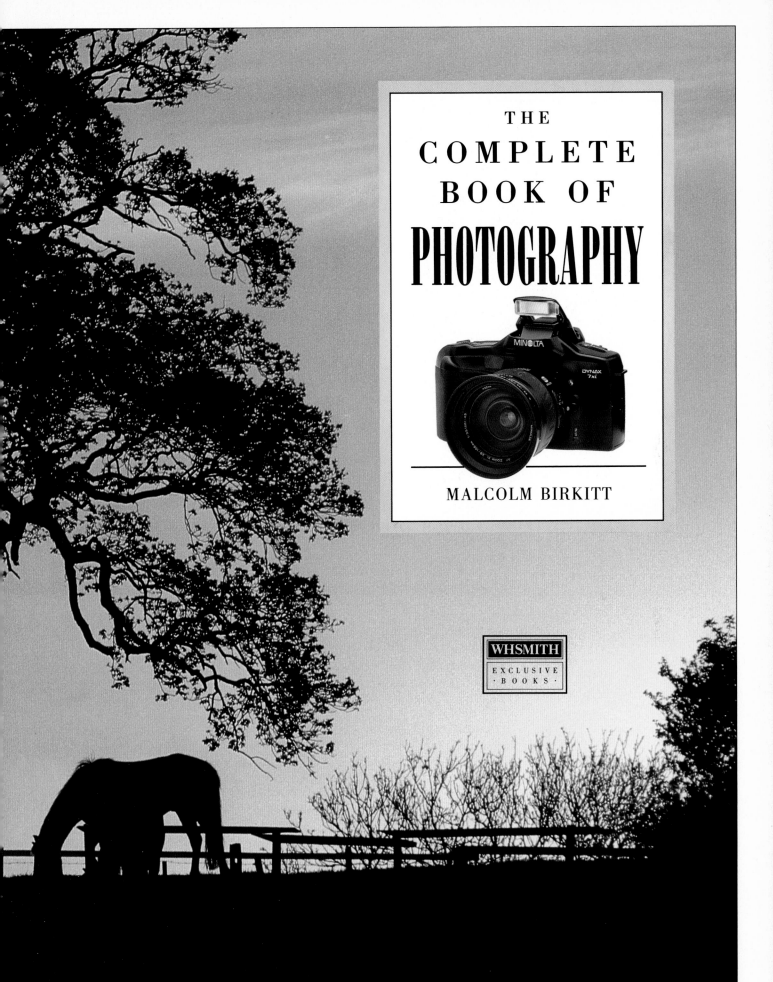

THE
COMPLETE
BOOK OF
PHOTOGRAPHY

MINOLTA

DYNAX 7xi

MALCOLM BIRKITT

WHSMITH
EXCLUSIVE
· BOOKS ·

This edition produced exclusively for W H Smith
Published in 1992
by The Hamlyn Publishing Group Limited
part of Reed International Books
Michelin House, 81 Fulham Road, London SW3 6RB

ISBN 0 600 57497 0

Produced and filmset by Icon Publications Limited, Kelso, Scotland
Story Editor: Shirley Kilpatrick BA (Open)
Production Editor: David Kilpatrick FBIPP AMPA
Icon Studio photography: Angus Blackburn, David Kilpatrick, Roger Lee
Graphics: Oxford Illustrators Limited and Icon Publications Limited

Contributing photographers (alphabetical order):
Malcolm Birkitt, Rex Butcher, Paul Dooley, Dave Ellison, Geoff Evans,
Derek Forrest, Fotopic (ACE Photographic Agency), Lee Frost, Charles Green,
John Guidi, Roy Hampson, Tom Hustler, David Kilpatrick, Shirley Kilpatrick,
Martin Lillicrap, Alan Lines, Christopher Lobini, Duncan McEwan, Tim Moat,
Marie O'Hare, Polaroid (UK) Limited, Geoff Redmayne,
Carroll Seghers (ACE), Geoff Stephenson, Mike Taylor, John Tinsley,
Richard Walker (ACE), Janet Walkinshaw, Kevin Wilson, Lawson Wood.

Produced by Mandarin Offset
Printed in Hong Kong

CONTENTS

INTRODUCTION

IF YOU were to believe all the advertisers' claims, buying a new camera will suddenly turn you into an expert photographer. This is not the case. New technology ensures a photograph each time you press the shutter, but the photographs produced are unlikely to be award winners unless the camera is given careful guidance.

In reality, three separate ingredients are needed to create successful and effective images – equipment matched to the task, a good idea, and the technique to see it all through. That's why this book is divided into three distinct sections.

The first of these deals with photographic hardware – cameras, lenses, flash, tripods and other accessories. The diversity of equipment now available can make purchasing decisions very difficult. Some insist the type or make of camera is irrelevant, while others maintain a high-grade, high-price model is essential for good photography. Neither statement is ac-

tually true. You can take excellent pictures on the simplest equipment – but in a limited number of situations.

To clarify matters, the Equipment section logically explains the options available, and describes what each item can, and cannot, do. The advantages of different camera types and formats are covered first, along with exposure modes, metering patterns and other features.

Later chapters examine the benefits of many different lenses, whether autofocus is desirable, plus how to choose and use filters, motordrives and camera bags.

Finally we advise on how a camera outfit can be put together. All this enables your current requirements to be closely identified, while not forgetting potential future ambitions.

The second section is concerned with the Techniques of photography. Despite their incredible wizardry, modern cameras still cannot tell you how to 'see' pic-

tures. It is still down to the photographer to select a subject, find the right viewpoint, compose the shot in the viewfinder and manipulate light to convey mood or atmosphere. These chapters are therefore designed to provide a grounding in photographic vocabulary and a grasp of the hands-on aspects of the medium.

It clearly pays a photographer seeking control over the picture-taking process to understand how to choose the right film and expose it correctly for different subjects. Camera handling, focusing methods and how to portray movement – all are covered. Though highly automated, no camera is 'intelligent', so it can't advise you how to manipulate colour, shape or pattern, or how to employ perspective to give a picture depth. This section also shows how to use artificial light sources, develop film and make a print.

Having chosen the right equipment and studied the basics of the photographic language, you now

need a subject to shoot to put what you've learned into practice. This is where the third section titled Projects comes in. Just wandering around looking for things to photograph rarely produces satisfactory work. Rather than leave pictures to chance, it provides a fund of ideas for you to start with.

The section is divided into a dozen chapters, each dealing with a major theme. Here we'll show you in detail how to take powerful portraits or candids, or how best to capture children, animals, landscape or sport. Other chapters reveal how to shoot still life or architecture, make effective pictures at night or while travelling, and tackle all kinds of special effects.

The three sections add up to a Complete Book of Photography. Armed with the information and images it contains, plus your own thoughts and ideas, great results are now within reach. I hope you enjoy it.

MALCOLM BIRKITT

DOES EQUIPMENT MATTER?

ONE of the most difficult aspects of selecting a camera is finding one which will suit your future needs as well as your present ones. Take a look at the four characters here, for example. They're all photographers, but each has vastly different aspirations. The woman on the top left is using a Polaroid instant camera because she wants to view pictures immediately. No other camera suits her purpose. The person next to her, just about to embark on a travelling-light trip, carries a zoom compact for maximum convenience and portability. To capture high-speed action down at the racing circuit, the photographer shown bottom left is employing a top quality motor-drive 35mm SLR with powerful telephoto lens fitted. Finally the fashion photographer on the bottom right has a substantial roll-film camera on a tripod, setting up for a location shoot.

What unites our four is that their cameras have been chosen for functional reasons – not because they've heard the name or like the colour! You may wish to take pictures of family and friends on a casual basis only, or specialize in serious portraiture for profit. Or your interest may lie in wildlife, architecture, sport, landscapes, or still life. Each type of picture demands a different choice of equipment, so selecting the right tool for the job is important. The more you get bitten by the photo bug, the more items of equipment are required. With the right equipment, you'll get the job done without wasting money.

That's something the SLR user has to bear in mind all the time. A compact camera tends to be self-contained; SLRs by definition are more flexible, with the facility to interchange a number of components. Lenses, prisms, screens, backs, motordrives and a host of other accessories can be attached. Flashguns and filters are almost essential additions. Larger outfits are often kept in a customized bag or case for protection; a tripod is vital to keep the camera steady for those low-light scenes, or enable maximum depth of field to be utilized. Some photographers also prefer to retain complete control over their images, by developing and printing film in their own darkroom.

All these topics are comprehensively covered in this chapter, with the purpose of each item of equipment clearly explained and its best applications described. That way you won't go down blind alleys when buying. Towards the end of the chapter we look at specialized cameras, and there's also a section on how to build up a cost-effective and coherent SLR system.

CHOOSING YOUR CAMERA

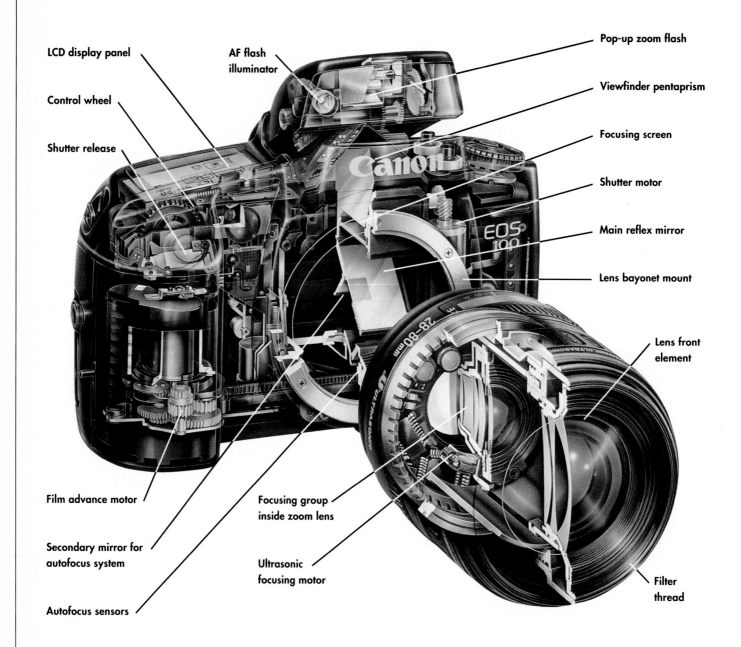

LCD display panel

AF flash illuminator

Pop-up zoom flash

Viewfinder pentaprism

Control wheel

Focusing screen

Shutter release

Shutter motor

Main reflex mirror

Lens bayonet mount

Lens front element

Film advance motor

Focusing group inside zoom lens

Secondary mirror for autofocus system

Ultrasonic focusing motor

Autofocus sensors

Filter thread

CAMERA selection can be simplified if you go back to the basic principles behind camera design. Irrespective of type, make or cost, all cameras fulfil one primary function – recording a scene by allowing a carefully controlled amount of light to fall onto the film surface. To achieve this, four components are needed – a lens, a viewfinder, some method of exposure control and a film transport system. If you know what you want from the four basic components you're well on your way to finding the right camera to suit your needs. Any other feature on the camera is just a refinement

and you can decide whether your photographic needs justify the extra expense.

Ideally, you should go for the most versatile camera you can afford. You also need to decide how much control over the finished result you want. If you want a camera where all you have to think about is the picture, go for an automatic model. If you want learn about picture-taking then automation isn't quite so important. You also need to consider how much weight you are prepared to carry around.

With compacts, consider whether a 35mm wide-angle as

often fitted is adequate, or whether you prefer a choice of focal length settings. Twin-lens compacts are a reasonable compromise, or further optical flexibility can be found with a zoom model at a higher price. High specification 'bridge' cameras offer the most versatility, though they hardly qualify as 'compact'.

If you want control rather than convenience when taking pictures, the usual choice is a 35mm SLR. These range from basic manual models and simple auto-exposure versions through to versatile multi-mode cameras which may be set to fully automatic

mode, yet can also provide some form of exposure override or the option of full manual operation. If you own an SLR, lenses may be interchanged and other accessories added to increase its scope greatly.

Higher image quality may be obtained with a roll-film camera. Some are constructed along similar lines to 35mm models, and aren't too far behind in terms of handling ease. Bulkier versions, however, are best left on a tripod in the studio. Large-format technical cameras deliver optimum picture quality, but are slow to set up and use.

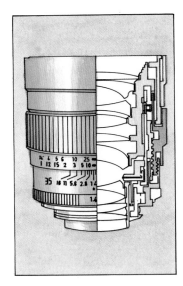

THE LENS

A lens consists of curved glass elements which bend light rays to converge on the film plane producing a sharp image of your subject. In the simplest cameras the lens is 'fixed' – you cannot alter its distance from the film plane. This limits the range of distances which can be brought into sharp focus, so these models rely on a small aperture to ensure adequate sharpness for most scenes. More advanced cameras give better results because the lens, or at least part of it, can be moved, or focused, to form a sharp image of subjects at a wider range of distances from the camera. Many compacts and some SLRs now have self-focusing or autofocus lenses. See Lenses, page 18.

THE VIEWFINDER

Two main types of viewfinder can be found in modern cameras – direct vision and reflex. The former, mainly used in compact cameras, takes up little room and is inexpensive, but shows a very slightly different image from that seen through the lens. For general use this is adequate, but can give inaccurate framing as the subject nears the camera – a condition known as parallax error.

In a reflex camera what you see is what you get because the image in the viewfinder is seen through the picture-taking lens. A mirror reflects the image via a pentaprism which turns the image the right way up and the right way round. The mirror flips out of the way when an exposure is made. With the reflex viewing of SLR cameras, you can frame a shot with care and know that the same image will appear on film, even with close-up subjects. You can also see what effect any attachment in front of the lens will have on the picture.

SHUTTER AND APERTURE

To regulate the amount of light reaching film, all cameras use three linked components – an exposure meter, an aperture iris in the lens, and a shutter. The exposure meter measures the brightness of the light falling on it and calculates how much of this light is required to expose the film correctly. The amount of light reaching the film is determined by the width of the aperture and the duration of the exposure. Again basic cameras offer the least flexibility – perhaps a couple of shutter speeds and a fixed aperture (giving a camera that performs well in only two lighting conditions; very sunny and quite sunny because the aperture is fixed to a small diameter for greatest depth of field). More expensive camera models offer more with an exposure meter, which either gives a reading for you to set manually or is electronically coupled to the diaphragm and the shutter to give the appropriate diameter and duration. The combination of a range of aperture settings and several speeds means the photographer is able to take pictures in many more lighting conditions. He can also decide whether he wants a fast shutter speed (and large aperture) to stop action or a small aperture (and slow shutter speed) for the greatest range of distances in sharp focus.

FILM TRANSPORT

Once an exposure has been made, the exposed frame of film needs to be replaced by an unexposed frame. A precise amount of film is advanced, so that a narrow unexposed border occurs between successive frames. Otherwise unwanted double-exposures or overlap of images will occur. Film may be advanced manually – by a lever or thumbwheel – or automatically. Some cameras have auto-winders or motor-drives built in; others offer them as accessories.

A small film format such as 35mm permits rapid transport of film into place, especially with a motor-drive. Roll-film is much larger in area, and therefore slower to travel through the camera.

COMPACT OR SLR?

COMPACTS

MOST precision compacts now have autofocus. In 'active' automatic focusing, a pattern of infrared light not visible to the eye is projected on to the subject. The angle formed by a line from the infrared source, to the subject, and back to a receptor is measured electronically and the information used to set the lens focus. This system works equally well in the dark. 'Passive' autofocus works by existing light and is not limited to subjects within the range of an infrared beam, but as most snapshots are taken at close range, often using flash, the active system is now the most popular.

SNAPSHOT The simplest cameras in 110 and 35mm formats are today's equivalents of the Box Brownie. The lens is fixed focus with a small aperture for reasonable sharpness. There's a basic flash unit built-in, film advance is manual, and exposure is set by sunny/cloudy symbols. These limitations mean that snapshot cameras are only capable of taking pictures in good light or by flash with the subject between five and fifteen feet away. They are, however, inexpensive and if you only want a camera to record the

A STARTING POINT
Many photographers begin with simple fixed-focus compacts like these.

family on a sunny holiday a snapshot camera may be adequate.

QUALITY COMPACT These cameras are also fitted with a lens of single focal length but of higher optical quality, which means that the maximum aperture can be larger without the image becoming degraded. They may use either symbol focusing or a simple form of autofocus so the range of distances that the camera can focus sharply is increased. Superior circuitry enables these cameras to expose pictures more accurately in most seasons and weather conditions or by flash. Some models have a simple form of exposure compensation which will produce the correct exposure in 'difficult' lighting conditions, and a choice

of 'intelligent' flash modes. Film loading, wind-on and rewind are all motorized. A wide choice of models is available.

TWIN-LENS COMPACT This is very similar to the quality AF compact models with the difference that a choice of two 'taking' lenses is offered. These are often 35 and 70mm or 40 and 80mm combinations, but other variations can be found including some useful 28mm wide-angle plus 45mm standard types. Viewfinder coverage changes automatically as you switch the lens. The extra lenses increase bulk and price, but add considerable versatility. Examples of twin-lens compacts include the Nikon TW20 and the Fuji Mini Wide.

ZOOM COMPACT The zoom compact is more versatile and more expensive than the twin-lens compact but the versatility in focal length is produced by a single zoom lens rather than two fixed focal length lenses – intermediate focal lengths can be set. The greater the lens range, the bigger the camera becomes. Models with 35-70mm lenses are most popular, but a 38-105mm version is capable of bringing more distant objects 'closer'. A coupled zoom viewfinder matches the focal length set. Several flash options increase the camera's scope.

BRIDGE CAMERA These cameras 'bridge' the gap between compacts and SLRs. They combine most of the versatility of an SLR with the simplicity of an automatic compact, sometimes in an unusually designed body. They have many advanced and automated features, a 3x or 4x zoom, a powerful, adjustable flash, and the ability to override the automatic exposure. The focal lengths available to bridge cameras are limited to those of the permanently attached zoom lens and are not as extensive as the choice available to SLR users. These cameras are classified as compacts but their size contradicts this description.

A CHOICE OF SIZE, FEATURES AND QUALITY
The Balda Mini 35 Plus is small and light, with manual focus, auto exposure, a superb lens and detachable flash. The Pentax Zoom 105R is very quick to use, with sequence motor-drive and many functions. The Canon Epoca 'bridge' camera is styled for one-handed operation.

SINGLE-LENS REFLEXES

MANUAL-ONLY These cameras contain all the basic SLR features – reflex viewing, focal-plane shutter, TTL metering and interchangeable lenses – but with few further additions. The shutter, aperture, focusing and film advance are all operated manually rather than automatically. Manual cameras are very reliable because the shutter continues to operate if batteries fail – only the metering facility is lost. Their prices range from some of the cheapest SLRs (Zenith 12XP) to the most expensive (Leica R6).

AUTOMATIC An electronic SLR can combine manual with one or more automatic exposure modes – usually the more you pay the greater the number of options. Aperture-priority auto is useful for controlling depth of field, while shutter-priority is preferable for action subjects. The simplest automatic SLRs have lever wind-on and simple dial controls, while the more advanced versions have features like integral winders and liquid crystal display panels. These cameras rely on a battery for shutter operation so you should always carry spares. Cameras of this type include the traditionally-

PROFESSIONAL VERSATILITY
The Pentax LX system was one of the first fully modular electronic pro cameras, and is also a rare survivor into the autofocus age. Here, a selection of the available replacement viewfinders is shown – more than any other comparable camera can offer.

styled Pentax P30T, the modern push-button Ricoh KR-10M, and the high-specification Canon T90. The latter uses an input wheel to speed up selecting data on the LCD display panel.

AUTOFOCUS These cameras have the same features as an automatic SLR with the added refinement of autofocusing lenses. Sensors within the camera body measure image contrast (see Lens chapter) and trigger motors which move the lens to sharp focus. AF technology has advanced considerably

since it was first introduced and it can cope well with most situations – but certain conditions like dull light, low contrast and moving subjects may still cause focusing problems.

The AF camera retains the option of manual focusing so it is possible to overcome any limitations. Inexpensive examples are the Canon EOS 1000, Minolta Dynax 3xi and Yashica 270. The Canon EOS 100, Minolta Dynax 7xi and Nikon F-801s occupy the medium price bracket. All cameras depend heavily on batteries.

PROFESSIONAL SLR These are rugged auto or AF SLRs, designed to cope with daily use in all weather conditions – some have special water-resistant sealing. Professional SLRs may also have extra features which either increase their speed of operation or increase their versatility. The Contax 167MT and Olympus OM-4Ti are fine manual focus examples, while the Canon EOS-1 and Nikon F4 are top-ranking autofocus system cameras.

SLR FEATURES

In addition to considering the options when selecting an SLR – manual or auto focus, traditional dial or push-button controls, and the number of exposure modes desired – prospective purchasers should also examine whether a camera has these worthwhile features:

DEPTH OF FIELD PREVIEW Also called a stop-down preview, this closes down the lens to the aperture at which the shot will be taken. Although the viewfinder screen is darker, the full zone of sharpness can be seen, and a clearer idea of composition is given as background and foreground sharpness are accurately

BASIC MANUAL FOCUS, AUTOFOCUS OR SUPREME ENGINEERING – WITH ONE THING IN COMMON
Ricoh's KR-10M is a good basic manual choice; the Minolta Dynax 7xi is state-of-the-art autofocus; the Contax 167MT is a non-AF thoroughbred. All three have one unusual function, auto exposure bracketing, built-in to the Ricoh and Contax, and added by a card to the Dynax.

shown. This feature also provides verification of the effect of filters, particularly soft-focus, on the lens.

EXPOSURE COMPENSATION This enables an automatic exposure to be biased in favour of under- or over-exposure, depending on the lighting conditions. It can be set in increments of third or half stops, and two or three stops either side of 'normal' exposure. It is used in situations when the meter is liable to be fooled (backlit, very light or very dark scenes or scenes with the sun in the picture) or to bracket exposures.

AUTO BRACKETING An automated version of exposure compensation is built into some advanced SLRs and the inexpensive Ricoh KR-10M. Three shots are taken – at the metered exposure, just above and just below it. Some models allow you to adjust the degree of under- and over-exposure. This feature is a way of guaranteeing at least one perfect exposure but if it

is used unnecessarily you may waste a lot of film.

MULTIPLE EXPOSURE A button or lever disengages film advance while the shutter is cocked, enabling a further exposure on the same frame. Certain cameras like the Canon EOS-1 permit the number of exposures to be pre-set.

AE LOCK is a button which 'holds' a meter reading in memory so that a picture can be recomposed without a lighter or darker element affecting the exposure. This feature is sometimes combined with a focus lock in AF models.

SELF-TIMERS (delayed action firing, putting a ten second delay in between pressing the shutter release and the camera operating) are often used by photographers to include themselves in group photographs. They also let the vibration from touching the shutter release of a tripod-mounted camera subside.

INTERCHANGEABLE FOCUSING SCREENS
Many SLRs have user-changeable focusing screens, though the process is tricky enough to persuade most people to leave this fragile part alone.

SPECIAL AF MODES New AF SLRs have brought special features connected with auto-focus and motorized zoom lenses. These include instant framing when the camera is put to the eye and aimed, and constant image-size with a moving subject, through links between focus and zooming.

SCREENS AND FINDERS Most good specification 35mm SLRs have interchangeable focusing screens. A few, such as the Pentax LX and Nikon F4, also have interchangeable viewfinders. Nearly all rollfilm SLRs (see next page) have both these features as a matter of course.

ROLLFILM CAMERAS
Three 120 rollfilm reflexes, all very different in construction and use – a professional's well-used motorized Hasselblad, often found second-hand at reasonable prices but sometimes in poor condition (they are the favourite camera for pro equipment hire departments); a Pentax 645, totally self-contained and handling just like a 35mm camera, popular with amateurs; and the Rolleiflex 2.8GX, a superbly-built traditional twin-lens reflex.

SPECIAL ZOOM MODES
The control on this Minolta zoom switches the lens from manual setting to auto zoom, a mode where the camera rapidly frames the subject.

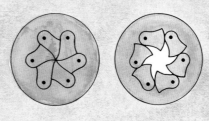

FOCAL PLANE AND LEAF SHUTTER
The focal plane shutter above uses blinds which cross the film gate, uncovering the film. The leaf shutter below uses blades which open and close, and is positioned inside the lens unit.

ROLL-FILM SLR

Roll-film SLRs are often modular in design, so that major components can be interchanged. This applies to viewfinders, film backs, modes of film transport and, of course, lenses and other optical accessories. They are slower to use because of greater bulk and lower speed of film advance but they are often more robust than all but the most expensive professional 35mm SLRs.

Hasselblad, Rolleiflex, Bronica, Mamiya, and Pentax are the major manufacturers, each with a range of cameras (in several formats in the last three cases). These cameras are rarely chosen by amateur photographers because of their lack of automation, high cost and heavy weight.

ROLL-FILM TLR

This is a traditional design employing a pair of matching optics, arranged vertically. The top lens is linked to the viewfinder, while the lower one exposes the film. Because you see a view slightly above that photographed, these cameras aren't recommended for close-up work, but the lack of a mirror mechanism makes them quiet. The are frequently used by wedding photographers because

expressions can be watched without interruption. New twin-lens reflex cameras are available from Mamiya, Rolleiflex, and imported from the east. With second-hand twin-lens reflexes, names like Yashica and Minolta can be added to the list.

RF RANGEFINDER

These cameras bring medium-format quality in relatively lightweight packages, but they are not as common as SLRs. Few components are interchangeable, so their construction is more compact than modular roll-film cameras. The rangefinder focusing Mamiya 6, for instance, accepts three compact lenses, but cannot switch backs or finders.

TECHNICAL CAMERAS

Cameras can be constructed like an optical bench, with lens and film standards linked by a light-tight bellows and provided with movements so the lens or film can be tilted, raised, lowered or swung. Studio cameras are built on a rail, with extensive movements. 'Field' cameras fold out from a portable box, with a baseboard instead of a rail, and have limited movements. Wooden field models are popular due to their light weight.

Two distinct types of shutter can be found in cameras – the focal plane type fitted inside 35mm and some roll-film SLR bodies, and the leaf-shutter seen mainly in compacts but also in a number of medium format SLRs. Both types use an identical system of shutter speed numbering, such as 1/30, 1/60, 1/125, 1/250, 1/500, 1/1000 and so on. These are fractions of a second, and each represents a halving of exposure, or a stop.

A focal plane shutter travels across the rectangular aperture of the film gate either horizontally or vertically. There are actually two blinds moving – the first exposes the film and the second conceals it. The interval between their movement determines the duration of the exposure and it can be

as brief as 1/8000 of a second.

Leaf shutters are sited in the lens adjacent to the aperture mechanism and resemble its iris-like construction. The shutter can be operated using either a control ring on the lens or a release sited on the body and mechanically (or electronically) linked to the shutter. This type of shutter is not capable of the high speeds reached by the focal plane type – 1/500 of a second is usually the maximum – but unlike the focal plane type it offers flash synchronization at all speeds. If the leaf shutter is contained in a lens which is interchangeable, shutter failure calls for the repair of the faulty lens and not the camera body, meaning that you can still carry on taking pictures with an alternative lens.

WHICH FILM SIZE?

MOST of today's cameras use one of three main film formats – 110, 35mm and 120 (roll film) – all of which can be loaded and unloaded from the camera in daylight. There are also various sheet and instant film formats.

The 110 film size, aimed at the snapshooter market, is a miniature film format measuring just 17mm wide. The film (and its numbered backing paper) is in a sealed cartridge with light-tight compartments for unexposed and exposed material, and a central exposure window. With each wind-on a new frame is available for exposure until the end of the film is reached, when the tension of the film prevents the wind-on lever from being operated. The cartridge is then removed and can be replaced. Film types can be changed mid-roll by removing a partially used cartridge and replacing it by another – only one frame of film will be wasted.

The most popular film size is 35mm, the format originating from cut lengths of 35mm-wide movie stock. Rows of perforations run along the edges of the film and engage with teeth which advance and rewind film; these holes limit

the image area to 24mm wide. The film is usually purchased in metal cassettes; a short length of film protrudes through a light-tight felt-lined slot in the side of the cassette for loading. The first few frames are wasted as the loose end of the film is attached to the camera take-up spool; the film is rewound into the cassette once exposed.

Roll-film – otherwise known as 120 – is 62mm wide. Image width is usually 56mm although this is often called 'two and a quarter' in inches or written as 6cm in metric, but the other dimension varies as several sub-formats are used, such as 6 x 4.5cm, 6 x 6cm, or 6 x 7cm. Like the much smaller 110 format, 120 film is attached to an opaque backing paper, longer than the film itself. It is this which is threaded onto the camera's take-up spool. Frame numbers are again printed on the backing material, though modern 120 cameras have motorized or lever-wind advance with no need to view the numbers through a window in a camera back. Once fully exposed the film is wound on so that the paper length protects the film before it is removed.

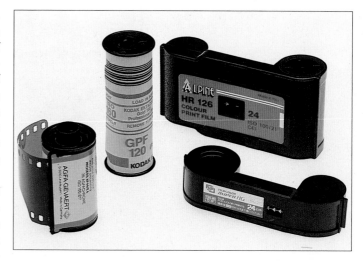

FILM TYPES AND SIZES
All modern films can be loaded and unloaded in daylight. Roll-film has a backing paper to protect it, 35mm comes in metal cassettes, and both 126 and 110 films come in plastic cartridges.

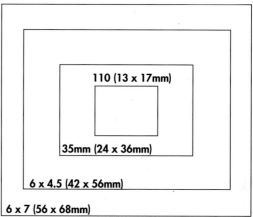

110 (13 x 17mm)

35mm (24 x 36mm)

6 x 4.5 (42 x 56mm)

6 x 7 (56 x 68mm)

FORMATS
Left, actual film areas from 110 to 6 x 7cm. Below, cameras which use these formats – pocket snapshot 110 (front), and from left (back) 6 x 4.5cm roll-film SLR, 35mm AF SLR and 6 x 7 field camera.

QUALITY COUNTS Which film format is best for you? For the person taking snapshots, 35mm is definitely the best option. Though 110 cameras are very pocketable, the format is so small that picture quality is only just acceptable even at enprint size. Sharpness is also affected by the flatness of the film when it is inside the camera, and the 110 cartridge has no precise means of holding the film in place. One or two very high quality 110 cameras have been marketed, such as the Pentax 110 SLR system and the Minolta Zoom 110 models, but the lack of precision in the plastic cartridge design limited their performance.

Having suggested that 35mm is the best format for the casual user, which format should the aspiring enthusiast go for? Here, too, 35mm is probably the best choice. This format produces excellent picture quality, especially when slow film and superior lenses are employed in combination. Above all, it is affordable and versatile – every imaginable type of film is available in 35mm.

Why, then, does anyone need a larger format? Roll-film is predominantly used by professional photographers and amateurs who enter exhibitions and competitions – those who need the best quality possible. The image area of the smallest popular 120 roll-film format is at least three times that of 35mm. This leads to superior enlargements with less visible grain and greater detail. Dust-marks and scratches on the original negative cause more trouble on 35mm than they do on 120 because they, too, are bigger when the picture is enlarged. The disadvantages of roll-film are the cost per shot and the necessity to re-load frequently because there are only 8 to 16 shots per roll of 120. Some pro cameras take size 220 film, which is double length and gives up to 32 shots, but only a few film types can be bought in this size.

As film format increases so does camera size, with 120 cameras being much larger (and more expensive). A roll-film system costs from two to four times as much as a 35mm system, and even when it is complete the camera is not suitable for all applications. A 35mm kit probably includes versatile zooms or a long telephoto lens; either of these lenses for rollfilm will stretch your budget and build unwanted biceps. The smaller 6 x 4.5cm and 6 x 6cm models can be hand-held, but aren't ideal for moving subjects. The bigger 6 x 7cm to 6 x 9cm cameras are normally confined to the studio.

FORMAT KING With its blend of image quality, modest equipment size and reasonable price, most photographers choose 35mm. Its sprocket holes mean that the film can be transported through the camera reliably at high speeds using an auto-winder or motor-drive without damaging the delicate emulsion. For action, sport, wildlife, candids and a host of other picture opportunities, 35mm is by far the finest format. Medium-format 120 cameras excel where quality – not speed or portability – is paramount.

INTERCHANGEABLE LENSES

HAVE you ever watched a magnifying glass concentrate the rays of the sun to burn a hole in a piece of paper? Then you've also witnessed the primary function of all photographic lenses – to bend, or refract, light. We use this ability of lenses to translate the three-dimensional real world into a two-dimensional representation on film. Lenses employed in modern cameras are far more complex than the simple magnifying glass. They are designed by computer and use combinations of several elements to eliminate distortion and colour fringing, or aberrations, and achieve optimum performance.

All lenses have a focal length – the distance from the centre of the lens to the point where focus is achieved. With the simple magnifying glass it is the distance between the lens and the paper which causes smouldering – all the sun's rays converge on one tiny spot. In a modern camera optic, the lens barrel holds the glass elements at the focal length from the film plane.

SLR LENSES

Compact cameras have increased in versatility in recent years with the advent of dual lens and zoom models but the only way to explore broader optical horizons is via the SLR route. With a single lens reflex the viewing of the subject takes place through the taking lens giving optimum accuracy and the ability to view the scene through whatever lens is attached to the camera.

As the SLR has become more sophisticated, so the range of lenses to fit it has grown also. Today most manufacturers produce a wide choice of optics, and some (Nikon, Minolta, Canon and Pentax) have created lens systems of extraordinary range.

Why do we need so many different lenses? With them, photographers can tackle every subject and produce every effect they want to achieve.

IMAGE MAGNIFICATION

Different focal lengths enable a photographer to adjust the size of a subject on film. A 200mm lens will produce an image four times the size of that produced by a 50mm. However the area of subject placed across the film format is reduced, because the telephoto lens also has a narrower angle of view. A lens of 1000mm, then, magnifies the same subject some twenty times, but records only a small part of it.

When the focal length of a lens is shorter than standard, the opposite occurs. When compared with a standard lens, a 28mm optic reduces the scale of everything in the shot, but there's more included, because the lens's angle of view is wider. At 20mm focal length, the scale of detail is smaller still, but a very wide angle of view is provided. For this reason, lenses shorter than 50mm are termed wide-angles. Those longer than 50mm are called long-focus or telephoto lenses.

APERTURES

All lenses have a variable iris, or diaphragm, to control the amount of light entering the camera. An aperture, or f number, is an accepted value of light, with settings which run as follows: $f1$, $f1.4$, $f2$, $f2.8$, $f4$, $f5.6$, $f8$, $f11$, $f16$, $f22$, $f32$, $f45$ and $f64$. This series of calibrated numbers is, in fact, a strict geometrical progression, with $f1$ being the widest iris opening and the other figures representing its gradual closure. As the aperture number rises from one figure to the next, the amount of light passing through the iris is precisely halved.

So an aperture of $f8$, for example, lets in 50% of the light passed at the $f5.6$ setting. Such a change is also termed one f-stop difference – a measurement of light we've already come across in the discussion about exposure control. Adjusting either the shutter speed or the aperture by one step will have exactly the same effect on light reaching the film. Control of these two settings enables metering systems to establish the right exposure on film accurately.

A SYSTEM LENS RANGE
A modern SLR system will include over 20 choices of lens; some makes offer double this number, ranging from new designs, compatible with every feature of the latest cameras, to older models with limited functions. Makers now change the 'look' of their lenses every two or three years. The kit above, for Minolta AF and Dynax SLRs, covers seven years and three camera generations as well as 16mm to 500mm.

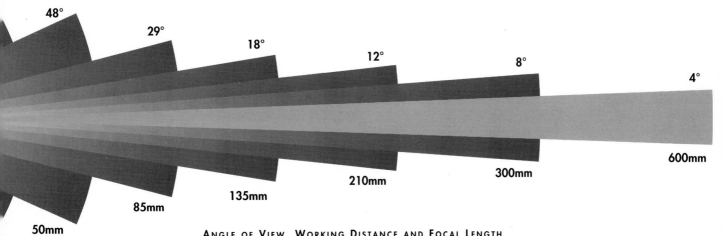

ANGLE OF VIEW, WORKING DISTANCE AND FOCAL LENGTH
This chart shows how a range of lenses (see the photographs overleaf for actual results) is used in practice.
Each lens in the series from 16 to 600mm takes a progressively narrower view of the world – but normally, you
increase your working distance with longer lenses. You might take exactly the same subject with a 20mm and
a 28mm, but stand a little further back with the 28mm. The longer lenses are used to be more selective, not
just to change the working distance, but you rarely use a 300mm as close as you would a 135mm.

LENS FOCAL LENGTHS

FOCAL LENGTHS

Lenses can be divided for convenience into categories like wide-angle and telephoto. The focal lengths given here all apply to 35mm SLR systems.

STANDARD LENSES Normal lenses, as supplied with the camera unless you buy a zoom, have a focal length equal or near to the length of the diagonal of the film size covered. For the popular 35mm format, this means the 50mm optic, giving an SLR viewfinder image magnification about the same as looking at the subject with the naked eye. The angle of view of a 50mm lens is 46-47°, and maximum apertures are often quite wide at ƒ1.7 or ƒ1.8.

FISH-EYE – 6MM-16MM These lenses have extreme angles of view, sometimes wider than the human eye. A fish-eye lens is so-called because its image is formed using a curved projection, like a security door-viewer, instead of geometrically straight lines like an architect's drawing. Using this 'curvilinear' image-drawing means that an angle of view of 180° or even 220°, which includes objects actually behind the camera, can be fitted on to a circle of film. Depth of field, even at full aperture, is extensive. Full-frame fisheyes provide an image which covers the full 35mm format, while circular image types create a round image 24mm in diameter in the centre of the frame. The fish-eye effect is easily recognized and is only effective on a limited number of subjects, so overuse should be avoided.

WIDE-ANGLES Lenses from 14mm-35mm are ideal for use in confined spaces, or when open vistas are required in a single picture. The magnification is reduced when compared with a standard lens, but if your subject is close to the lens a wide-angle can emphasize the closer parts, for example

the nose in a portrait or the knees of a seated subject. There is considerable depth of field (sharpness in depth, from near the camera to the distant view) especially at the shorter focal lengths between 14 and 21mm. Sometimes termed superwides, these specialized wide-angles may produce stretching or distortion of the image towards the edges of the frame, but record the picture with straight lines unlike the fish-eye designs.

TELEPHOTO – 85MM-300MM With longer focal lengths than the standard lens, tele lenses give magnified views of a subject. Lenses up to 300mm are not so large that the camera has to be mounted on a tripod to use them, and the degree of magnification provided (up to 6x) causes few problems with holding the camera steady. They often have a reasonably wide maximum aperture, so short shutter speeds can be used to avoid camera shake, but this reduces their already limited depth-of-field. Telephotos are useful for bringing distant scenes closer, and for the way they appear to compress perspective.

Long lenses from 75 to 100mm are often called 'portrait' lenses and may not actually be telephoto designs, as the word telephoto means a specific optical grouping which results in a compact lens, often physically shorter than its focal length in millimetres. A 300mm telephoto will often be only 200mm long.

TELEPHOTO – 400MM-2000MM Longer lenses are like looking at a subject through a pair of binoculars. Due to their considerable bulk, these heavy optics are best attached to some method of support such as a sturdy tripod. Image magnification is high, making them ideal for inaccessible subjects or those that are too dangerous to approach. Depth of field is extremely shallow, especially at wide apertures, and camera shake is a constant risk.

ZOOMS

Zoom lenses offer variable focal length. 'Adjustable telephoto' lenses were made in the early 1900s, but zooms became popular in the 1960s. 'Zoom' means the lens holds its focus as you change magnification. Earlier 'varifocal' designs needed re-focusing after every small change in image size.

Zooms now rival fixed lenses in terms of compactness, aperture range and image quality. The main attractions of a zoom are its versatility and convenience. A 70-210mm tele-zoom does the work of 85mm, 135mm and 200mm traditional telephotos, while a 28-85mm stands in for 28mm and 35mm wide-angles, 50mm standard and 85mm 'portrait'.

50MM

210MM

85MM

300MM

135MM

600MM

With a zoom, an image can be re-framed several ways with the photographer standing in the same spot. Complexity is the zoom's disadvantage; standard lenses normally have five or six elements, but a zoom can have three times as many. Extra glass adds weight, and increases problems due to internal reflection of light or misalignment during manufacture.

MIRROR LENSES

Also known as catadioptric lenses, mirror lenses are one method of reducing the bulk of a powerful telephoto. Instead of a straight-through path, the image forming rays are 'folded' by means of mirrors within the lens barrel. The most popular focal length for mirror lenses is 500mm, but you can

also find 250mm, 300mm, 600mm, 800mm and longer designs.

Hand-holding a mirror lens is made easier as using mirrors rather than lenses cuts down the weight as well as the size. As it is difficult to fit an iris diaphragm within this type of lens, the aperture is both fixed and rather slow – usually $f8$. Depth of field is minimal, and light intensity can only be re-

duced by adding neutral density filters at the lens's rear. A visual characteristic of the mirror lens is that defocused highlights take on a ring-like, or doughnut, appearance. The effect is clearly seen when a sunlit or watery backdrop is included in shot.

MACRO LENSES

Specially computed to give optimum performance at very close subject distances of a few inches, both standard 50mm and longer 90mm to 105mm macro lenses are available, the latter providing a greater working distance between lens and subject. This is handy to avoid blocking your own light, or frightening off a jumpy subject!

Most macros focus right down to 1:1 or life size. This means that a subject an inch long, such as an insect or stamp, is also an inch long on the 35mm frame of film. At half-life size, or 1:2, the same subject would be half an inch long. Macro lenses typically have an $f2.8$ maximum aperture, and cost two or three times the price of a standard lens.

The term 'macro' applied to zoom lenses normally means close focusing, to around one-quarter life size, without any of the special corrections for sharpness at such close distances which a true macro lens is expected to have.

TELECONVERTERS

Add-on telephoto converters provide a way to extend the reach of a telephoto or zoom lens for an SLR without stretching your budget too far. They're also available for a handful of compacts.

An SLR converter or extender is a small optical device which increases focal length by between 1.2x and 3x, depending on the specification. It fits between the body and lens, and couples with the camera's metering system. A 2x model converts a 135mm lens to a 270mm, or turns a 70-210mm into a 140-420mm lens. While doubling subject magnification, it also absorbs two f-stops of light in the process, so setting $f8$ on the lens means getting $f16$ on the film. TTL metering systems automatically take this into account. A small loss of image quality may occur, particularly in the corners of the picture.

MAKING AN IMPACT WITH EXTREMES

Your camera outfit will probably include lenses between 28mm and 210mm. Real eye-catching shots can be taken with lenses most people never get to own – fish-eyes and mirror lenses. If you don't want to lay out hundreds for a real fish-eye, there are many low-cost fish-eye converters available which do the job well enough for the occasional shot with impact. Independent lens manufacturers produce low-cost mirror lenses of good quality. The extremes of focal length are more affordable than you thought.

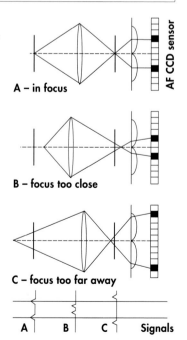

FISH-EYE AND MIRROR
A low-cost fish-eye converter turned a regular 50mm standard lens into an 8mm circular image fish-eye for the shot above. The picture was originally a 22mm circle in the middle of the 24 x 36mm frame. Left, a 500mm $f8$ mirror lens has created bright 'doughnut' rings from out of focus sparkling water.

AUTOFOCUS LENSES

Have you ever wondered how an autofocus lens works? How does it reach a sharp image so quickly and accurately? The camera sensor looks for the area of highest contrast in a scene – so does the human eye. Edge effects are the best indicator – a sharp border between dark and light areas indicates contrast is at a maximum, and the shot is sharp. If the division between light and dark is less pronounced, contrast is lower and the subject is out of focus.

Modern SLRs use charge coupled devices (CCDs) which emit an electrical signal in direct proportion to the amount of light falling upon them. A microprocessor scans the output of a row of CCDs, and senses the various signals strengths. When the signals are similar, focus has not been achieved, so the lens motor is commanded to turn the focusing barrel.

But how does the lens know which way to turn? This is the clever part. Correct focus is achieved by a method called 'phase difference detection'. Light entering the camera from a subject in focus passes the film plane equivalent distance, then diverges to form two images a precise distance apart on the row of CCDs. The camera microprocessor recognizes this as the electronic equiva-

AF CCD sensor

A – in focus

B – focus too close

C – focus too far away

A | B | C | Signals

lent of a 'sharp' image. When the lens is focused beyond or in front of the subject, the spacing of the two images on the CCDs alters, to either wider than or narrower than the correct spacing. With this data, the camera knows which way to turn the lens.

AUTOFOCUS MODES

As with auto-exposure, autofocus in SLRs can operate in different ways or modes. Currently there are four types of focusing method:

ONE SHOT The camera focuses on a subject placed within the AF sensor's range. Shutter release is only possible once optimum focus has been reached. A single exposure may be taken, then the finger must be removed from the shutter button and pressed again to take another picture.

SERVO This mode allows sequences of shots to be taken of a moving subject, with the lens refocusing after every frame. The shutter may be fired even if the subject is not rendered sharply.

PREDICTIVE This is a refined version of servo mode, which is also useful for subjects in motion. Refocusing of the lens occurs after each exposure, guided by the camera's CPU which predicts the direction of travel and moves the lens accordingly.

TRAP Here the lens is prefocused upon a point. When a subject in motion passes through this area, the shutter is released as optimum focus is achieved – an AF mode seen only in Yashica SLRs to date.

PHASE DETECTION
When the subject is focused correctly on the film plane (A, diagram on left) the AF sensor records peak output in two zones. Out-of-focus images B and C record peak outputs away from these zones – and the camera can tell which way to adjust the focus.

LENS HOODS
Shades or hoods prevent the image of a lens being impaired by a bright light source – usually the sun. Non-image forming light, otherwise known as flare, degrades the image. Looking through the viewfinder, a pale haze is apparent, lowering contrast and reducing colour saturation. In extreme cases, a series of images of the lens diaphragm can be clearly seen. To avoid flare, fit a suitable lens hood. This must be chosen to suit the focal length precisely. Too long a hood will intrude into the picture area. The left hand hood is a Cokin filter-holder universal hood designed to work with most lenses, while the rearmost bellows design is an adjustable Ambico Shade. The short hood is for a wide-angle zoom, the 'bat-wing' hood fits a 20mm ultra-wide, and the rubber hood is another universal adjustable design, from Hoya. It folds back on itself for wide angles and pulls out fully for telephotos.

INSTANT FRAMING
Increasing communication between the lens and camera body in AF SLRs means that new lens functions are now possible. The latest Minolta Dynax and Pentax Z-series models sport facilities which provide a lens setting suitable for a compositional starting point, or return to a memorized focal length at the press of a button. In this action shot, the photographer could follow the subject with the lens set to a wide view, keeping it central in the finder. When the shutter was pressed, the lens instantly zoomed in to capture a close-up.

MODES AND METERS

ALL but a handful of cameras for the 35mm format feature an integral exposure meter. Compact models are the easiest to use because all the major camera functions are automated giving you time to concentrate on composition. If your photograph is to record an event you are taking part in, an automatic compact is going to be the least distracting.

35mm SLRs, on the other hand, give the photographer the option of greater control over metering and exposure settings. Through the lens (TTL) metering operates whatever lens is fitted, providing greater exposure accuracy. The silicon metering cell lies within the camera body, either below the mirror or up in the prism housing. Many SLRs permit the metering area to be varied, enabling unusual or tricky lighting situations to be carefully measured. Manual and semi-automatic exposures are possible with an increasing number of additional exposure modes which calculate the aperture and shutter speed settings to suit various situations.

Camera manufacturers now fully exploit the extraordinary capabilities of the SLR's computer central processing unit. Analog inputs, such as the film speed index or the amount of light passing through the lens, are converted into digital form and processed with other information at lightning speed. The resulting data is used to govern shutter speeds, apertures and other operational aspects.

With a choice of metering patterns and a range of exposure modes to select from, a photographer can set up an SLR to cope with almost any lighting situation and picture possibility.

IN-CAMERA MEASUREMENT
Through-the-lens (TTL) light metering is accurate because it measures the light which will actually form the image on the film. It also works with automatic dedicated flashguns, metering flash exposure from the film itself. Subjects like butterfly close-ups can be taken quickly without any tests or calculations, with perfect results guaranteed every time.

EXPOSURE MODES

MANUAL Marked 'M' on controls or in displays. In the traditional method of exposure control, the meter measures the light reflected off the subject and gives an indication in the viewfinder of current settings, plus those which will result in correct exposure. The photographer has the option of using the indicated settings or adjusting them slightly for awkward lighting conditions when the meter is liable to be fooled into giving a 'false' reading.

APERTURE-PRIORITY Marked 'A' or 'AE'. This semi-automatic mode provides control over the depth of field in a photograph. The operator chooses an aperture, and the camera provides an appropriate shutter speed according to the available light. In a portrait, for example, ƒ2.8 might be selected to give a shallow zone of focus, concentrating attention on the subject. For a landscape study, ƒ16 may be set to keep the entire scene from foreground to background sharp.

SHUTTER-PRIORITY Marked 'S', or 'EE' on some older camera models, this semi-automatic mode governs how sharply a moving subject will be recorded. A high shutter speed is chosen to freeze motion, or a slower speed to create deliberate blurring of the subject during the exposure. Whatever shutter speed is chosen, the camera selects a suitable aperture to give correct exposure.

PROGRAM Marked 'P' – or unmarked if the only mode – this fully automatic mode decides both the shutter speed and the aperture, according to a set of conditions known as a program. Refined versions can emphasize shutter speed or apertures, and some take into account the focal length of lenses to shorten the shutter speed and avoid camera shake when telephotos are fitted.

PROGRAM SHIFT Based on Program mode, a 'shift' thumbwheel or switch lets the photographer change the automatically set shutter speed and aperture to a combination giving the same actual exposure, but favouring faster or slower shutter speeds and corresponding wider or smaller apertures. Until cancelled, the camera continues to adjust the exposure automatically with the shift remaining active.

BULB Also called brief time or 'B', this setting will keep the shutter open for as long as the release is pressed. Often used to record the light trails of moving subjects in night exposures, it is marked 'B' on controls or LCD displays.

TIME A similar mode to 'B' or Bulb, 'T' or time opens the shutter with the first press of the shutter release, and does not close it until the release is pressed a second time. The camera can be left unattended with the shutter open.

DEPTH-OF-FIELD AE This is a mode in Canon EOS SLRs which permits the near and far points of a scene to be accurately pinpointed to give a controlled zone of sharpness. Other cameras have similar functions which depend on add-on accessories or cards.

AUTO BRACKETING An additional mode built in to various maker's top models, or added by an expansion card to Minolta SLRs, this sets the camera to take three (or more) frames in rapid succession at normal, under-, and over-exposed settings.

PIC Some SLRs and many compacts indicate the selected programmed exposure modes by a *pictogram* in the viewfinder or on a top-plate LCD display. For example, a flower indicates a close-up mode, a mountain landscapes, a face portraits and a running figure an action mode. Suitable exposure programs are set in each case.

METER WEIGHTING

To cope with difficult light, many different built-in metering patterns have been developed by each manufacturer, *weighting* different zones of the viewfinder. Some 35mm SLRs provide a choice, but you have to understand when to switch from one weighting to another.

Computer analysis of thousands of amateur pictures is used to design new metering systems, which are often intelligent enough to recognize typical patterns of light and dark, switching automatically. Other systems have the meter linked to autofocus, so that the focused subject is the meter target.

WHOLE SCREEN Takes the entire screen area into account, and averages the readings – also called average reading. Works well if there is a reasonable distribution of light and dark areas.

CENTRE-WEIGHTED Reads from the whole picture area, but gives more emphasis to the central area placed in the lower half of the frame. This is designed to avoid a bright sky tricking the meter into under-exposure.

EVALUATIVE Measures the light value of one part of the screen and compares it to another – usually the central portion and the outer area. If the outer areas are brighter, more exposure is allowed. More sophisticated versions measure a number of smaller segments, then compute the exposure accordingly.

PARTIAL Exposure calculations are based on a small part of the central screen area – often 6-8° of the total screen – ignoring the outer areas. Accurate providing the main subject is also centrally placed.

SPOT Measures a narrow 1-3° angle in the centre of the screen. Can be very accurate if this area coincides with the main subject.

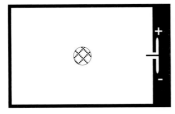

AVERAGE METERING
This simple manual SLR viewfinder shows correct exposure when the needle is centred. The meter reads from the entire screen area.

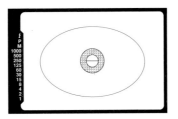

CENTRE-WEIGHTED
An aperture-priority auto SLR has an LED read-out of the shutter speed set by the camera: over 80% of the meter reading is based on the zone shown in the diagram (but not in the finder).

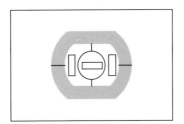

MULTI PATTERN
One of the first 'intelligent metering' AF SLR viewfinders has markings for three focusing zones and central 'spot' metering. The grey area and its clear centre are divided up into segments which the camera can auto-select, according to the response of the focus sensors, and can compare.

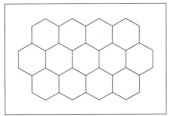

STATE OF THE ART
Fourteen meter segments follow moving subjects, measuring contrast, and even switch on fill-in flash when shadows are harsh.

SEPARATE METERS

Sometimes the meter built into a 35mm SLR is not accurate enough, or doesn't provide enough information about readings taken. Some rollfilm and large format cameras don't incorporate a meter. In either case, a separate or hand-held exposure meter may be used. It can take a reflected light reading similar to a 35mm SLR or compact, though generally with a narrower angle of view.

The main advantage of a separate meter is its ability to take an incident light reading – camera meters cannot. A reflected reading is taken from the camera position and measures the light bouncing off a subject; an incident reading is taken from the subject position towards the camera and measures the light falling on it. A translucent cover, or receptor dome, is fitted over the metering cell in this case. This type of reading, though slower to use, provides greater accuracy.

A second type of separate meter is the spot meter which narrows the acceptance angle, often to just 1°. This takes precise reflected light readings, as it can be trained on a small or important part of the scene. Some general meters also accept an accessory which permits a spot or narrow angle reading to be taken.

HAND-HELD LIGHT METERS
The Gossen Spot-Master (left) costs more than most cameras but is capable of fine-tuning exposure precisely using a viewfinder with a metering area, an electronic measurement analyzer, and a graphic display. The Spot-Master is capable of displaying a scale of shades of grey 'zones' and you can select which zone you want the metered area to match in the final picture. The Minolta Flashmeter IV (centre) is about the same price as a good AF SLR, and can meter continuous light or flash in any combination; it will also control and set a Minolta camera remotely, and has attachments for microscopes and technical cameras. The Gossen Sixon 2 (right) is a typical basic hand-held meter, and reads continuous light only – ideal as a back-up or for quickly checking your camera readings.

MOTORIZED FILM WINDING

MANY 35mm SLRs incorporate an auto-winder or motor-drive, or can be fitted with one. The main advantage of automated film advance is that a series of photographs can be taken in rapid succession. Separate drives often have a hand-grip to allow single-handed operation, and many cameras with integral motor wind have retained this feature in their body-shape. Manual winding on can mean taking the camera away from your eye, missing action shots or accidentally changing a careful composition. Motor winding eliminates all these problems. Motorized film loading and rewinding, found in all AF SLR systems and most compacts, only take a few seconds and you can have your camera back in action rapidly when the time comes to load a new film.

Motor-drives are frequently associated with sports photography but they are useful for all types of photography. In a portrait session the expressions of the sitter can be continuously watched, and instead of fiddling with the camera the photographer can build a greater rapport with his subject – or a 'paparazzo' press cameraman can quickly fire off a few frames of a publicity-shy celebrity!

There are several types of motorized add-on winder available, depending on the make and type of camera you own.

By the term 'auto-winder' we normally understand a motor which advances automatically between each shot, but does not necessarily allow a continuous sequence to be taken by holding the shutter down. The term 'motor-drive' normally covers any mechanism which does allow a continuous sequence.

Recently these terms have become slightly confused, and makers often call anything with a relatively slow 'frames per second' (fps) rate an auto-winder, reserving the motor-drive term for advance rates of 3fps or faster, regardless of continuous shooting.

ADDING A MOTOR

The Pentax LX modular camera, left, starts off with no motor-wind. You can add an auto-winder, shown fitted to the bottom of the camera, which provides a continuous shooting speed of 2 frames per second or single-shot mode. For sports shots, you can replace this with a 5 frames per second motor-drive (right). The pistol grip holds the batteries needed to power the baseplate-attached motor. Most new AF SLRs have the basic auto-winder built in, and professional models achieve motor drive speeds without attachments.

SPEEDING UP FILM ADVANCE

The Canon EOS-1 professional AF SLR, left, has a built-in winder, which uses the camera's main batteries and runs at 2.5 frames per second. This is the typical specification used by most AF SLRs, and has the disadvantage that a single power source may in some cases be supplying the drive, metering, auto focus, shutter and flash. By adding the booster unit shown here, which includes its own power supply, the EOS-1 can double its shooting rate to 5.5fps and conserve the power of the built-in batteries, as the booster takes over from these. This feature is invaluable to professionals who can not afford to lose shots changing batteries.

AUTO-WINDER A motor which, immediately after each exposure, winds on the film and cocks the shutter ready for the next shot. Some auto-winders, even those in pocketable compact cameras, have single-shot and continuous modes. Speeds range from 1 frame per second up to 2.5fps. Auto-winders are incorporated in most compact cameras and all current AF SLRs.

Battery-powered accessory winders can be attached to the base of many manual wind-on SLRs. They link up to the camera's wind-on mechanism through electrical contacts and a drive linkage.

Because auto-winders don't have fast advance rates, they use less battery power than motor drives, and typically need four size AA (MN1500) cells. Many built-in winders run from the lithium cell which powers the entire camera – winder, exposure metering, autofocus, and flash.

BOOSTER An add-on accessory can increase the firing rate of some cameras' integral motor-drives, primarily by increasing the available battery power and taking the load off the inbuilt power supply. For example, the Canon EOS-1 SLR can fire at two and a half frames per second in standard trim, or 5.5fps with its booster attached. The Nikon F4 has a similar motor-drive attachment which boosts the speed of its built-in winder. A booster can be removed to save weight and bulk and refitted when a faster rate of film advance is needed.

MOTOR-DRIVE Rapid motor-drives can be either integrated into the camera body, or added as a system accessory. Motor-drives give a faster firing rate than auto-winders, in the range three to six frames per second, so they're more suited to applications where high-speed shooting is required. They

may offer a choice of low- or high-speed firing, and most are also able to advance film one frame at a time at slower rates, like an auto-winder. Some cameras, such as the Contax RTS III, have extremely fast motor-drives entirely built-in with no need for a booster.

Using a motor-drive at a fast firing rate of five frames per second, it's possible to run through a 36-exposure film in a little over seven seconds. This facility is only required by photographers who shoot action subjects regularly, where the action cannot be predicted or may be unrepeatable.

Accessory motor-drives are heavy due to the hefty mechanisms and batteries. Motor-drives are often noisy which may be a point against them if you are trying to shoot wildlife, though the Contax, Nikon F4 and Canon EOS 100 show that this can be significantly reduced by clever design.

ROLL FILM WINDERS
Winders are also available for Hasselblad, Bronica, Pentax, Rolleiflex and Mamiya medium-format cameras. Because roll film is larger than 35mm, firing rates are slower, around one frame per second. The Pentax 645 and Rollei 6008 feature integral winders, while Bronica and Mamiya models like the Mamiya 645 (above) have add-on grips or baseplates.

HOW FAST ?
Whether you need auto-wind or motor-drive depends on the subject. For shots of people, right, an auto-winder is ideal, each shot being timed according to expression or pose. In the studio, flash units are often limited to one shot per second, so an auto-winder is adequate. Sports photographers need more speed; for the sequence below, a Minolta Dynax 7xi was used. This camera runs at up to 4 frames per second without needing any add-on devices, and allowed automatic focusing to track the rider with a 100-300mm tele-zoom lens.

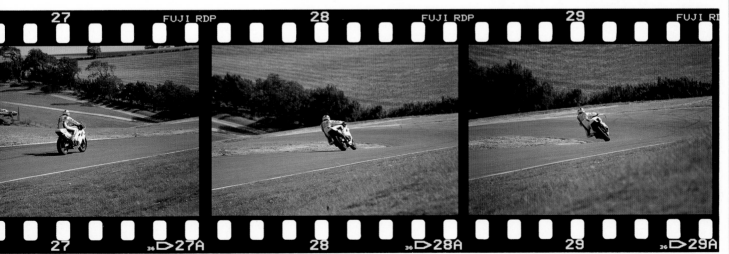

ELECTRONIC FLASH

PICTURES are often taken in less than perfect ambient lighting conditions and electronic flash is often used to improve the situation. The flash may either be used as the only light source for the picture or it may be used to 'fill-in' unwanted shadows. Three main forms of flash equipment are produced: built-in; self-contained battery operated flashguns; and studio flash which is powered by the domestic electricity supply. In the United States, all electronic flash is referred to as 'strobe'. Elsewhere, 'strobe' is only used for very rapidly firing or repeating flash used for multiple exposures, motor-drive or special effects.

In all flashguns a capacitor holds a high voltage charge. When the picture is taken the energy is discharged through the flashtube in a burst of high-intensity light lasting for 1/1000 to 1/10,000 of a second. The capacitor is then recharged, causing a short delay before the flash can be fired again. An indicator light glows once full charge has been reached.

On-camera flashguns usually measure the light being reflected back from the subject through a sensor cell and halt, or 'quench' flash output when the exposure is correct. Sophisticated SLRs offer TTL off-the-film flash metering for ultimate exposure accuracy.

COMPACT FLASH

Most compact cameras feature a fully automatic integral flash which is turned on manually, or automatically, in low light. The flash unit is fixed in a forward-facing position, and provides a beam of light covering the lens angle of view – in zoom models the angle of illumination varies to coincide with the focal length in use. Flash power is moderate, because of the need for miniaturization and the possibility of early battery exhaustion. High-grade compacts feature a number of exposure modes for flash versatility:

AUTO MODE fires the flash when the meter senses that ambient light is insufficient.

FILL-IN does the same thing in backlit situations, to pump light into shadowy areas.

FLASH OFF mode is useful to record natural light, or when flash is prohibited.

SLOW-SYNCH combines a burst of flash with a long shutter speed to light a main subject and reveal background details.

VARIABLE POWER flash avoids over-exposing subjects which are too close to the camera.

STROBE fires several flashes in quick succession to record a sequence or multiple image.

RED-EYE PRE-FLASH uses a low power flash which fires just before the main exposure, to close the iris of the eyes of the subject, just before the main flash is fired.

TYPES OF FLASH
Flash units range from built-in on compact cameras, through very small prism-top units for SLRs, to multi-function dedicated guns and specialized ring flashes (above).

SLR FLASH

Some recent 35mm models have taken a leaf out of the compact book, by incorporating a mini-flash into the prism housing. The most sophisticated versions link the flash coverage automatically to the focal length set on a zoom lens. Most SLRs, however, employ an accessory flashgun in the familiar hot-shoe position, and these are available in a wide range of power outputs and specifications including auto-zoom.

Basic models have fixed flashtubes facing forward, while others enable the reflector to be tilted or swivelled, for softer bounce lighting. Zoom flash units normally cover the lens-range between 28 and 85mm. Twin tube guns provide direct and bounce

GUIDE NUMBERS

The power of all camera-integral and accessory flashguns is stated as a Guide Number, related to distance in meters or feet and film of ISO 100. If a small flash unit in a compact camera has a GN of 80 in feet, that means a subject 10 feet from the camera can be exposed at $f8$ ($80 \div 10 = 8$). If the subject moves to a point 20 feet from the camera, the required aperture is $f4$ ($80 \div 20 = 4$). This neatly illustrates that doubling the subject distance requires a fourfold increase in flash power – $f4$ is two stops or four times more exposure than $f8$.

Add-on flashguns usually have GNs in the region 56-110/ft, while hammerhead units have outputs ranging from GN 110-320/ft. This kind of power allows a wide choice of apertures, or the flashtube can be aimed at a wall or ceiling to soften the light falling upon a subject.

lighting in combination, and units with AF pre-flash allow auto-focus in the dark.

Powerful and versatile 'hammerhead' units can be attached to SLRs using a bracket. These use clusters of batteries in the vertical handle, or a separate battery pack. The increased output of these units is offset by less manageable handling qualities. All add-on flashguns can be combined with other accessories, such as reflectors, bounce cards and non-optical colour filters, to modify the light.

Some flash units are designed for specialized photographic purposes. The ring-flash, for instance, features a circular flashtube which is placed around the lens. It gives shadowless frontal illumination which is often better than sidelighting for macro close-ups.

Very few flashguns now have manual exposure using a calculator dial. Most flashguns use an integral sensor to measure light output or link up through the hotshoe to an internal sensor which reads the light actually falling on the film (called TTL-OTF, or through-the-lens, off-the-film, flash control).

Any kind of coupling through the shot, even just to set the shutter speed to flash operation automatically or show that the flash is fully charged by an LED in the viewfinder, is termed 'dedicated' flash. It's important to be sure that your flashgun is correctly matched to your camera if dedicated functions are to work properly.

Variable power output means that a selection of auto apertures can be chosen, to ensure the subject is within the range of the flash. Output is quenched when enough light has been delivered onto the subject (sensor controlled). Many models give a flash confirmation signal to show that the exposure was complete. Manual exposures may also be fired, usually at full power or fractions of that figure. TTL-OTF gives virtually foolproof flash

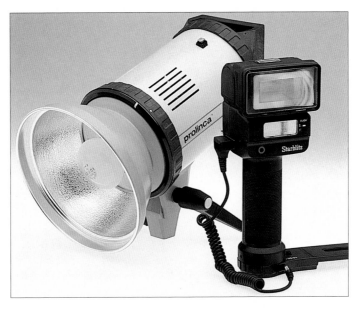

PROFESSIONAL FLASH

For more power, professionals use twin tube hammer-head flashguns with large handle grips to hold battery packs. The twin flash tubes, one low power aiming permanently forwards and the other high power adjustable for bounce, provide fill-in and modelling in a single unit. Exposure is automatic. In the studio, AC powered flash with built-in modelling lamps is preferred (in background, above) for extra power and total control of the image, as the lighting effect can be previewed. The smallest such units are the same power as a large camera-top or hammer-head gun; large units may be hundreds of times more powerful

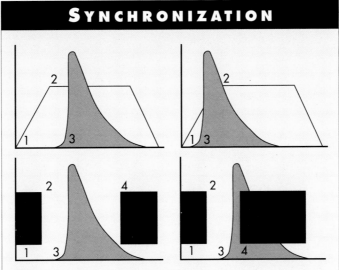

SYNCHRONIZATION

Flash synchronization may fail for different reasons, depending on the type of shutter used. A leaf shutter once released (top left diagram, point 1) gradually opens fully (2) and electronic flash should be fired (3) during the fully open period. Early flash synchronization (top right), built in to some cameras for use with flash bulbs, puts 3 before 2 – and the flash fires before the shutter is open, resulting in under-exposure. With a focal plane shutter, a speed of 1/125 (bottom left) may fully uncover the film frame before closing (point 4). If flash is used at 1/250 (bottom right) the second blind is already covering half the film when the flash fires.

exposure, and is ideal for difficult applications such as macro or multiple flash situations.

STUDIO FLASH

For optimum creative control studio photographers use electronic flash to light their subjects. Two main types of flash are available – the monobloc, where the power pack and flash tube are combined in one assembly; and studio flash where the lights and the power pack are separate units. Both types employ a tungsten modelling lamp placed at the centre of the circular flashtube to show the lighting direction and quality – an advantage over hand-held flash systems.

Power output and versatility are the main criteria for studio flash – apart from lights used on location, portability isn't that necessary. The lowest power units have an output roughly similar to that of a hammerhead portable flash, but a more powerful output is available further up the price scale. Why is this necessary? Because studio photographers tend to use medium or large-format cameras, the lenses of which must be well stopped down to create plenty of depth of field. Light tends to be well diffused too, absorbing much of the flash energy.

Flash units are placed either on stands, or hung from the ceiling in established studios to leave the floor uncluttered. Integral or add-on slave cells are often used to synchronize a number of flash heads, ensuring they fire simultaneously. This is a neat solution as there are no synch cables lying around to trip up the unwary.

Flash-heads accept a wide variety of attachments, including reflectors, umbrellas, softlites, snoots and honeycombs. All these modify the harsh nature of direct flash, to give a variety of lighting effects. Exposure is measured with a handheld flash meter, capable of sensing the rapid burst of light and giving a read-out of the f-stop required.

CHOOSING FILTERS

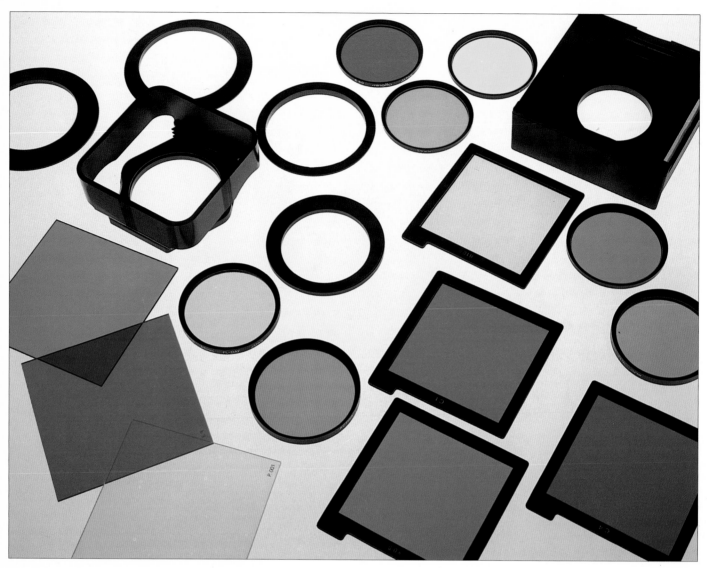

FILTERS placed in the optical path – usually in front of the lens – enable the image recorded on film to be manipulated in a number of ways. A coloured filter absorbs part of the light passing through it so it can alter the quality, colour and intensity of the image produced by the lens creating a wide range of effects, from subtle enhancement of a shot by one filter, through to highly creative treatments involving several filters used simultaneously.

Filters may be used correctively, to make the image recorded on film look more like that seen through the eye, or they can be used 'artistically' to produce special effects. They can also be used to enhance reality, by adding colour to a dull sky or subduing blemishes in a portrait.

The versatility and relative cheapness of filters have made them very popular with photographers and a large number of filter types and systems have grown to cater for this demand.

Filters are most frequently attached to SLR camera lenses because their effect can be observed through the camera viewfinder. Some compact cameras also allow filters to be fitted but, as the subject is viewed by a separate optical system, the precise effect on the image cannot always be accurately assessed.

FILTER TYPES

Optical filters are manufactured from either glass, resin or gelatin – though unofficial versions can be created from almost anything, in-

cluding ladies' stockings, petroleum jelly, cellophane and even sticky tape. Glass versions are expensive but resist damage. Gelatin types are the best optically as they are very thin and introduce less distortion, but they are also prone to scratching and easily damaged by damp. Many filters are now produced from resin – cheaper than glass, harder than gelatin, but the optical quality is inferior and colours not as precisely controlled.

Most filters are attached to the front of the lens. The exceptions are for lenses with large front elements such as powerful telephotos and fish-eyes (the former have a filter slot towards the rear and the latter often have a dial to set internal filters). Filters that fit the front of the lens may be either the

traditional rim-mounted circular types, which screw into a thread at the front element, or rectangular ones which fit into a holder or bellows hood. If a lens outfit consists of several different lens diameters, circular versions must be purchased for each individual size or stepping rings used which may cause cut-off at the corners.

Filter holder systems are more versatile because they allow the position of the filter to be adjusted in relation to the lens. They also fit different lens diameters so they can work out cheaper. A hood can be clipped on the front of the holder to shade the front surface of the filter from flare. With the increased depth of the holder, it is important to ensure that image cut-off doesn't occur with wider angle lenses.

FILTERS FOR BLACK AND WHITE

There are many filter colours intended only for use with black and white films. Much to the confusion of beginners, they are more brightly coloured than filters for use with colour film. This is because strong colours have distinct effects on how the black and white film records different hues of the original scene in terms of different greys on the print. A deep red filter which would ruin a colour picture has the effect of making all the red shades in a scene look very light in a black and white print, and all the blue shades much darker than normal. If you were to photograph a red balloon against a blue sky, the red filter would show a white balloon on dark grey. Without a filter, black and white film would show a grey balloon on a pale sky.

The basic rule to remember is that a filter of a certain colour lightens that colour's tone in the final print, and renders other colours in darker tones. This is why a yellow filter is popular for landscapes – it darkens the blue of the sky by just the right amount, creating contrast with white clouds, but does not alter many of the other tones in the picture. Orange has a stronger effect but results can look slightly artificial, and red makes it stronger still, with very high contrast. Blue is rarely used in monochrome except to add a little depth to lips and skin in portraits taken by tungsten light. Green can improve outdoor portraits and landscapes. Neutral grey graduated filters are useful for landscapes as the denser upper part of the filter helps to reduce contrast in a scene where a bright sky is included in the composition.

Original scene in colour

Normal black and white shot

Black and white with filter

+ 2x
Yellow

+ 4x
Orange

+ 8x
Red

All filters absorb a portion of the light passing through them. Filter factors marked '2x', '4x' mean 'two times' and 'four times', and indicate what additional exposure is required to compensate. A filter rated at 2x requires twice the normal unfiltered exposure, or plus one stop to be added to the exposure; a 4x filter needs two stops extra, an 8x three stops, and so on.

Though TTL metering takes filters into account when they're fitted to the lens, this method isn't always accurate, as the meter sensor may be fooled by strong colours. A better solution, if time permits, is to take an exposure reading without the filter attached, then recalculate the exposure with the filter factor.

FILTER TYPES

FILTERS FOR ALL FILMS

Some filters are useful with black and white, colour negative and colour slide films alike. The UV/Haze filter and Polarizer are almost essential in a well-planned SLR outfit, but Neutral Density filters are rarely needed. They are most often found as part of a mirror lens kit, to change the working aperture of the lens, which has no other form of aperture control.

UV/Haze A plain ultra-violet filter is colourless, and equally useful for black and white. It protects the lens, often fitted permanently, and eliminates a bluish haze in very distant views sometimes caused by excess UV light. It's essential for sea views and at high altitudes. Black and white film records this haze as loss of detail and overexposure in the distant view.

Polarizer Polarizing filters do not affect colour, but allow light vibrating in one plane only to pass through – ordinary light moves in all directions. A rotating mount lets you turn the filter until the

best position is reached to cut down the polarized-light component you want to eliminate. Polarized light in normal scenes includes most reflections, surface sheen on rocks and leaves, and a high proportion of sky-light on a clear day. This filter allows the view through a window to be seen without reflections even if the camera is at angle to the glass, and reduces the reflections off other shiny surfaces such as backlit water or polished wood. It can also deepen the blue of a clear sky covering a broad zone roughly at right-angles to the sun, and generally removes glare from surfaces, boosting colour saturation as a result.

Neutral density (ND) filters also do not affect image colour, but simply reduce the amount of light being transmitted. They come in a range of strengths; ND 0.3 or 2x requires an increase in exposure of 1 stop, ND 0.6 or 4x requires 2 stops increase and so on. They are used when the available light is too bright, to use a wide aperture, or to extend the shutter opening time to create a particular effect.

CUTTING THROUGH REFLECTIONS
A polarizing filter can eliminate specular reflection, the kind seen on both the paintwork and windshield of the car in the left-hand shot. With the filter fitted, right, the paint is brighter and you can see the driver.

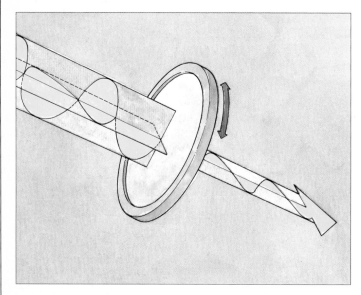

HOW A POLARIZER WORKS
Light entering the filter (from the left, above) vibrates in many directions. The filter is like a picket fence; if you pass a skipping-rope through the fence, you can make up-and-down waves in it, but not side-to-side waves. Rotating the filter selects the direction of vibration it lets through.

IMPROVING COLOUR SATURATION
The top photograph was taken without a filter on a February day. Most people know that a polarizer darkens the sky, but it also brightens the colour of foliage. The bottom picture was taken with a polarizer, and produces a darker sky and greener tree – turning winter into summer.

SHOOTING BY ARTIFICIAL LIGHT
Colour film used in tungsten lighting produces a strong orange cast (left) which cannot be corrected fully during printing. Using an 80A blue filter corrects the result (right) but two stops extra exposure is necessary.

COMPENSATING COLOURS

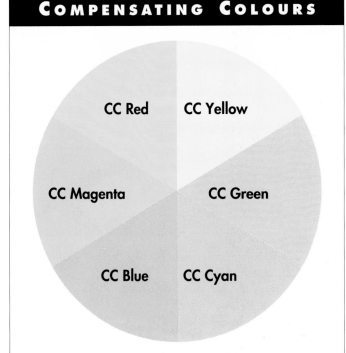

To correct colour casts caused by lighting, you should use a CC *compensating* filter of the colour opposite (complementary) on the wheel above to the colour you want to reduce or remove. Casts can be produced by reflected light. A portrait taken outdoors in the shade of trees, with a green sunlit lawn all round, will normally have a strong green cast. A magenta

CC series filter can correct this. If a room has predominantly blue decoration and carpeting, a light red CC filter can prevent this from spoiling skin tones. CC filters are useful when copying old originals which have faded and show a colour cast, or correcting out-of-date film batches. It takes some experience to judge the strength needed, and you may have to shoot some tests.

FILTERS FOR COLOUR

Filters for colour film have more subtle colours than those used for black and white, and are intended for use with the more accurate (in terms of colour rendition) transparency film. Effects filters can be used with colour negative but there is a danger that any effects you have deliberately introduced may be interpreted as a 'colour cast' by the printer and it will 'correct' the prints, destroying your effect.

SKYLIGHT Unlike UV/Haze, Skylight filters are slightly warm-coloured and need an increase in exposure by around one third of a stop. They are used as permanently-fitted filters, just like UV, and improve colour shots on dull days or when blue skies give 'cold' shadows. Skylight 1A is slightly yellow; Skylight 1B, pinkish and with a stronger effect.

COLOUR COMPENSATION These specialized filters, starting a little stronger than Skylight, are available in various colours to correct minor colour-casts present in slide film or lighting set-ups. The CC filter series includes green, red, yellow, magenta, cyan and blue and strengths are normally given in CC values, the weakest being CC05 which needs around one third of a stop extra exposure. CC filters are very rarely used outside the professional studio or film set; 'compensation' means what it says, making up for failings in film or lighting. Strong CC filters such as CC30M (magenta) can be used for effect or mood pictures. They are never needed for colour negative/print film.

COLOUR CORRECTION Similar to compensation filters, the correction ranges are used to adjust slide film to shooting under various kinds of artificial lighting or at different times of day. They're rarely necessary with print film.
    The internationally recognized

Wratten scale of filters, from the warmest amber to the deepest blue, runs as follows:
    85B, 85, 85C, 81EF, 81D, 81C, 81B, 81A, 81, (neutral), 82, 82A, 82B, 82C, 80D, 80B, 80A.
    The warm-coloured Wratten 81 and 85 series filters are used to reduce colour temperature, making light which is too blue lose its cold cast. In bright mid-day sun, subjects shot on transparency film often have too strong a blue tinge for a Skylight filter to correct; an 81A (pale salmon colour) will do the job.
    The cool or blue Wratten 80 and 82 ranges increase colour temperature, so that a shot taken by evening sun or theatre stage lighting will look neutral instead of having an orange cast.

COLOUR CONVERSION The most powerful filters in the correction range 'convert' from one kind of lighting to another. Films are normally balanced for use in daylight or electronic flash, but you may want to shoot pictures using tungsten photofloods, video lights or domestic lighting. Wratten 80B corrects daylight colour film – slide or negative – for use with photoflood bulbs, Wratten 80A for use with video lights. There are some special slide films made for use under tungsten lights. To use one of these in daylight, a Wratten 85B is necessary.
    A special filter, coded FL-D and called Fluorescent to Daylight, is used to convert daylight film to accurate colours under domestic fluorescent lighting. This filter is a salmon pink colour, but it's only a rough guess on the part of the maker, as tubes vary so much. You can use CC filters to make up 'packs' for different types of tube. A typical daylight tube needs around CC50M and CC50Y together, but some special tubes designed for accurate colours need as little as CC10R. Warm white tubes usually need CC40M + CC40Y, cool white tubes don't need the yellow filter.

SPECIAL-EFFECTS FILTERS

SPECIAL EFFECTS

A wide range of effects filters is available, enabling subtle or garish changes to the original image.

SOFT-FOCUS filters reduce contrast and sharpness by varying degrees, by spreading highlights into shadows. Some filters have their effect at the edges drawing attention to the unaffected subject in the centre of the picture. Diffusion filters blur the image; true soft focus filters only 'spread' the highlights, but cost much more.

GRADUATED FILTERS have a transparent lower half and a coloured or grey upper area, to alter an image partially. A gentle transition from colour to clear areas,

plus the proximity of the filter to the lens, hides the 'join', especially if it is positioned to coincide with the horizon or another suitable division in the composition.

CROSS-SCREEN (or 'starburst') filters have a number of fine lines etched onto the surface, creating localized flare in the image. The parallel lines intersect at 90°, 60° or 45°, creating four, six or eight rays for each point source of light. Rotating the filter alters the angle of the rays. They are often used for street lights at night, or with the sun in the frame.

MULTIPLE-IMAGE PRISM filters create overlapping images of the same subject. Versions producing three or more images are avail-

able, arranging them in clusters with a central image surrounded by others, or in parallel layouts. Best used with strong, graphic subjects against plain or dark backdrops. Prisms which are very thick do not create multiple images, but give strong colour fringing and abstract distortions.

DIFFRACTION FILTERS can produce effects similar to starburst or cross-screen, but with patterns of spectrum-coloured light instead of simple stars of white flare. Some will also create streaked or multiple images, often with rainbow colours and some softening of focus. They are expensive because they use holographically recorded patterns of very fine lines moulded on a plastic sheet.

SPLIT-FIELD FILTERS Not filters, but a form of lens, these consist of a powerful close-up lens cut in half to occupy only half the frame. This enables a very close subject to be sharply rendered in the bottom of the picture, with other subjects at normal distances in the top. Careful composition is essential to position the 'join' over a blank area of sky, horizon or straight line in a building, and you must use a fairly wide aperture to keep this join soft. Unfortunately, close-up lenses (whether cut in half or not) give their best results at very *small* apertures.

There are many other kinds of special effect filters and attachments – too many to list, as new types are designed frequently.

NIGHT SPARKLE
A starburst filter livens up a night-time city view

SOFTER SKIN
Portraits can be improved by using a soft-focus filter

FILTERS ON FLASH
Filters to colour the light from flashguns do not have to be optically perfect – moulded plastic is often used for clip-on types – or cheap theatre spotlight 'gels' can be cut up and taped to your flashgun. Using different colours on two or more flash units, or mixing coloured flash with existing light, can produce some exciting results.

ACCESSORIES

CAMERA systems may include many accessories which increase the versatility of your camera. If you want to go beyond taking straightforward snaps, you need to make sure that the camera you buy is designed to work with these various items.

CLOSE-UP EQUIPMENT

Several accessories are made to enable cameras to focus closer than normal – some extend the focusing range a little way beyond the shortest distance marked on the scale, while others let you take pictures so close that the image on the film is larger than the subject itself.

REVERSING RING An inexpensive, thin adaptor ring screwed into the filter thread of the 50mm lens can enable it to be reverse-mounted on the camera. The lens is then capable of focusing on closer subjects than when it is 'normally' mounted, reducing the minimum distance from 60cm to about 12cm. Metering is possible in manual and aperture-priority (stop down) modes only.

EXTENSION TUBES Different lengths of tube are placed between the lens and camera body, increasing the lens to film distance. Automatic types use the same mount linkages as the lens retaining aperture and metering functions. No optical elements are incorporated, so lens definition is unchanged, but stopping down the aperture is recommended for optimum performance. Extension tubes for use with 35mm cameras often come in a set of three units of increasing length – these can be used individually or in combination, giving magnifications up to 1:1 or life-size.

BELLOWS Extending bellows also fit between the lens and camera body, but they are more versatile than extension tubes because the magnification range may be con-

ACCESSORIES FOR CLOSE FOCUSING
There are ways of making an SLR focus closer than the eighteen inches or so provided by standard lenses. Extension tubes and bellows (foreground) give progressively higher magnifications. A self-contained slide copier, centre, consists of a tube with a lens in the centre and a slide holder at the end, and is a painless solution to one particular close-up problem. A microscope adaptor, rear left, fits your SLR to any standard microscope.

tinuously adjusted. Again linkages are maintained in auto versions, though metering should be done at the lens working aperture. They can give greater magnification than extension tubes, especially when used with a true macro lens, but the greater bulk and increased light loss also mean that a tripod is necessary for sharp pictures when bellows are attached to the camera.

CLOSE-UP LENSES Simple convex lenses, in a range of focal lengths, can be attached to the front of the camera's lens via the filter thread. Calibration is in dioptres, or light-bending power – a +1 dioptre lens has a focal length of 1 metre, while a stronger +4 version is rated at 0.25 metre. A combination of two +1 dioptre lenses gives a focal length of 0.5 metre. These lenses are easy to use because the camera's TTL metering is unaffected and the lens focusing ring operates normally. The distance scale, however, becomes inaccurate. These lenses are an inexpensive way of getting close to your subject and they are best used with a standard 50mm or longer focal lengths, and the aperture well stopped down.

COPYING ATTACHMENTS

Various copying devices are available for different subject sizes and distances. For flat artwork, a four-legged stand or adjustable column, similar to that used on an enlarger, can be used in a vertical arrangement with the camera directly above the subject. Certain tripods are also suitable for this.

For high volume· copying of 35mm transparencies, a specialist slide copying unit with its own flash system, such as the Bowens (Bogen) Illumitran, can be used. A cheaper alternative is to use a small tube-like unit containing a simple lens, fitted to an SLR body by a T2 lens-mount adaptor. The slide is held in a slot in front of an opal light-diffusing screen at one end. No focusing is required. 'Zoom' models let you crop the slide up to 2x magnification, with the slide carrier allowing movement to select the area enlarged.

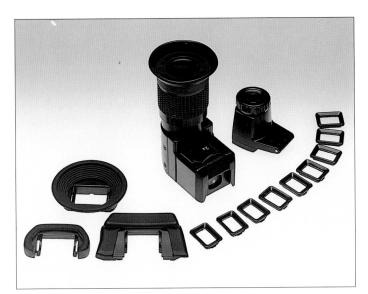

A CLEARER VIEW
SLRs have an accessory slot or thread for fitting magnifiers, eyecups, right-angle viewfinders and eyesight correction lenses to the viewfinder eyepiece. This Minolta range includes (from the left) three eyecups; a periscope type rotating angle finder for using the camera close to the ground or on a vertical copy-stand; a 2x flip-up magnifier for critical focusing; and a set of eyesight corrector lenses in clip-in frames.

INTERCHANGEABLE CAMERA BACKS
Many 35mm SLRs, like this Contax, accept replacement camera backs which either imprint data or add special control functions to the camera.

DECK OF CARDS
Minolta's Dynax 7xi camera, left, showing the hinged 'palm door' which opens to allow cards to be slotted in, together with a selection of expansion cards and special holders to protect them.

CAMERA BACKS

Interchangeable backs enable a photographer to switch film type readily and without wastage, even mid-roll. A colour and a monochrome shot of the same subject can be taken in rapid succession, or a Polaroid taken to check lighting and composition, without needing several cameras. Extra backs can also be pre-loaded and rapidly fitted once a film has been completed. This saves time – it is much faster than rewinding a partially or fully exposed roll. Film backs have a sheath or blind to keep them light tight when not on a camera and this is removed before exposures are made.

Currently only one 35mm SLR has rapidly interchangeable film backs – the Rolleiflex 3003. This camera has the modular design often used for larger roll-film cameras rather than 35mm cameras. Interchangeable camera backs for medium-format models accept regular length film (120), double length (220), bulk versions, 35mm and panoramic formats, plus Polaroid backs.

The ability to change a camera's back adds to the complication of its design and this raises the cost of the camera substantially. Users of 35mm cameras may find it cheaper to buy additional camera bodies.

DATA BACK System 35mm SLRs allow the conventional hinged film back to be replaced by a similar unit incorporating a data imprint device. A miniature light source prints pre-set details such as the date, time, exposure data or a message onto a corner of the frame.

CONTROL BACK Version of the data back with additional functions often incorporating a timer (*intervalometer*) which fires the shutter at pre-programmed intervals, so a sequence of time-lapse pictures can be taken every hour, for example. Other backs add functions like auto-bracketing exposures or extra program modes.

REMOTE CONTROL

A standard feature of a number of small compacts, this small unit enables the camera to be remotely fired from a distance, typically 15 feet. One 'party-goers' model is fired by clapping your hands or shouting.

More sophisticated and expensive systems are available to fire SLRs placed in dangerous or inaccessible places. A transmitter unit can send a pulse (either infrared, ultrasonic or radio) to a receiver mounted on the camera, and the shutter is either tripped directly in the case of electronic shutters, or using a solenoid trigger if a mechanical release is involved.

EXPANSION CARDS

Minolta Dynax SLRs feature a unique system of programming the camera, by inserting a small 'card' into a slot. Each 'card' contains electronic exposure instructions for the camera's central processing unit, increasing the range of effects which can be achieved using pre-programmed settings. Minolta has devised a host of modes and creative options, and a further advantage is that the system can be expanded infinitely.

BAR-CODE READER

A small light pen reads a series of bar codes corresponding to various picture types, and inputs the data into a receptor on the camera body. A programmed exposure can then be taken. It's currently unique to Canon cameras, though other SLR makers may follow.

TRIPODS AND SUPPORTS

MOUNTING your camera securely on a tripod enables you to take shake-free pictures at all shutter speeds. Camera shake takes the edge off the sharpness of hand-held pictures even when exposures are made at exposures between 1/60 and 1/250 of a second. The camera shake warning on most automatic cameras only comes into operation when unsharp pictures are a certainty so, if you don't use some form of camera support, your pictures may still suffer from camera shake, even when the camera implies that you can hand-hold.

A tripod allows you to set a small aperture for increased depth of field in a landscape scene, even in poor light. The blur of subjects in motion can be recorded against a sharp backdrop, and indoor and night scenes easily handled.

If you mount your camera on a tripod when photographing portraits, you no longer have to remain behind the camera and you can make your sitter feel more at ease. Good portraits can be taken using available light from windows using shutter speeds of 1/8 or 1/4 of a second, a short time for the sitter but not for a photographer hand-holding the camera.

A tripod enables you to keep the subject accurately framed for several shots with different exposure or lighting when shooting close-ups and still-lifes. The closer you get, the greater the need for a tripod; macro photographs, where the subject is life-size on the film, are almost impossible without one.

With a tripod you can use long telephoto lenses that are difficult to hold steady, and magnify camera shake. Many tele and zoom lenses have a separate tripod bush at their point of balance, when fitted to an average SLR body. Always use this bush rather than that on the camera, as the weight of the lens will strain the lens-mount. Fit the lens to the tripod, then mount the camera on the lens, and don't carry the whole assembly by the camera strap!

CHOOSING A TRIPOD

You should put as much care into choosing your tripod as you would into any other major photographic purchase. It's no use buying a model which is so big and heavy that it'll never see the light of day after the first back-breaking trip, and a tripod that is too flimsy to support a camera firmly is equally worthless. The right tripod will be light enough to carry all day if you want to, but rigid enough to cut any vibration caused by gusts of wind.

The legs should open out to form a wide base, with around a 45° angle at the top. All tripods have telescopic extending legs, but some have one or two sections, others up to five.

A good compromise is a three-section leg, with an extending centre column. This can be geared with a small 'wind-up handle' for very precise adjustment; it is best if the tripod reaches eye-level with only an inch or two of the column extended.

Check that the leg section locks – levers, screw knobs or rings – are sturdy and easy to use even in the cold or with gloves on. Fully erect the tripod, and look for play in the joints when you apply pressure to the platform from above. Worthwhile features to look out for are cross-braces between the base of the central column and each leg.

Don't forget feet – those fitted to a tripod are crucial. Inexpensive models tend to wear fixed rubber boots, which protect the leg's end and give reasonable grip.

Better models combine a ground-spike with a rubber pad for

HARD-WORKING ENGINEERING
A tripod and its head should be solid, functional and firm like this Italian Manfrotto heavy-duty design.

indoor use, either by reversing the foot or screwing the rubber pad down to conceal the sharp spike. Some special tripods for landscape and natural history use, like the Benbo, have the widest telescope section at the bottom of the leg, sealed in a U-shape so that the tripod can stand in water.

Most tripods have a fixed 'pan and tilt' camera head which allows horizontal rotation (panning), vertical tilt and, on all but the most basic models, a third axis to switch between vertical and horizontal compositions with the camera level.

A removable head can be an advantage. On some models, the head can be taken off and fixed underneath the apex of the tripod, on the bottom end of the centre column, to suspend the camera close to the ground. A ball and socket head gives more freedom in positioning the camera and takes up less space when travelling, but the best of these costs more than complete tripods.

Look out for quick-release mechanisms, to unclamp the camera rapidly or switch between different camera bodies, so you can quickly lock and unlock two or more SLRs using different film or lenses to shoot the same subject.

GOOD DESIGN POINTS

A good amateur tripod should have a high proportion of the following desirable features, if not all of them:
● Individually adjustable legs with locking at any angle, to cope with uneven ground or staircases
● Built-in spirit levels both at the apex (shoulder) and on the pan and tilt head itself
● Scales marked on the pan head for panoramas, and on the tilt movement to allow you to repeat settings precisely
● Additional screw threads to attach the removable head to the bottom of the centre column or near the base of a leg (a good example of a design like this is the Slik 88G)
● A tilting centre column (see below) to position the camera near the ground or above artwork for copying
● Locking clamps and fittings which don't stick out when the tripod is folded up – the best designs collapse with all the sharp or vulnerable parts safely aiming inwards
● Eye-level height without using the centre column – even better if eye-level height is managed with just two of the

FEATURE SPOTTING
This Susis tripod design has triangular legs so the clamps don't stick out, lockable leg-brace struts, feet which switch from spike to rubber pad, a centre column, and a compact single control for the pan and tilt head.

three leg sections extended
● A wide range of possible camera heights and lockable leg splay angles
● Shoulder strap lugs, a fitted strap, or a carrying case
● Dual-purpose feet with ground spikes normally covered by rubber pads, until these are screwed back or reversed for outdoor use

BUILT-IN WADERS
The Benbo tripod design has upside-down telescopic legs, fattest section at the bottom, so that it can be sealed against water. A large Benbo tripod can be used in water so deep that you need fishing waders to operate the camera. This is the smaller amateur 'Trekker' model.

CLOSE APPROACH
This lightweight Velbon tripod – a typical Japanese design which has been made for many years – has a centre column with a rack mechanism and adjustable tilt, so that the entire camera head can be suspended close to the ground for macro shots, and carefully adjusted using the geared column movement.

ALTERNATIVE SUPPORT

Between hand-holding and tripods are a range of other possibilities to avoid camera shake. The closest relation to our three-legged friend is the monopod – a telescopic tube like a single tripod leg. Providing steady downward pressure is applied, exposures of up to 1/8 sec or even 1/4 of a second can be made. Monopods are ideal for supporting high-power telephoto lenses and let you swing the camera round freely to follow action.

Pistol grips, with a trigger operated cable release, are best with motor-driven cameras and longer lenses where your other hand can support the front of the lens. Some pistol grips are extended to form a rifle-style shoulder stock.

Chest-pods, chains which you place under one foot and pull taut, bean-bags which you can rest on a wall, auto-pods with a sucker to stick to a partly-opened car window, ground spikes and even tree screws (outlawed by natural history photographers) are all sold as alternatives.

Pocketable universal camera supports combine a G-clamp with a miniature tripod and pistol grip. One can be slipped into a camera bag, and will hold a camera securely to a door, table, or railings when a flat surface at the right height is not available.

POCKETABLE STABILITY
The small group of camera supports above, with a veteran monopod in the foreground still fine after years of service, is a selection of the clever designs for camera-bag tripod alternatives. The Minolta tripod in the centre costs as much as some full-size models; the camera clamps, despite their token tripod legs, work best when firmly clamped to a solid object. The tubular type on the left doubles as a pistol-grip.

SHUTTER RELEASES AND CABLES
The black fabric cable (upper left of picture below) is a normal mechanical design; the brown tube with a black squeeze-bulb is a silent pneumatic release. In front is a Minolta electric cable release for autofocus SLRs.

TRIPOD DOS AND DON'TS

●The lower the tripod, the greater its stability. Tripods at their maximum height are more prone to shake.

●Choose a firm platform for the tripod – avoid soft ground, sand and polished surfaces where possible.

●When using a tripods' leg extensions, use the thickest sections first, then the thinner ones if more height is required. Resort to the centre column only when the full leg extensions have been used.

●On uneven ground, use the leg extensions to get the camera level first. This is a better method of working than using the pan and tilt head, as it still leaves you the full range of head adjustment.

●Keep the tripod head above the centre of the triangle formed by the feet – the centre of gravity. On a slope or stairs, place one tripod leg directly under the platform.

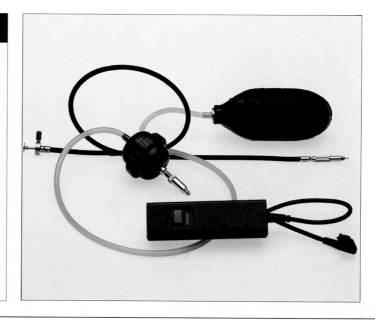

SMOOTH RELEASES

Even when a camera is tripod mounted, it can still suffer from vibration if you press the shutter release directly. A flexible cable release avoids this problem. It screws into a tapered socket in the shutter button or on the camera body; a plunger like a hypodermic syringe at one end pushes a pin out of the other to trigger the camera's shutter. Mechanical cable releases range from a few inches to around two feet.

Pneumatic releases use a rubber squeeze-bulb and flexible tubing to do the same thing, over a distance of ten to twenty-five feet. Modern cameras often have an electrical release socket which allows any length of electric release or a choice of wireless remote triggers. The lowest-cost models are ultrasonic. Infrared triggers work from greater distances but obstructions may cut them off; radio remote releases work even through walls, but are not permitted in some areas.

Delayed action 'self-timers' are popular because you can put the camera on a tripod and join the group you are photographing. The camera won't fire for about 10 or 12 seconds. The self-timer is also a good substitute for a cable release if the subject is static. Compose the shot on the tripod, set the timer, press the shutter and wait. By the time the shutter fires, any trace of vibration from touching the camera will have died down.

If you use the self-timer, light entering the viewfinder eyepiece of an SLR camera may influence auto exposure metering. When your eye is up to the camera the effect is negligible, but if the camera is aimed downwards on a tripod with the sky above, with your eye away from the finder using the timer to fire the shutter, this stray light may cause serious under-exposure. Shade the eyepiece with your hand if the camera has no built-in eyepiece shutter (or supplied eyepiece cap).

REWARDS OF PATIENCE

A good tripod opens up new worlds by freeing you from the constraints of light. Time exposures, ranging from the slow speeds on your camera between 1/15 and 1 second or more to several hours on 'B', record changing light and the movement of the subject to create a uniquely photographic image. If you are prepared to seek out your subjects, wait for the light, and compose your shots carefully you can achieve results like this. This photograph was taken using a Hasselblad 6 x 6cm SLR on a heavy Gitzo Studex tripod, using Ilford black and white film, carefully printed on fibre-based Agfa paper. In case you think results like this are only obtained by professionals or college-trained fine artists, the photographer is a retired dentist whose hobby is to make first-quality prints for exhibitions and competitions.

BAGS AND CASES

WHETHER your photographic outfit consists of just one camera or a large collection of camera bodies, lenses and accessories, some method of carrying your equipment is essential. A bag or case fulfils at least three important functions:

- It keeps an outfit together and makes it more easily portable
- It provides protection from the elements, such as heat, rain, snow, grit and dust
- It cushions equipment from the inevitable knocks and shocks

WHICH TYPE AND SIZE?

The type and size of bag you choose will depend upon: the size of your current system (bearing in mind any additions which may be made in the future); whether you prefer a soft or a hard outer material; and how much you can afford.

Clearly, it would be unwise to buy a bag which fits the camera kit you own now without an inch to spare. An equally foolish purchase is an oversize bag with your equipment rattling around in the bottom. The ideal solution is somewhere between the two, to allow for future expansion. Many photographers own more than one bag, using one for a small, portable outfit and a second larger bag to transport their complete kit.

Prices vary from minimal for a basic small outfit bag to greater than some cameras for a large, high quality holdall. The former offers little protection, but may be adequate for the occasional photographer with just a handful of items. The extra expense may be justified if you own an extensive range of valuable equipment – each item can be stored in its own compartment thus greatly reducing the possibility of it being damaged.

When selecting a bag for your own needs, you must carefully weigh cost against quality. Extra

A RANGE OF CASES
Hard alloy, rigid fabric-covered plastic, real canvas, Cordura shoulder bags and pouches – many options.

money spent on a stronger bag is rarely wasted – its greater durability may work out less expensive in the long term.

OPTIONS

EVER-READY CASE For those who prefer to travel light with a compact, or an SLR with just one lens, the ever-ready case (ERC) is ideal. Such cases may be supplied as standard with some compacts, or are available separately as an accessory. By undoing a couple of clips or a Velcro fastener, the camera is available for picture-taking. Ever-ready cases are usually designed to fit a specific camera body but there may be flexibility in the lens choice if the case has a specially extended 'nose'.

SLR versions are traditionally made of vinyl and comprise two pieces – the lower portion fits snugly onto the camera base and is held in position by a screw inserted into the tripod bush,

while the top section covers the lens and camera top-plate. Camera cases where the front can be detached are better; they avoid the possibility of it inadvertently appearing in your photographs.

ADVANTAGES
- compact
- portable
- low cost

DISADVANTAGES
- uses limited – any other equipment must be carried separately
- ERC must be removed to load fresh film into camera

SOFT LENS POUCH Produced in various sizes, individual pouches provide padded protection for individual lenses, with a draw-string or Velcro flap to keep the item secure inside. Use them inside other bags for extra protection.

ADVANTAGES
- Small and portable
- Good adjunct to ERC
- Fits neatly around lens

DISADVANTAGES
- Two or more can be awkward to carry
- Outfit not kept together

SOFT BAG These popular bags are available in a vast range of styles and sizes. Smaller versions have a main compartment which is large enough to accommodate an SLR with a standard lens together with an additional lens or a flashgun, and further storage pockets for smaller accessories, filters or film. Larger soft bags not only have larger compartments, but also have more compartments and pockets available so it may be easier to organize your kit. Special features to look out for include: detachable pockets, tripod straps, a carrying handle and a padded shoulder strap for extra comfort.

Exterior materials used for soft bags are: vinyl; proofed nylon weave; canvas; or Cordura. Better quality bags have an exterior covering comprising two layers of fab-

A Practical Jacket
On a bike, on horseback, walking or climbing – a photographer's vest

ric with a shock absorbing layer sandwiched between them. This gives extra protection and it also helps the bag to retain its shape over a long period. A darker exterior colour will show fewer signs of wear and tear, and will attract less attention.

Internal dividers are fabric-covered cardboard on cheaper bags, or rigid foam on better quality makes. Velcro fasteners on the edges of each panel permit an infinite number of internal arrangements to be set.

Look for a bag with good all-round protection. The base should be generously padded with a rigid insert to cushion equipment from shocks. It should also have a raised durable (usually metal) foot at each corner to keep the bag clear of dirt and damp. The main compartment and other pockets should be covered by flaps which prevent rain getting in and small items falling out. Exposed zips can leak, so avoid them.

Shoulder straps warrant close attention. The width should be at least two inches – any narrower and the strap will cut into your shoulder when the bag is full – preferably with a non-slip shoulder pad, although these can be purchased separately.

It is far more secure to have a continuous strap which travels under the bag rather one that is attached to the sides. There should be reinforcing stitching on the bag sides. Check other stitching at the seams to ensure the bag has been well made, and make sure all zips are free running.

Advantages
- Huge choice available
- Comfortable to carry
- Permits shots 'on the run'
- Interior panels flexible

Disadvantages
- Stored equipment needs separating panels
- Smaller items can be 'lost'
- A large bag can be very heavy when full

Hard, Shaped Bag Rigid shoulder bag are less popular than soft bags. They are usually made of canvas, leather, or vinyl, and reinforced by heavy duty cardboard. Their outer shape is fixed so these bags, unlike their softer counterparts, take up the same space regardless of whether they are empty or full. This is not the case with their interiors which can be freely rearranged using adjustable, padded dividers.

A hard bag gives excellent protection (some have a watertight seal around the rim), and smaller items can be easily located. Further security is provided by a lock clamping the lid to the main body of the case. These bags, however, are quite bulky and hard-edged, so they're less comfortable whilst being carried on the shoulder.

Advantages
- Good level of protection
- Items can be securely stored in separate compartments
- Easy accessibility
- Lockable

Disadvantages
- Quite expensive
- Bulkier than soft bag of same capacity
- Compartment sizes may not fit your gear

Alloy case Alloy cases tend to be either large and brief case-shaped or even larger and box-shaped. Both types usually have a pair of locks, a carrying handle on the lid, and strap eyelets on the sides to accept a shoulder strap. The case's corners are reinforced to prevent damage and crushing. The most expensive cases have a watertight gasket seal around the rim. Silver and black finishes are available, the latter being less eye-catching to the potential thief.

The interior may have slot-in padded dividers which can be moved around to fit your equipment, or a dense foam block which can be cut to suit. Some foam blocks are pre-scored. Alloy cases are so tough and durable you can stand or sit on them if necessary, especially if they have an inner shell of strong plywood.

An alternative to the alloy case is the injection-moulded high density plastic airline transit case, with a gasket sealed rim and pressure valve. Kinetics, Pelican and Andiamo cases of this kind will all protect equipment against immersion in open sea and heavy transit handling. In all other respects they are similar to alloy cases.

Advantages
- High standard of protection
- Foam insert can be custom tailored
- May be used as seat or step

Disadvantages
- Heavy and bulky
- Briefcase-type has to be placed on horizontal surface before opening
- May be obtrusive

Photo vest A sleeveless jacket with plenty of pockets and pouches enables you to carry your outfit the same way a fisherman does. The pockets are zipped or have Velcro fasteners, to provide virtually instant access. Protective padding is limited to the main pockets, and both the camera kit and wearer may be injured by a fall. The individual compartments mean that equipment is protected from it neighbours. A photo vest does have the advantage of allowing the photographer to remain relatively unencumbered while carrying a comprehensive kit.

As an alternative, try belt-bags or 'fanny packs' in conjunction with a couple of smaller soft bags – slinging equipment on both shoulders and at your waist to distribute the weight.

Advantages
- Quick access to items
- Lots of smaller pockets for accessories and film
- Good for action if not too heavily laden

Disadvantages
- Expensive
- Limited capacity

BUILDING AN SLR SYSTEM

COMPACT cameras are self-contained. The SLR camera, in contrast, is only a part of a system together with lenses and other accessories. Putting together a well-balanced outfit can be a daunting process with many considerations to take into account.

SCOPE VERSUS COST

Would you rather allocate your entire budget to a multi-function SLR with just one lens – or would it be better to spend less on a simple camera with an extra lens and, perhaps, a flashgun? Much depends on whether you want to keep on adding to your outfit.

It you have a clear idea of where your photographic interests lie the range of possibilities should be simplified. If close-ups of flowers and insects are your interest, then a macro lens and sturdy tripod will be high priorities. If your interest centres on action subjects, such as racing cars or athletics, an outfit built around a fast motor-drive SLR and a powerful telephoto would be a good starting point. Portraits are best shot with a short or medium-power telephoto, and a wide-angle is a versatile lens which has its uses in most fields of photography. Most people, however, want to tackle a cross-section of subjects, in which case a reasonably versatile SLR plus a zoom or two would be a good choice.

NEW OR USED?

If new equipment is beyond your scope, look for second-hand bargains. Local papers, photo magazines and camera dealers are all sources of individual items or complete outfits. The risk with used equipment is that you don't know whether it has been carefully treated or abused, though close inspection usually reveals all.

With new boxed equipment there are fewer risks and in the unlikely event that the equipment does turn out to be faulty it will be

INSIDE THE EDITOR'S CAMERA BAG

A good way to see a balanced outfit is to look at a real kit which has been built up over a few years by someone you know. The editor of The Complete Book of Photography was packing a Tenba shoulder-bag ready for a photographic trip. Here's what it contained: two well-used Minolta 9000 bodies, without auto-winders or motor-drives, to keep the outfit light when travelling. A 50mm ƒ2.8 macro lens instead of a standard 50mm, to provide extra close focusing; a 24mm ƒ2.8 wide-angle; a 75-300mm ƒ5.6 long tele zoom; a high quality 7-element Teleplus 2x tele-converter which turns this into a 150-600mm ƒ11 combination for dramatic sunsets and occasional tripod-mounted long tele shots; one powerful Minolta 4000AF flashgun, bulky but capable of tackling any subject; a 20mm ultra-wide angle ('I would prefer a 17mm with the 24mm, but there isn't one available'); Minolta polarizing filters and close-up lenses, a stack of assorted other filters screwed together to save space, an electric cable release, table-top tripod, lens brush, foil pouched camera wipes, spare batteries. Not included in the bag, a Benbo Trekker tripod.

TWO REAL OUTFITS

The system above was taken straight off a dealer's second-hand shelf, with a case and low cost tele-zoom in addition to the Olympus OM-10 body, 28mm, 50mm and 35-70mm Olympus lenses and flash, for the same price as the lowest-cost AF SLR in the shop. The kit below is an extreme – an expensive pro Nikon F4 body, 35-70mm AF zoom, highly specialized 16mm fish-eye and very fast 135mm ƒ2 soft focus portrait lens. The cost of this outfit, new, would be ten times the kit above.

MIXING OR MATCHING?

If you buy a complete kit from one maker, with lenses from the same factory as the camera body, you don't just satisfy vanity. Though all modern lenses are good, each makers uses different types of glass and lens coating. The colour balance and contrast of a Tamron lens will be a close match for another Tamron, but won't be exactly the same as a Sigma or Minolta lens. Some budget kits are sold with a pair of independent lenses and a top-make body. This is fine, as the lenses are usually from the same maker. You can build a whole outfit using nothing but Sigma lenses, for example. If you mix your lens makes, the results may vary. It is not so important to stick to your camera maker's own flashgun. Good fully dedicated independent brand flashguns work well, and have no effect on picture quality.

covered by consumer rights legislation or warranties. It's possible to shop around for the best deals on any item, but don't expect your neighbourhood dealer to be too pleased if you ask the benefit of his advice and then buy cheaper elsewhere. The lowest price may mean the worst service.

VALUE FOR MONEY

A good SLR system can be built for a modest total by selecting inexpensive items at every level. Even the cheapest SLR is capable of excellent pictures. The budget independent lens manufacturers sell wide-angles and zooms which cost a fraction of major camera manufacturer's counterparts and, though not built to the same exacting standards, provide optical quality which isn't that inferior. Independents are often cheaper for accessories like flashguns, camera bags, filters and so on.

MIDDLE GROUND

Equipment prices can represent excellent value because this is the most competitive part of the market – pricing is especially keen among the rival makers, to the benefit of buyers. A mid-range SLR coupled to top-grade lenses offers premium value and excellent reliability. Later, a higher specification camera body can replace the original item, yet still accept the same lenses.

QUALITY CONSCIOUS

By purchasing expensive equipment all from the same camera system you are certain of the highest standards of construction, performance and compatibility. Most manufacturers have at least one top-performance SLR body, with an extensive range of dedicated lenses and accessories, so you need not stray from the system when putting an outfit together, but the total cost may be more than you expect.

LENS OPTIONS

ZOOM OR PRIME Zooms offer fine value as they are more versatile, often handling the same tasks as two, three or more fixed focal length lenses. For general photography zooms are the best bet. They are, however, a compromise so, if your shots are only usually taken at a single focal length, you may get better quality for a lower price from a fixed focal length lens. For instance, a standard 50mm lens would be better than a 35-70mm zoom if many pictures are to be taken in low light conditions without flash because the 50mm has a faster maximum aperture. The fast maximum aperture would mean a brighter screen for easier focusing and faster shutter speeds can also be used to reduce camera shake. On the other hand, the short zoom provides a choice of subject magnifications, without changing viewpoint.

FOCAL LENGTHS When an outfit consists of two or more lenses, adequate spacing of focal lengths is important. If a 50mm standard has been supplied with your 35mm SLR, choose extra lenses carefully. A 35mm wide-angle is perhaps too close to the 50mm in terms of angle of view, so a 28mm or 24mm would be a better choice – even more so if you have a 35-70mm zoom instead of a 50mm. If you want to go wider still, a 17mm lens makes a good partner to a 24mm, while a 20mm teams well with a 28mm.

With telephotos, an 80-200mm or 70-210mm zoom is a versatile addition to the 50mm. Longer 75-300mm tele-zooms are also available, though maximum apertures are slightly slower. Mirror lenses, usually 500mm ƒ8 design, offer a powerful telephoto lens of compact proportions. If you need faster maximum apertures, 200mm and 300mm ƒ2.8 apo-tele designs enable fast shutter speeds to be used, but these lenses are very large and heavy as well as expensive.

SPECIAL EQUIPMENT

BESIDES all the 'routine' equipment mentioned in the previous pages there are a number of specialized cameras and optics which could be worth considering for a special assignment, or as light relief from regular equipment.

DISPOSABLES

Fuss-free snapshooting is provided by the inexpensive, disposable camera. Essentially it's an ISO 400 film cassette surrounded by a rudimentary camera body. The only controls are a shutter release and a thumbwheel to advance to the next frame. Focus and exposure are both fixed – the lens aperture of around ƒ11 is fast enough for most situations. A hole in the body acts as a makeshift 'viewfinder'. Once the film is fully exposed, the camera is returned to the d & p outlet where it is dismantled, and the film removed for processing. Some models now boast an integral flash, while others may be used underwater to a depth of 12 feet.

PANORAMIC

Cameras with very wide angles of view which produce narrow horizontal, or panoramic, pictures. Models include cheap and disposable cameras like the Kodak Stretch which, with its fixed focus 25mm ƒ12 lens, fires at a constant 1/100 of a second on ISO 200 film. Panoramic AF compacts include the Minolta Riva Panorama, with a 24mm ƒ4.5 lens. Both these models use a 'stretched' processing service to produce their long thin prints.

The Widelux and Horizon models, using 35mm film, both use a lens which moves in an short arc to cover a 24 x 58mm format. The most expensive panoramic models are the professional roll-film cameras, such as the Linhof Technorama and Fuji G617, which both produce a negative 6 x 17cm (two and a quarter by six and a half inches).

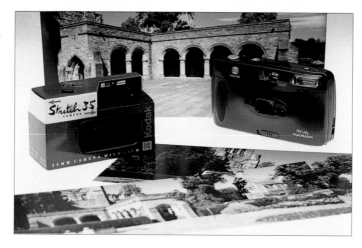

DISPOSABLE AND PANORAMIC CAMERAS
Kodak's Stretch 35 is a disposable panoramic camera making 3.5 x 10" prints as seen here. Minolta's Riva Panorama is a precision version.

INSTANT PRINTS
Polaroid instant cameras are bulky but produce colour prints on the spot.

HIGH-PRICED PRECISION
The Contax T2 is an autofocus compact, but has a titanium body shell and offers effective manual control of exposure and focusing.

INSTANT

Instant pictures are produced on Polaroid's instant film, a refinement of the process invented in 1947 by Edwin Land, the son of a Connecticut scrap metal and salvage dealer. The main drawback to this type of film is its high cost. A wide range of cameras is available, from simple budget models with fixed focus lenses and a basic integral flashgun through to sophisticated autofocus Image models with a high-quality flash unit. Their top-range 'Image' cameras fold for compactness, can accept filters and have an overridable exposure system.

Snapshots with a Polaroid can be fun, but these cameras have more serious uses. They can be used as a visual notebook with countless industrial and record applications.

PRECISION COMPACT

Not all top grade compacts are autofocus zooms. Minox, Leica, Contax and Rollei produce very high precision, palm-sized cameras. Minox are known for their sub-miniature 'spy' cameras, but they also build 35mm models with manual focus and a 35mm lens concealed behind a fold-down flap for compactness. Film advance is by thumbwheel. A scaled-down Minox flashgun is also available.

Contax, with top quality 35mm SLRs, also produce a T2 compact. This camera has a 38mm lens, AF or manual operation, and exposures are programmed or aperture-priority. The T2 has an integral flash, exposure compensation and automated film advance.

Leica's Mini has a German-made Elmar lens and many automated functions in a lightweight package. The Rollei 35 Classic is a modernized version of a 1960s camera – the optical (40mm Sonnar) and engineering quality of this camera are extremely high but it is also the most expensive compact camera in the world.

DURABLE

Cameras with built-in weather protection are increasingly popular. The ability to shrug off rain, snow, sand and bumps is an important feature for outdoor types. Special sealing technology and rugged construction keep the elements at bay, while larger-sized controls give ease of handling, especially for those wearing gloves. Typical compacts are the Yashica T3 Super, and the colourful Pentax PC-606W, both with 35mm lenses. Konica's Off-Road features a 28mm wide-angle.

Nikon's Nikonos camera goes one further, being a fully-fledged underwater model with oversize controls and a choice of six interchangeable optics. It can shoot to a depth of 50 metres, thanks to a series of O-ring barriers, but performs equally well above the water. The Minolta Weathermatic DL has two lens focal lengths and works down to 15m depth.

STILL VIDEO

This medium, still in its infancy, sidesteps conventional silver-based film photography. Instead of using film and chemical processing to create a picture, SV cameras convert optical information into electronic data, and then store them on a small magnetic floppy disk. This absence of the processing step means that pictures can be played back almost instantly, on a monitor or TV set. Hard copies or prints can also be produced via a special printer.

Like video tape, an SV floppy can be re-used if required. In this instance, the disk is wiped clean of information, and previous pictures lost. Many major manufacturers are developing SV cameras and associated hardware, ready for the still video revolution. Some, like Canon and Sony, have already tested the market. The quality of electronic images needs to improve before the medium receives universal acceptance.

RUGGED AND SPLASHPROOF
The Konica Off-Road won't work underwater, but is shockproofed and will stand up to splashes. Its large controls are easy to use with gloves.

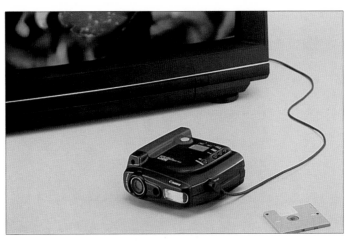

PICTURES ON THE TELEVISION SCREEN
The Canon Ion or Xapshot cameras use computer diskettes to record their images, which are usually played back on your domestic television screen. In-store printing points in major photo shops and hi-fi dealers produce low cost colour prints from the disks, with a choice of lots of small pictures on one print, or a single image filling the frame.

SHIFT LENS

These lenses have been developed to overcome the problem of converging verticals, which occur when a lens is tilted up to include the whole of a tall building. Shift, or PC (perspective control) lenses have the ability to move the lens off-axis by a tilting or shifting motion. By keeping the camera back in a vertical plane, and raising the lens slightly, the sides of a building will remain parallel. Shift lenses are expensive due to their complicated mechanisms and because they require greater covering power (the image circle of acceptable quality) than a normal lens. Some shift lenses also have a pivoting movement, which is useful for controlling depth of field. Most major 35mm SLR lens ranges have one or more shift lenses. PC lenses are also available for medium-format cameras.

SOFT-FOCUS LENS

Simple diffusion can be produced by using filters but more control of unsharpness is offered by special soft-focus lenses, usually of moderate telephoto length. These give a blend of focused and unfocused detail, depending on how many aberrations are permitted to enter the mix. This gives a slight spreading of highlights and some softening of detail. Such lenses are commonly used to create flattering (and characterless) portraits. Examples of soft-focus lenses are the Pentax 85mm $f2.8$ Soft and the Canon EF 135mm $f2.8$ s/f. Each permits a variable degree of softness to be set; the best effects are usually seen when the lens is set from $f2.8$ to $f5.6$.

AN OFF-CENTRE LENS
Perspective control or shift lenses have a mechanism to move the lens upwards so the frame can include a tall building without tilting the camera backwards. A PC lens gives parallel verticals, a tilted lens makes them 'lean back'.

HOME PROCESSING

ALL FILMS, whether monochrome or colour, can be processed and printed at home if you want to have full control over the production of your pictures.

The first step is to process the film using the appropriate series of chemicals at a regulated temperature. For this a light-proof developing tank for one or more films is required, with either a special light-proof bag with elasticated armholes, or a properly blacked-out room to ensure total darkness when the film is being loaded. The cylindrical tank holds a spiral reel with a groove to hold the film surfaces apart so that chemicals can reach all of its surface. Tanks and spirals are made either of plastic or of stainless steel.

A clean hot and cold water supply, plastic or glass storage bottles, measuring cylinders, a funnel and a thermometer are also required for mixing and keeping the chemicals, and preparing them at the correct temperature. A countdown timer is also handy.

Once the development and fixing is completed, you will need running water at a temperature between 60 and 68°F, or enough water for six or seven successive tankfuls, followed by drying in a dust free atmosphere if possible. Drying cabinets are available, but a clothes-line across the room at 6ft height will do fine. Clips with weights in have a dual purpose, one at the top holding the film on the line, one at the bottom keeping it hanging straight. Once dry, films should be cut into strips and stored in transparent files in an album.

THE DARKROOM

The centrepiece of any darkroom, whether a permanent space or temporarily housed in a bathroom or kitchen, should be the enlarger with its paper supplies, paper easel, lenses, focusing aids and timer or colour analyser. All these pieces of equipment occupy the 'dry' side of the darkroom.

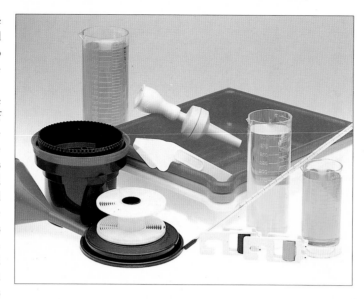

WET BENCH EQUIPMENT
Plastic developing tanks are universally popular because of their ease of loading and use. You also need measuring cylinders, a water filter, funnel, thermometer, and film clips before you process films. For paper processing, three dishes and print tongs are also necessary. All these products are from Paterson.

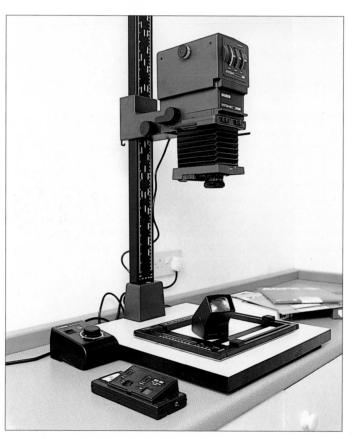

A UNIVERSAL ENLARGER
Kaiser's basic enlarger assembly can be adapted to almost any format, or converted to a copy stand. Here it is assembled for enlarging rollfilm 6 x 7cm format with a 90mm enlarging lens, paper easel, focusing aid, and exposure timer. In the foreground is a Durst DES 100 colour analyzer, and beyond the baseboard, colour and monochrome papers.

A second separate area, or 'wet' side of the darkroom, is where the paper is processed to make the latent image visible. Black and white is normally processed in a set of open trays; colour, in a drum or an enclosed tank. You also need facilities for washing the paper once the processing cycle is completed.

THE ENLARGER

When setting up a darkroom many people make the mistake of buying a high grade enlarger, then adding a cheap enlarging lens almost as an afterthought. This is not a wise decision if you have invested extra money in purchasing superior camera lenses, because the cheap enlarger lens will not be capable of carrying that extra quality to your print. Choose a focal length of 50mm for 35mm negatives, or 80mm for the 6 x 6 format. More expensive lenses feature a wider maximum aperture for improved image brightness and focusing on the baseboard.

When choosing the format of your enlarger it is worth bearing in mind that one which accepts 35mm only is adequate for today's needs but it doesn't allow for future expansion. In addition, enlargers equipped to handle 6 x 6 or 6 x 7cm film as well as 35mm are more sturdily constructed and often have a superior range of features. You can buy one equipped for 35mm only but upgradeable.

Two main types of enlarger illumination can be found – condensor and diffusor. Prints from condensor enlargers are very sharp, popular with monochrome workers, but show dust or scratches. Diffusor-lit images are of lower contrast, but conceal defects and are favoured for colour work. Some makes, such as De Vere, Durst and Fujimoto, offer both. Other aspects of enlarger design to watch for are maximum enlargement size, smooth operating controls, good heat dissipation, and a quality negative carrier assembly.

ANCILLARIES

Contact printing frame Holds negatives in neat rows under a clear sheet of glass, and also has a slot to take a single sheet of printing paper. The film and the paper are held together under slight pressure to produce positive images from negative strips. Contact printing can be done by using a plain sheet of glass but this is more difficult and the image will not be as sharp because the film and the paper are not held as flat. Some transparent negative files can also be 'printed through'.

Masking frame or easel Flat platform to hold printing paper, with adjustable leaves to mask different sizes. Gives a neat white border to exposed prints and keeps the paper perfectly flat.

Focus magnifier Greatly enlarges the image projected on the baseboard. A small mirror reflects light back onto a screen, where a magnifier allows you to check whether accurate focus has been achieved.

Test strip device Produces a range of print densities on a sheet of printing paper, to aid exposure calculations.

Timer Electronic timer can be placed between the enlarger and power supply to give pre-programmed exposure durations as soon as the enlarger is switched on.

Shading & printing-in tools Shading tool used to 'hold back' the light on part of the image that would otherwise appear too dark in the finished print (dodging). Printing-in tool allows more light onto a part of the image that would appear too light (burning in). Experienced darkroom workers use their hands to create the appropriate shapes. This is more versatile but requires a great deal of practice.

Essentials for the Darkroom Bench
Darkroom accessories save time and improve results. In this photograph, from front to back, are an Ilford film-cassette opener (vital!), a Kaiser rotary trimmer for cutting paper, a Paterson 35mm contact-printer, cotton gloves to avoid fingerprints on negatives, a Kaiser focusing negative and texture effect negatives which can be sandwiched with your original shot. On the baseboard are three Photax safelights, fitted with orange (for black and white), deep brown (variable contrast) and dense green (colour paper) safelight filters.

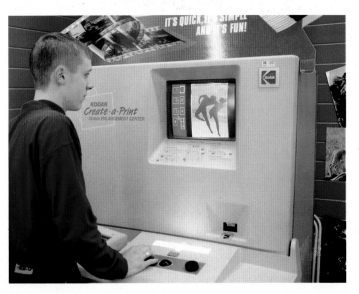

Safelight Monochrome printing papers are unaffected by orange light, so a safelight of this colour may be permanently left switched on. Gives a low level of illumination in a darkroom which won't fog printing paper, but allows the operator to see what he's doing.

THE WET SIDE

Exposed printing paper is carried to this area for processing. Monochrome workers traditionally use a set of three trays for chemicals, though the deep tank design is becoming popular. Here paper is fed into vertical channels containing the solutions, thus saving space and heat loss. In either case a set of tongs stops contamination of the paper.

Colour workers use a processing drum, which must be loaded in darkness, but an increasing number now own automatic bench-top colour processors where the paper is simply fed into a slot and emerges as a finished dry print. This costs about the same as a complete SLR outfit, and may need professional plumbing-in as well as care in maintenance. The latest drum processors, though still loaded in the dark, are fully automatic with programmed chemical changing and step timing.

Custom Printing
People using colour negative materials have another option in the form of one of the many Kodak Create-A-Print machines sited in shopping malls and photo specialists. It accepts 35mm only, with a maximum enlargement of 17x. The image is viewed by the customer on a video monitor, and can be tilted to correct compositional error, and adjusted for colour and cropping, Create-a-Print produces a print in under five minutes. Four print sizes including a panoramic format are available, up to a maximum of 11 x 14".

TECHNIQUES

MODERN equipment is highly efficient, and automation sometimes removes the need to concentrate on technicalities. But no technology is completely foolproof, so obtaining effective pictures still requires craftmanship and a grasp of various photographic techniques. If the word 'technique' puts you off, don't assume that it means 'technical'. Your grasp of technique should cover knowing what materials to use, which lenses to fit, what exposure settings are best for the shot in hand.

This year's SLR model will not make you a better photographer although it will probably reduce the number of bad shots lost through lack of know-how. A lens focused on ten feet and settings of 1/125 at $f8$ produces the same picture on an old manual SLR as it does on the latest autofocus programmed model. What matters is the subject in front of the camera when the picture is taken.

Few people explore the full potential of their existing cameras and lenses, but many keep expanding their systems in the hope that better equipment will mean better pictures. Money is far better spent on film and processing, so that more pictures can be taken and a greater number of techniques tried. Equipment should only be bought to fill an identified need.

This section of the book is all about using the equipment you already have in the best way. It's also about learning various visual skills, and developing a feel for the language of photography.

The opening chapters deal with basic camera handling, metering and focusing techniques – essential to produce sharp, correctly exposed images. Film choice is also important, so the merits of colour negative, colour transparency and monochrome emulsions are discussed, together with aspects such as film format, the relationship between speed and grain, and why films are balanced for different light sources.

We show you how to work in various types of natural lighting; why selecting the right viewpoint is important; how to compose an image to best effect, and how to freeze or blur a moving subject. Find out how to use different kinds of perspective to make images three-dimensional, to manipulate colours and convey different ideas, to show texture and shape.

There's plenty of useful advice on using artificial light creatively, and how to handle the unique tonal characteristics of black and white photography.

We show you in step-by-step detail how to develop your own films, and make prints. These skills give you ultimate control over your pictures. Basic care of your equipment and guidelines on filing or storing photographs, and a little advice on selling pictures as a freelance follow. Finally, everyone makes mistakes, or at least they should when learning – turn yours to advantage by discovering what caused the problem, and making sure they're not repeated.

FILM TYPES AND CHOICE

FILMS can be divided into two main types – colour and black and white – which are available in a range of speed ratings. To choose the right film to load in your camera you need to consider, the nature of lighting available, the camera settings needed for the type of shot being taken, and what kind of finished result is desired.

Most people want a colour photograph – after all, that is the way we perceive the world around us. For everyday snapshots, colour negative film is the preferred solution, as the film is more tolerant to exposure error and prints produced from it are inexpensive, easy to handle and view. Colour transparency film (also called slide and reversal) gives superior colour saturation and is more suitable when quality is paramount. It is used for projection and publishing purposes by professional users, and by scores of discerning amateurs. A smaller band of photographers prefers black and white film for its gritty or graphic characteristics, and because it can be easily processed and printed at home.

There have been considerable advances in film technology in recent years, bringing increasingly fast products and enhanced performance, but the basic structure of photographic film remains unchanged. All types of colour film have three emulsion layers, interleaved with a filter so that each is sensitive to just one colour of light. Black and white films have a single light layer equally sensitive to all colours.

COLOUR NEGATIVE film is very tolerant to exposure error. Faults such as colour casts and film density can be corrected because the production of a positive image is a two-stage process (development of the orange/brown negative, followed by its printing on paper). This makes it easier for pictures to be taken under a wide variety of illumination sources without worry. Any number of duplicate prints can also be made from the original negative at low cost. This type of film is ideally suited to the casual user or snapshooter, as well as applications where a print is the required end product.

COLOUR TRANSPARENCY film produces a positive image in a single stage. It exhibits brighter, cleaner colour, higher contrast and reveals less grain – no print can match the brilliance of a transparency projected onto a screen. Transparency materials are, however, less tolerant to exposure error than negative materials, though many photographers deliberately underexpose their pictures by a third or half one stop to give the image greater colour saturation. The colour of the light source is just as important as light intensity. Most slide films are balanced for daylight, and work well in bright sunlight during the middle hours of the day. Overcast conditions, low light or alternative sources of illumination make filtration necessary to correct colour rendition. Tungsten-balanced transparency films are also available to counteract the need for blue filters.

BLACK AND WHITE film (also termed monochrome) is traditionally silver-based, but has recently been joined by a chromogenic or dye-based emulsion which owes much to colour negative technology – Ilford XP2. This emulsion is developed in regular C41 colour negative chemistry, has terrific tolerance to exposure error and very low grain even at considerable enlargement.

Conventional black and white film has undergone innovations of its own recently, resulting in a crop of films which also challenge the orthodox grain/speed relationship, though not as much as XP2. Monochrome films can be used in any light source without filtration, and remain the quickest material to process and print when speed is of the essence.

INSTANT film is made only by Polaroid – the inventors and patent holders – and Fuji. A variety of colour and monochrome types are available, in print, negative and transparency formats. Each relies on diffusion of the image from one part of the film to another, after the two have been pressed tightly together by rollers. Instant cameras use a single sheet material, whereas many professional films for use in Polaroid backs are of the peel-apart type. 35mm colour and monochrome materials can be used in conventional cameras, but the slide version is of low quality and incapable of sizeable enlargement due to the pattern of lines on the image. With all Polaroid films the ability to view a picture immediately is very valuable to the snapshooter and professional user alike.

INFRARED film is available in colour and monochrome, both with extra sensitivity to invisible wavelengths. It is manufactured by Kodak (35mm only, both colour and monochrome) and Konica (120 and 35mm, monochrome only). Ektachrome film delivers strange colours which bear little relation to reality. Black and white versions must be loaded and unloaded in total darkness. Best results occur when the film is exposed with a visually opaque filter (which lets through the infrared wavelengths), but a deep red filter makes it easier to use. Exposure readings are awkward, as light meters are not suited to infrared measurement. But a general guide to film speed is given with the film packaging, and generous bracketing is suggested.

As lenses bring infrared light to a different point of focus than visible light, an adjustment to the focus setting is needed. Some lenses have an infrared mark next to the normal focusing index; if not, stop the lens well down to a small aperture.

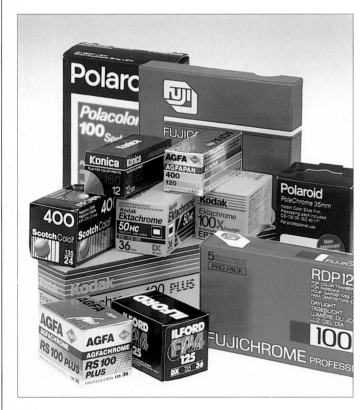

FILM TYPES
You can pick from dozens of different film types from 'own brand' low cost colour negative material to refrigerated professional transparency stock in multi-roll packs.

WHICH BRAND OF FILM?

Choosing which film depends on the type of photography you undertake and upon your own personal preferences. It is best to experiment with several brands to see which you prefer in terms of colour rendition and contrast. Photographers may choose to use one film type to retain consistency in their results, but it is generally better to use different films for different purposes, matching emulsions to a range of applications.

The major film makers – Kodak, Fuji, Agfa, Konica and Ilford – can be relied upon to deliver optimum results, though there are substantial differences evident between products in the same sector. Fujichrome colour transparencies tend to be 'warm', for instance, producing bright and breezy colours which are not necessarily accurate. Its great rival Kodachrome gives greater colour fidelity, but comparatively 'cool' image colour. Other brands should also be experimented with, to try alternative image character or save a little money!

PROFESSIONAL film differs from a regular emulsion in that it is kept at the factory after production to age, and periodically tested for optimum performance. When this state is reached, it is released in a refrigerated state to dealers. The film must be kept in this condition by dealer and photographer, and processed immediately after exposure. Providing this approach is adhered to, professional film produces slightly superior results. If the film is not kept at ideal conditions it will produce results equal to conventional film.

SHOWING THEIR COLOURS
Different makes of film produce different results; they show most on subtle colours, not bright ones. The top version is taken on Kodak Ektachrome 200 film, the bottom shot on Fujichrome 100. Study the greens, yellows and browns.

FILM SHARPNESS

Several factors contribute to the impression of sharpness in an image. What makes choosing a film tricky is that individual emulsions vary in the amount of each characteristic they possess. Some of these factors are subjective, such as the amount of fine detail given. Others can be accurately measured:

GRAIN ranges from fine through medium to coarse, depending upon the speed of the film. Slow films are least grainy, while fast emulsions feature a more visible grain structure, which tends to break up the image and reduce apparent sharpness. Some films exhibit good speed yet the grain is crisp, which helps retain an impression of sharpness.

RESOLUTION indicates how much fine detail a film can capture. The higher the resolving power, the sharper the result. Film is not the only factor, however – the resolution of the lens used is equally important.

ACUTANCE measures how crisply sharp edges or sudden changes of tone are imaged. Imagine taking a photograph of a chess board. With a film of high acutance, each square will seem to have a very sharp 'edge'. A film with low acutance has a soft transition from white to black.

CONTRAST works the same way as on your television. Picture two chess boards, one with black and white squares, and a second with light grey for the white squares, dark grey for the black. Though the acutance of the image where white meets black or grey is identical, the higher contrast image looks sharper because the contrast between white and black is higher than light grey and dark grey.

ABOVE: HIGH SPEED, LOW DETAIL
Very fast colour film – ISO 1000 or over – has more grain, less vivid colours, lower fine detail sharpness and lower contrast. This can be used creatively to convey mood and atmosphere, especially at dusk, when the human eye responds in this way too.

BELOW: FINE GRAIN BLACK AND WHITE
The opposite end of the scale is slow monochrome film, like the Kodak T-Max 100 used for this tripod-mounted shot taken on an Exakta 66 rollfilm single reflex, and printed on fibre-based paper for maximum sharpness and detail.

FILM SPEED RATINGS

All films have a speed rating, or a particular sensitivity to light. Details are printed on the film packaging and cassette. Film speed is measured in ISO (International Standards Organisation) numbers, with typical examples being ISO 50, ISO 100 or ISO 400. Film rated at ISO 100 is twice as sensitive to light as one of ISO 50, and four times faster than a film rated at ISO 25.

Slow films of ISO 25-64 give very fine grain and optimum picture quality. However low light levels may prevent a suitable combination of aperture and shutter speed and make hand-holding inadvisable. Here the camera should be attached to a tripod. Medium-speed films rated ISO 100-200 represent a good compromise between speed and grain, and can be used in a variety of lighting situations without sacrificing too much quality. Duller light usually demands fast films of ISO 400-1000 if the camera is to be hand-held, though this also means the image will be quite grainy and have moderate definition. Ultra fast films of ISO 1600-3200 permit shooting in poor lighting and, though grain is readily apparent, resulting images are perfectly acceptable.

POLAROID'S INSTANT 35MM SLIDE FILM
One special film, which does away with the need for darkroom or processing lab, is Polaroid Polachrome 35mm instant transparency film. The film is in a normal 35mm cassette, and once exposed it is placed with a developer cartridge in a small desktop processor. This winds the film out of the cassette into contact with a developer gel. After a minute, the film is rewound. When you pull it from the cassette, a fully developed dry colour picture can be seen. It is darker than a normal slide and has a distinct pattern of fine lines forming the image when projected.

INFRARED COLOUR
Kodak's Infrared Ektachrome film is available to special order. It records the infrared reflectance of the scene in false colours. A normal slide (top) shows autumn colours. Infrared Ektachrome used with a yellow filter picks out healthy vegetation in purple, dead leaves in blue. It can be used to spot forests suffering from drought or disease, in aerial surveys, before the eye can distinguish any change in leaf colour. Photographers most often use it for surreal effects. It must be processed in Kodak's E4 chemicals by a specialist colour lab.

KODACHROME FILM
Unlike E6 slide films, Kodachrome films have the dyes added during development. They are very stable dyes, making Kodachrome suitable for long-term storage without fading, but in most countries only one Kodak processing plant is able to handle development.
This picture of St Albans was taken exactly 30 years before this book was published by an amateur photographer living in London. His daughter would have disposed of them but decided to give them to a photographic collection. The colours of the Kodachrome slide are just as bright as one taken today.

CAMERA HANDLING

NO MATTER how good your camera is, you will never get good pictures from it unless you know how to use it properly. You stand the chance of ruining pictures through camera shake, and missing valuable photographic opportunities as they occur in front of you because you are too slow adjusting the camera settings. To enable you to react promptly to situations, learn all about your camera and lenses, and practice various handling techniques.

GRIP

Photographs are often taken at eye-level but many other heights and positions should be tried to bring variety into your photographs. The following stances should prove comfortable and provide stable support to avoid camera shake.

In the standing position for normal horizontal shots, use your right hand to grip the side of the body and press the shutter release, and your left hand to cradle the camera/lens and focus – try holding it from underneath rather than from above. Press the viewfinder eyecup against your face and keep your elbows tucked neatly into your body. For vertical format pictures, place the right hand over the top of the camera with the shutter release uppermost, so the left hand again bears most of the load. Depending on personal preference, an alternative here is to support the camera using your right hand, with the shutter release below the lens.

When kneeling, raise your left knee and support the left elbow vertically upon it to brace the camera. Remember that your elbows form a tripod if you squat on the floor and place them on your knees, or sit on a chair and lean forward onto a table with your camera at eye level. If lying prone for a low angle shot, place both elbows on the ground to form a stable platform. In crowds or when an obstruction is encountered, the

camera can be supported by two raised arms for a higher viewpoint. If the camera has an interchangeable prism, remove it and shoot with the camera body upside down so that the focusing screen can be seen.

Holding your camera steadily while leaning against a handy lamp-post or wall also helps eliminate shake. Most cameras feature a flat baseplate, so reasonably sharp time exposures can be taken by placing the camera on a table and using the delayed action self-timer release.

For panning, stand firmly with your legs apart, and tuck your elbows in to support the camera. Pre-focus on a spot the subject will pass through, then frame it in the finder as it approaches; follow its motion by swivelling from the hips. Continue with a follow-through pan even after the shutter has been fired.

HOLDING IT STEADY
Two-handed grip – one hand on the body grip, the other supporting the lens – always helps keep a camera steady. Tucking your elbows in, resting on a firm surface, putting your legs slightly apart, or kneeling down can all help. When panning to follow action (right) don't swing the camera, swing your whole upper body with a swivel from the hips.

CUTTING CAMERA SHAKE

Camera shake can be avoided when hand-holding by remembering a simple rule. Unless you have very steady hands or are expert at hand-holding, use a shutter speed higher than the reciprocal of the focal length used. For a 50mm lens, the minimum recommended speed is 1/50, which rounds up to 1/60 sec on the scale of recognized shutter speeds. A 28mm translates to 1/30, the longest setting of a 70-210mm zoom would be 1/250, and a 500mm mirror optic needs 1/500.

FAR OR NEAR FOCUS?
If the subject is fairly small, the AF system may find it hard to decide whether to focus on the distant detail (top) or foreground (bottom). In this case, either manual override or focus lock will solve the problem.

INFINITY LOCK
Shooting out of an aircraft window (left), the glass and plastic layers are often so dirty that autofocus cameras try to lock on to these instead of the distant view. Infinity lock, fitted to many compact models, forces the camera to focus on the far distance regardless of glass, wire netting or similar obstacles.

FOCUSING

Focusing a lens not only gives a sharp image, it can be used to create emphasis. When a wide aperture is set to give shallow depth of field, a lens focused on the main subject makes this the centre of interest, while other obtrusive areas are rendered out of focus and therefore less important.

In most photographs the subject is quite obvious, but often there are many subjects in the scene. You need to decide whether you want some or all these to appear sharp. In fairly bright conditions and with a static subject you can take several shots increasing the depth of field so that everything is sharp, or restricting it so that just a part of the scene is in focus. If light levels are low and a slow-speed film is being exposed by a telephoto lens, selective focusing is often the only option.

For moving subjects, it is advisable to familiarize yourself with the direction in which a manual lens focuses – does the barrel turn clockwise or anticlockwise to reach infinity? This knowledge helps focusing become a reflex action when something happens quickly in front of the camera.

Reflections in windows, mirrors and water pose an interesting focus problem. The reflected image is actually further away than the surface which carries it, so it may not be possible to render both sharp when depth of field is restricted.

AUTOFOCUS HICCUPS

The built-in autofocus systems of compacts and SLR cameras vary in quality, but even the most sophisticated versions are far from perfect. When a subject is placed away from the centre of the viewfinder frame, as in a portrait of two people standing side by side, the AF sensor may 'miss' the intended subject. Instead it passes between the people and focuses on the background instead. A small number of cameras like the Konica Aiborg and Canon EOS 10 now feature selectable AF sensors, but most AF models have a focus lock. With the latter, focus can be set on one of the subjects, then the picture recomposed.

Low contrast or dull light conditions can also fool the 'passive' AF systems used in SLRs. Here the lens will hunt for the subject, racking back and forth. Sometimes the only solution is to switch to manual focusing.

MOVING SUBJECTS

Focusing on a subject in motion, especially one heading directly towards or away from the camera, is one of the stiffest tests of camera handling competence. The mistake usually made is to try and adjust the camera's focus as the subject moves – a better method is to pre-focus on a point, and then take the picture as the subject moves through it.

When you first try this technique shots tend to be taken a fraction too late – a sharp subject is seen in the viewfinder, and only then is the shutter release pressed. The delay between making the decision to shoot and pressing the button is long enough for the subject to travel beyond the point of focus. To obtain sharp results, the movement of the subject has to be slightly anticipated, and the shutter released just before the subject reaches the prefocused point.

Taking a sequence of action pictures calls for rapid repetition of the above technique. After one shot has been taken at a certain point, the lens is quickly re-focused to a closer point and you wait for the subject to move into focus.

FLARE

This is usually avoided but on some occasions it can be used creatively. Flare is caused by bright, non-image forming light reflecting around in the lens, usually caused by the sun or a bright light inside or just beyond the picture frame. Flare is often seen as a string of patches of light, but can also degrade image contrast generally by weakening shadow density.

Lens manufacturers try to make lenses less prone to flare by coating the front element with a special material, and making the internal surfaces of the lens matt black. You can help by shading the lens with your hand, but take care to not get your hand in shot – study the viewfinder to check!

PRESET FOCUS
A predictable path followed by a subject can help you get pin-sharp pictures without even looking through the viewfinder. Mount the camera on a tripod, compose the shot so that you know exactly how much is included, and pre-focus on a particular spot such as a mark on the road or track. An instant before the subject arrives there, fire the shutter.

TAKING FLARE OR LEAVING IT
Flare is a photographic fault caused by light entering the lens from an adverse angle, and reflecting off the glass elements or metal components inside it. You can use flare creatively, as with the shot of the steam engine below. Here the flare goes with the impression of smoke and speed.

Serious flare (inset) is often encountered if you shoot into the light with a compact camera and dirty lens, and can't be spotted in the viewfinder.

To eliminate visible flare when using an SLR, hold your left hand so that it casts a shadow on the front element of the lens, but is not included in the shot (left). Here the photographer is using a 28-135mm zoom with a very large front element and no lens hood. Shading the 72mm diameter front glass in backlighting is absolutely vital for a flare-free shot.

USING EXPOSURE CONTROLS

APERTURE and shutter speed control the amount of light reaching the film. They can combine to give correct exposure, but each also has a significant effect upon the nature of the image produced on film. Understanding how apertures and shutter speeds alter your photograph will mean that you can select the appropriate combination to get the effect you want.

SHUTTER SPEEDS

Shutter opening times, or speeds, control the duration of exposure which determines how movement appears in a picture. A high speed, in the order of 1/1000 to 1/2000 of a second, would be selected to freeze fast action such as a speeding racing car. But this isn't the fastest shutter speed possible – some SLRs can now manage a fastest setting of 1/8000. Slower shutter speeds such as 1/30 or 1/4 may be chosen to induce deliberate blur in a moving subject, allowing some motion to occur while the shutter is open. Flowing water, for example, takes on completely different appearances when photographed at different speeds.

It is easy to learn which speeds will stop movement in subjects you tackle frequently (see box on opposite page). You may be surprised to learn that a tennis serve can be faster than an express train, and combined movements are often encountered – the top of a rolling wheel, for example.

Other speeds are worth knowing. The movement of the moon, when seen through a telephoto lens, can be enough to make it record as a slight blur if you give too long an exposure. The right exposure for a full moon (regardless of sky brightness) is 1/125 at ƒ8 with ISO 100 film. This will be sharp with lenses up to 500mm only. Always use a shutter speed

MOON SHOT
The moon is only this large in a 35mm frame with an 800mm lens, and a shutter speed of 1/250 is essential to stop it blurring.

at least one-quarter the value of the focal length of the lens – with a 2000mm lens, you would need 1/500 to keep the moon sharp.

SHUTTER SPEED CHOICE:
Stickle Ghyll in the English Lakes – left, 1/100 at ƒ11. Centre – 1/8 at ƒ22. Right – 1/2 at ƒ22 with a polarizer.

CONTROLLING MOVEMENT

For stationary subjects, all shutter speeds give the same effect. Moving subjects, however, can be rendered in many different ways. Five factors influence how the image appears; the speed the subject is travelling at, its direction in relation to the camera, the camera to subject distance, the focal length, and the shutter speed employed.

A car travelling at 50mph on the horizon appears to be moving relatively slowly, while the same vehicle passing within a few feet of the camera seems to hurtle past. The latter requires a far faster shutter speed to capture a sharp image.

If the car approaches the camera head-on at 50mph, its speed appears less than when it's travelling at the same speed across the field of view. The head-on shot would need a shutter speed of 1/250 for a sharp image, compared to the 1/1000 needed to freeze the side-on action.

A car travelling at 45° to the camera would require a shutter speed between the two previous settings – 1/500 – to achieve the same level of sharpness.

DIRECTION OF ACTION
A vehicle crossing the frame at 90° needs a fast shutter speed or panning (top). At 45° it can be stopped with less panning, or a slower speed. Coming head-on, it can be sharply frozen even at 1/125, so you can take this kind of picture on a dull day.

WHAT SPEED?

You can work out roughly what shutter speed is needed for a subject if you know how fast it is travelling and how far away it is. The actual calculation demands that you convert everything to metric values, and is rather obscure. It is better to memorize or make a note of some typical situations which you are likely to photograph, and work out the right setting on the basis of these. The shutter speeds below are for subjects comfortably framed, filling around two-thirds of the shot – moving across the picture. For movement at 45°, one speed slower is OK; for movement towards the camera, two speeds slower.

Walking man: 1/125
Jogger/runner: 1/250
Sprinter: 1/500
Car (urban speed): 1/1000
Car (highway): 1/2000
Formula 1 racer: 1/4000

Panning with the subject reduces the need for a fast shutter speed, as does increased distance, so that it fills only a small part of the frame. Any attempt to enlarge a small part of the negative, however, is just the same as filling the frame. You can't use a slower speed with a distant subject and expect it to be sharp when you blow it up.

In practice, very fast moving subjects rarely fill even two-thirds of the picture area. It is not possible to frame them accurately. Speeds of 1/8000 are rarely needed except for special effects, or capturing fast motion at close quarters.

DEPTH OF FIELD

APERTURES

Lens apertures control image brightness, and govern the amount of the scene that can be sharply rendered. This ability to adjust the zone of sharp focus is a powerful creative tool, enabling the photographer to isolate one subject, or keep all elements in a scene sharp. In a landscape composition, total sharpness from foreground to the distant horizon may be desired, in which case a small aperture (or large f-number) of $f16$ or $f22$ would be used. For a portrait, a wide aperture (or small f-number) of $f2$ or $f2.8$ might be set to give a shallow zone of focus, throw the background out of focus and concentrate attention on the subject.

DEPTH OF FIELD

Defined as the distance between the nearest and furthest areas in a scene that are within the limits of acceptable sharpness, the zone of depth of field is distributed roughly one-third in front and two-thirds behind the point focused upon. Three separate factors govern depth of field – subject distance, focal length and lens aperture.

Depth of field is reduced as camera-to-subject distance decreases, and becomes very shallow indeed in close-ups. So objects near to the camera require more accurate focusing than distant subjects. Focal length also affects depth of field – the longer the lens, the narrower the zone of focus becomes. So wideangles always give greater depth of field than telephotos. Aperture setting is the third factor – the basic rule is that the wider the aperture, the shallower is the zone of focus. Stopping down to a smaller aperture automatically increases depth of field.

Maximizing depth of field is an important technique, especially for the hand-held camera. Focusing on infinity with a 50mm lens will render distant subjects, and other

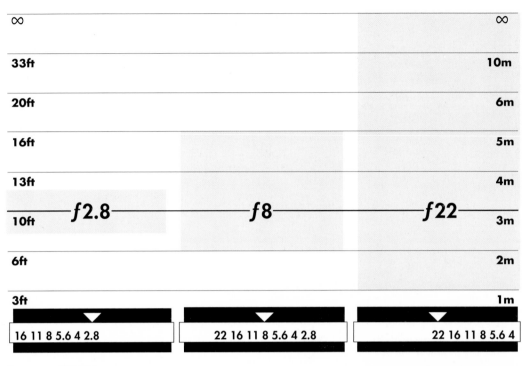

DEPTH OF FIELD RANGE
With a lens focused on 10ft/3m (above), the depth of field shown by the coloured zone at $f2.8$ will be limited (left) but extensive at $f22$ (right). Most lenses have a scale marked with f-numbers, below right, which can be read off against far and near distances of the ft/m focus scale.

areas up to about 20 feet from the camera, sharp at $f11$. But the zone of sharp focus can be further extended by altering the focus setting to 20 feet; this is the *hyperfocal* distance. Now depth of field extends from around 10 feet through to infinity at the same $f11$ aperture.

Most SLR lenses have a depth of field scale built in, enabling the zone of sharpness to be determined for various aperture settings. Sharp focus extends either side of the distance to which the lens is set. Smaller apertures are placed further from the central index, indicating additional depth of field.

A telephoto lens focused on a subject 20 feet away and set to $f8$ has less depth of field than a standard lens trained on the same subject and employing the same aperture. A wide-angle lens set to 20 feet and $f8$ will have a larger zone of focus.

WIDE-ANGLES from 20mm to 28mm have so much depth of

field that at small apertures, even subjects close to the camera can be sharply rendered while distant subjects are also in focus. Colourful flowers can be used to frame a building, or an interesting rock included to add foreground interest to a landscape composition.

TELEPHOTOS, on the other hand, have limited depth of field, especially as focal length increases and wider apertures are set. The technique of differential focus is best employed, to make the main subject stand out from other parts of the scene. With a portrait, a cluttered backdrop appears less intrusive when out of focus.

Clearly it's an advantage to have a lens capable of a variety of aperture settings. Wide apertures are useful for working in low light conditions where a high shutter speed is required. Smallest apertures for 35mm and roll film SLRs tend to be $f22$ and $f32$, as any narrower iris design results in diffraction of light passing through

the tiny aperture, and a rapid drop off in quality.

All lenses tend to give optimum image quality when stopped down to small apertures, as only the central part of the lens elements are used. At maximum or full aperture, the very edge of the lens is being used, light has to be bent further, and lens faults or aberrations become evident.

The viewfinder brightness does not change when you adjust the aperture ring on your SLR because the camera is made to operate at maximum screen brightness for compositional and focusing ease. It only reverts to the taking aperture a fraction of a second before the shot is taken. However, many advanced SLRs feature a depth of field preview facility. When this button or lever is pressed, the lens is stopped down so that the image on the focusing screen can be seen at the pre-set aperture – you can check depth of field, the effect of filters and other compositional details and know that is how they will appear on film.

DIFFERENTIAL FOCUS

Using a very shallow depth of field, to throw a confusing background completely out of focus while leaving the subject sharp, is called differential focusing. The subject must be fairly close to the camera, so it is reserved for close-ups, still lifes and portraits – especially when taken outdoors. A rollfilm camera using film larger than 35mm has less depth of field, and differential focus is easier to obtain at normal working apertures such as $f5.6$ and $f8$. If you use a 35mm SLR, it may be necessary to switch to a very fast shutter speed to achieve the right result in bright conditions.

DEEP FOCUS

A wide-angle lens on a 35mm camera, in contrast, produces the extreme depth of field shown below. Everything from the foreground a foot or so away from the lens to the far distance is recorded sharply. To produce results like this, you need a lens of 24mm or shorter focal length, and must 'stop down' to $f16$ or $f22$. Exposures of around 1/30 may be acceptable hand-held, but use a tripod for anything longer.

EXPOSURE AND METERING

ALL PHOTOGRAPHIC films require correct exposure to produce optimum results, and this is achieved by setting the appropriate aperture and shutter speed. In compact cameras and many SLRs exposure control may be fully automated which does not encourage the photographer to think about, and adjust, the factors which influence exposure measurement – subject brightness, contrast and tone. If, however, you spend a little time learning how to control these factors you will be rewarded with better photographs.

SHUTTER AND APERTURE

A short exposure to a bright subject can make just as effective a picture as a long exposure to a dimly lit one. That's because apertures and shutter speeds enjoy a reciprocal relationship, so 1/500 at ƒ2.8 gives the same exposure value (sometimes marked EV on light meters or cameras) as 1/125 at ƒ5.6, or 1/30 at ƒ11. This law only fails to apply when the exposure is extremely brief or of long duration. This is termed reciprocity failure, and can be corrected by extra exposure.

Usually light levels allow a range of shutter speed and aperture settings which will produce correct exposure. The photographer may choose a particular combination to create a certain kind of image, such as favouring a higher shutter speed to freeze motion, or using a small aperture to produce maximum depth of field.

Camera exposure meters are designed to produce an average mid-tone. Problems arise because subjects are not of average brightness. Given sufficient duration, pictures taken of a white cat in a coal cellar or a black cat in a totally white room will render both animals an average grey. The 'correct' exposure is always the one that makes the subject appear the way you want it. Many people bracket exposures and choose the best shot later, or prefer a high or low key result in comparison to the metered exposure.

When a subject is harshly lit – by sunshine from one side, for instance – it contains a full range of tones from highlight to shadow. This brightness range of around 1:250 lies beyond the recording capabilities of most films. Negative materials typically have a contrast range of 7 stops, or 1:125, while transparency emulsions are only about 5 stops or about 1:40. Therefore if the exposure is taken

A LIGHT SUBJECT
Average metering will deal well with this subject despite its extreme contrast. A spot meter reading, however, would have to be taken from the grass – not the car (too light) or trees (too dark).

from the highlights, shadow detail disappears, whereas if the exposure is biased towards the shadows, the highlights over-expose. So for high contrast subjects, a conscious decision has to be made about which part of the picture information to sacrifice, unless a compromise setting is used. With slide film slight under-exposure is usually given, as deep shadow is regarded as more acceptable than washed-out highlights.

Light meters incorporated into cameras use the reflected light method to take exposure readings. SLRs employing the TTL system are more accurate than compacts, as only the light entering the lens

To take a silhouette, position your subject to block the sun, or against a bright sky or background. Expose for the sky tones by taking a meter reading from them. This renders the subject dark or black.

is read. The entire viewfinder area is not covered, as the brighter sky area at the top would influence the meter into under-exposure of the main subject positioned lower in the frame. So a range of metering patterns feature in different SLR models, adjusting the area scanned by the metering sensor. The main types are covered on p25, 'Modes and Meters', in the Equipment Section, which shows that increasingly selective patterns are available. The spot metering option is the most accurate of all in tricky lighting conditions, providing the small sensor area is aimed to read the important part of the subject.

METERING ACCURACY

Before taking a picture, examine the entire viewfinder image to assess the final composition. Work out how the scene is lit and decide which are the critical subject areas. If there is a roughly equal distribution of light and dark tones, or if the subject and the background are of similar brightness, then an average reading will suffice. When a significant area of the picture is light-toned, but the main subject is dark, an average reading will result in over-exposure. Likewise a predominantly dark scene with a small, light-toned main subject leads to underexposure. To avoid these common errors, take a meter reading from the important subject area only, or dial in some exposure compensation.

There are occasions when it is difficult to approach your subject, to take an accurate meter reading. You may not wish to disturb the person whose candid portrait you are taking, or the action may be too dangerous to be near in the case of a racing car. In this case, find a similarly lit object elsewhere and take a reading from that. This method can also apply when the important area of the subject is small, but your camera is only equipped with a general centre-weighted meter.

To obtain a suitable exposure of a high contrast scene, take readings from the highlight and shadow areas, and halve the difference. With the light source in the viewfinder frame, the brightness range becomes much greater than the contrast span of film. So you must decide if the light source is important, or the area it illuminates. In a backlit portrait with sun visible in the background, the subject's face is still the most important element in the shot. Take a meter reading close to the face, ensuring the shaded area is metered.

In a night scene, street lights and car lights may be only parts of the scene bright enough to appear on film, and shadow details disappear. Over-exposing for the bright light sources is not satisfactory, because they're not the principal subject. Meter these light sources and the areas they illuminate rather than any deep shadow areas – a parked car's roof should give a suitable exposure.

With automatic cameras, employ the exposure meter lock if possible, or set the camera to manual mode. Alternatively use the backlight button, exposure compensation dial, or reset film speed setting to a slower rating. The high contrast that occurs with backlight can also be reduced by fill-in flash or reflectors.

VERY LOW LIGHT

Most SLR metering systems have a
fixed range of light sensitivity,
regardless of the film speed used.
The low-light limit is normally a
shutter speed of 1 second with an
ISO 100 film. If you use a fast lens
such as a 50mm $f1.4$, this allows
you to take meter readings by
candle-light. With a compact
zooms the maximum aperture is
often $f5.6$, and the meter will give
accurate readings until well after
sundown, when the street lights
are lit, and of well-lit buildings
after dark. Loading faster film will
not help; if the camera takes
readings to 1 second with ISO 100
film, it will only take readings
down to 1/4 with ISO 400, or
1/15 with ISO 1000. One way in
which a fast film will help,
however, is in ensuring a shutter
speed you can reasonably hand-
hold or support in low light. The
photographer chose ISO 1000 film
for the dusk view of Venice, right,
with the camera pressed firmly on
the parapet of the Rialto Bridge to
ensure a sharp result with a 1/8
exposure. The fast film adds grain
and muted colours to the picture,
but you need to enlarge shots like
this to a good size to see the effect
– it is totally lost in an enprint. Fast
films can also prevent compact
cameras from automatically
switching on flash operation.

NATURAL LIGHT

THE WORD photography literally means light (the Greek word *photos*) writing or drawing (*graphos*). Light creates the image on film, so an understanding of how the qualities of light may vary is essential for anyone wanting to take exceptional photographs. Light varies in quantity, in colour and with time, so making effective use of it calls for a mixture of technical and aesthetic skills, and an appreciation of how different conditions can be utilized to create pictures of different moods.

There is only one source of natural light – the sun – though it can be modified in many ways before reaching the earth's surface. What you see when the sky glows red after sunset, is wreathed in unbroken cloud on overcast days, or during moonlight at night, is diffused or reflected sunlight.

The main factors to consider when taking pictures in natural light are its direction and quality, and the orientation of camera and subject in relation to it. The camera angle is infinitely variable – it can, for example, be directed towards the light source, be placed at right angles to it, or for least shadow follow the same axis. Certain subjects such as landscapes or buildings have fixed positions, so the light falling upon them has to be accepted (though the viewpoint can be changed). In other cases, such as an outdoor portrait, the subject can be moved to face the light, or turned away from it.

LIGHT QUALITY

Each day the sun moves in an arc across the sky, its height varying with the hour, the season and the observer's geographical position. As the sun rises, the intensity of its light increases quickly, then changes little until late afternoon when the intensity drops rapidly. This is because sunlight passes through the earth's atmosphere and as the sun's angle becomes more oblique, the distance that light has to travel through the

atmosphere increases. So the greatest changes of lighting quality occur early and late in the day.

During these hours, the angle of the sun is also low. This throws the texture and detail of the ground into relief – hedges, furrows, hills and vegetation all cast strong shadows. Morning and evening light are therefore favourites with landscape photographers, who do not like the flat overhead sun of a summer mid-day. Winter, spring and autumn sun is lower

but may lack the strength of summer evening light.

Weather variables such as clouds, haze, fog, rain, mist and snow also affect light quality. Atmospheric pollution is now a factor to be reckoned with as well.

THE SUN'S PASSAGE

The course of a day sees many changes in light. These three pictures document daylight at different times on the stones of the rings of Callanish in the Isle of Lewis. Left, an image in full sunshine with a strong blue sky. Top, a lower sun but a naturally cool pale sky near the horizon, in backlighting. Above, a stone lit by flash after dusk, with the sunset colouring the sky and the shadows.

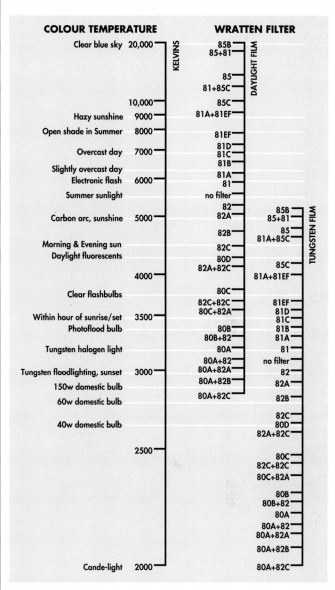

COLOUR TEMPERATURE

COLOUR TEMPERATURE	Kelvins	WRATTEN FILTER — DAYLIGHT FILM	WRATTEN FILTER — TUNGSTEN FILM
Clear blue sky	20,000	85B	
		85+81	
		85	
		81+85C	
	10,000	85C	
Hazy sunshine	9000	81A+81EF	
Open shade in Summer	8000	81EF	
		81D	
Overcast day	7000	81C	
		81B	
Slightly overcast day		81A	
Electronic flash	6000	81	
Summer sunlight		no filter	
		82	
Carbon arc, sunshine	5000	82A	85B
			85+81
		82B	85
Morning & Evening sun		82C	81A+85C
Daylight fluorescents		80D	
	4000	82A+82C	85C
			81A+81EF
Clear flashbulbs		80C	
		82C+82C	81EF
Within hour of sunrise/set	3500	80C+82A	81D
Photoflood bulb			81C
		80B	81B
		80B+82	81A
Tungsten halogen light		80A	81
		80A+82	no filter
Tungsten floodlighting, sunset	3000	80A+82A	82
150w domestic bulb		80A+82B	82A
60w domestic bulb		80A+82C	82B
			82C
40w domestic bulb			80D
			82A+82C
	2500		80C
			82C+82C
			80C+82A
			80B
			80B+82
			80A
			80A+82
			80A+82A
			80A+82B
Cande-light	2000		80A+82C

Both natural and artificial light sources are slightly coloured, although the eye adjusts to see them as being white. The colour varies with the wavelength of light and is measured by colour 'temperature' – the range of colours exhibited by metal as it is heated, on a scale of Kelvins. Heated metal first glows a deep red; as the temperature is increased it turns orange, then white, and on through the spectrum to a bluish colour. Light sources of a high colour temperature, such as a clear sky (10,000K) or electronic flash (6000K) look blue. Sources low on the scale include candlelight (1930K) and sunset (3000K) which look red. Noon Summer Sunlight is rated at 5500K, and most films are matched to this.

Correction filters are available to ensure that daylight or tungsten light balanced films record colours naturally regardless of the time of day or light source. The left hand scale above shows the Kelvins for each major lighting condition. The two right hand scales show the Kodak 'Wratten' filters, singly or in combination, needed to give correct colours in this lighting.

LIGHT DIRECTION

Photographers are usually advised to take pictures with the light source coming over their shoulder onto the subject and this is sound advice – up to a point. During the middle hours of the day this type of frontal lighting works admirably with colour film, but less well with monochrome as shadows are minimized. Very low sun can create quite dramatic conditions, though watch for encroaching shadows, including your own, appearing in shot. A slight change of camera angle can remove them from your composition.

Side lighting is better if texture and modelling are important criteria. The sun lights about half the subject, leaving the remainder in shadow to emphasize its form. This means contrast is high – often beyond the limits of the film – and you need to decide whether the highlights or the shadows should be recorded.

Shooting directly towards the sun subdues colour and further increases contrast but it can produce attractive atmospheric backlit images. The boldest of these is the silhouette, which should be a relatively simple shape to work effectively. If the camera is pointed slightly away from the sun, or the sun is masked by a building or tree, detail and texture begin to reappear, giving a quite different effect. A favourite silhouette background is a sunset – easier to shoot than a sunrise because the path of the sun can be anticipated, and it saves you getting out of bed at an unearthly hour.

WARNING! Preserve your eyesight. When shooting into the light, do not look directly at the sun, especially with a powerful telephoto lens fitted to your SLR.

WEATHER CONDITIONS

Outdoor photographers must take account of the weather, whatever

LIGHT THROUGH RAIN
For rain to show properly in a photograph, it must have the light coming through it, and there should be a dark background to set it against. Edinburgh (above) is frequently seen in this light, and the volume of water falling has made its own impact.

A BREAK IN THE CLOUDS
Rays of sunshine breaking through dark clouds, especially at sunset, make a dramatic photographic opportunity (right). Shoot quickly, taking many frames at different exposures, as the effect is fleeting and auto exposure is hardly ever reliable.

country they take pictures in. A broad range of lighting effects are produced by variations in the climate. At the start and finish of a clear day, low sun gives a warm light of moderate brightness. This hits the landscape at an oblique angle to produce a range of dramatic effects. With low sun coming over your shoulder, the light is even but shadows are not very pronounced. Low sun at a 90° angle gives warm colour, good modelling and heavy shadow, while shooting towards a low sun can provide strong reflections over water.

Noon sun on a day clear of cloud might seem an obvious time to be taking pictures, as people are up and about and activities are taking place. A brighter light of more consistent but entirely different quality is evident. Though the increased intensity enables a fast shutter speed and wide aperture to be used, its character is

diminished. There is less texture and greater contrast between highlight and shadow areas. The high position of the sun gives shadows a strong outline – this is fine for some buildings but rarely for portraits as the brow and nose cast shadows over the eyes and mouth. Landscapes also suffer as the dominant horizontal aspect is flatly lit with little texture. However, colours are bright and plenty of detail is apparent.

White fluffy clouds create a good contrast with blue sky on a sunny day, but if scattered cloud is moving quickly and intermittently covering the sun, this can produce significant changes in conditions and light levels. This weather can give dramatic, momentary effects, however. It's advisable to take meter readings for both the bright and duller conditions before taking pictures.

Overcast skies with unbroken cloud cover act as a giant diffuser

giving soft, shadowless light of low intensity. There is less textural interest as shadows are reduced or absent, and subjects lose modelling. This type of light is easy to meter, and complicated subject shapes can look better here than in harsh sunlight. Reflective surfaces also appear flatter. Thin cloud softens shadows, without removing them altogether. It also reduces contrast, and therefore makes a good light for outdoor portraits.

Particles of dust, pollution or water vapour scatter sunlight and create hazy conditions. Water vapour is neutral in colour and looks white from a distance, while dust and pollution scatter UV wavelengths to create bluish scenes. All types of haze make the landscape appear further away, and lightens shadow for a softer effect. Remember muted colours can make equally as attractive a picture as a vividly coloured scene.

With telephoto lenses, haze emphasizes distance, depth and atmosphere, but washes out detail, colour and crispness. This effect can be reduced by using filters.

Mist and fog are quite unpredictable and greatly reduce contrast and colour. But these conditions can be turned to your advantage – though the subject is harder to see clearly, it can give superbly impressionistic pictures. Dust and sand are also photogenic sometimes, when the wind keeps them swirling. But photograph these conditions from a distance if at all possible, as the small particles can ruin your camera equipment.

Rain is often accompanied by grey or dark brooding cloud, so light levels are low. Rain can look like mist when slow shutter speeds are used. To record rain on film effectively, try shooting it backlit with a darker backdrop – the light coming through the rain will show it up as streaks. Storms can look very dramatic, often with a rainbow if the cloud cover is broken.

Shafts of sunlight breaking through against a dark sky are well worth photographing, though speed is essential as the light changes quickly. Also look out for the after-effects of storms. When sunlight hits falling rain, a rainbow occurs. Its colour intensity and arc size depend upon the size and quantity of raindrops. To take a whole rainbow, you'll need a 28mm or 24mm wideangle. Slight under-exposure is recommended to emphasize its colours.

To photograph lightning, shoot at night and place the camera on tripod, leaving the shutter open for several flashes.

Snow, like rain, is often recorded as streaks. Faster shutter speeds will show it as more recognizable blobs. Settled snow becomes very reflective and fools most reflected light meters. To achieve correct exposure, give two stops more exposure than the metered reading indicates, or bracket exposures. The texture of snow looks best under low-angled sun early or late in the day.

LIGHTING WITH FLASH

ELECTRONIC flash, either built into the camera or added as an accessory, provides a means of illuminating a subject when there is insufficient ambient light. It can also act as a fill-in light for contrasty scenes where the main subject is in shadow.

Flash is often used for portraits but this demands care because, when fired straight at someone from the camera position, this rarely gives a satisfactory picture. The light is harsh in quality, reveals little form and therefore tends to produce unflattering results. Most compacts and a number of 35mm SLRs have integral flash units that are fixed facing forwards. When a subtler portrait is desired, the only option is to diffuse the light by taping a piece of translucent material over the flashtube. This scatters the light output a little, brings a touch of modelling to the face and softens shadows. Direct flash can suit other subjects, however, by heightening colour and creating a striking image.

The ideal flash position for portraits shot with a single portable unit is slightly to one side and higher than the lens axis – this gives a good mix of highlight and shadow, plus plenty of shape and detail. A flashgun may be fired from here if it can be connected to the camera by a long synchronizing cable, but most units are designed to operate from the hotshoe.

Basic camera top flashguns normally have fixed forward-facing flashtubes, so the only easy option is to diffuse the light with an attachment. Be very careful not to damage dedicated zoom flashguns.

One method to soften the light of larger flashguns fired directly is to fit a miniature soft-box over the head. These collapsible units are made of black, opaque material apart from the translucent screen ahead of the flashtube. Attachment is by Velcro tabs stuck on the side of the flash, so the accessory can be quickly removed.

DIRECT FLASH
Flash on the camera produces a harsh result, with bright colours but sharp nose and chin shadows.

BOUNCE FLASH
Bounce flash off the ceiling from a reasonable distance gives much softer light and no shadows.

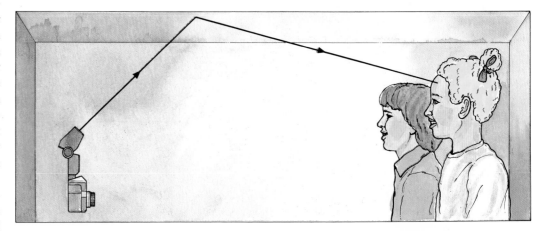

BOUNCE ANGLES AND CALCULATIONS
Bounce flash calls for a ceiling of reasonable height – around 10 feet – and a the use of a standard or short telephoto lens. If the ceiling is the minimum statutory height (often the case in new houses) ask your subjects to sit down, and kneel or sit yourself. If you are too close, the bounced flash will come from a vertical overhead position and form very dark eye shadows. If you are too far away, the angle of the flash head may allow some direct flash to spill on to the subject. The ideal set-up is an angle of around 45°, as above, so the subjects are illuminated more or less from the front. It is also possible to bounce flash into the corner behind the camera to light the whole room.

BOUNCE

Flashguns of higher specification permit the flashtube to be tilted, and sometimes swivelled, while the light sensor remains pointing forwards. Now it is possible to point the flashtube upwards or sideways and away from the lens axis, so that light output can be bounced off a surface onto the subject. This has two effects – it simulates using a light source of larger area to give a softer light, and it makes the lighting direction less frontal, improving modelling. Bounce flash requires greater power than direct flash for the same subject distance. This is because the light travels further to reach the subject, and a portion is scattered or absorbed.

Bounce techniques may be tried indoors if there's a handy wall nearby, or if the ceiling is low enough. In these instances, be wary of strongly coloured decor, as the bounced light may then give the subject a colour cast. Flash can also be bounced off a small white reflector attached to the gun itself, which gives excellent portability. A more static set-up involves fixing one or more sheets of white card in strategic positions, to bounce the flash onto a subject fixed in position.

Though it has many advantages, bounce flash also creates one or two lighting problems. When the flash output is bounced at an acute angle off a ceiling, for example, shadows under the nose and chin can look unsightly. Many guns now incorporate a smaller secondary flashtube under the main tilt and swivel unit, to fill in these shadow areas. They also add a pinpoint of light to the eyes which gives a pleasing sparkle in a portrait.

FILL-IN

For high contrast lighting situations, a burst of fill-in flash is most useful. The flash throws light into the shadow area of a subject, lowering the contrast between it and brighter parts of the scene. This allows both aspects to be recorded on film – without the flash, exposure would have to be tailored to one or the other. The technique is often used for 'contre-jour' (into the light) portraits. With fill-in flash, detail can be seen in a person who would otherwise be silhouetted against a sunset, or in front of a window for an interior portrait.

The aim with fill-in flash is to balance the available light with artificial light introduced by the gun. There is no precise rule for calculating this ratio because the degree of fill-in required varies with each picture taken. The narrow latitude of colour transparency film, however, imposes a limit of 1:4 – that is, the ambient lighting should be a maximum of four times the light emitted by the flash. Some prefer a ratio of 1:2, where the flash is half that of the natural light.

Some modern flash units give automatic fill-in, but the technique may also be manually controlled. To light a subject at a ratio of 1:2, double the film speed on the flash control panel; if the camera is loaded with ISO 100 film, set ISO 200. Now choose an aperture given by the flashgun, such as *f*8. Take a reading of the ambient light, to give *f*8 at a certain shutter speed, and check that this is not faster than the camera's maximum flash synchronization speed. If it is, choose a smaller aperture and repeat the process. Now dial in the aperture and shutter settings on the camera. The flash will provide a fill-in light half as strong as the ambient level.

There's no need to restrict fill-in to portrait subjects. It can work equally well with interiors which include windows. Usually the contrast between the light shining through the window and the dark interior is again beyond the latitude of film. Introducing flash lowers the ratio enabling both areas to be recorded. For interiors a lower lighting ratio than for portraits is used – perhaps 1:4 – and calculated as above except that the film speed should be multiplied by four. This gives a subtle, natural-looking lighting effect where the use of flash is not immediately apparent.

SLAVE TRIGGERS
Slave cells enable other flashguns to be triggered by the on-camera unit, for a two or multiple light outfit. The secondary guns can be used to fill-in the main flash, light the background or provide a rim light.

NATURAL LIGHT
With the light behind the subject, much detail is lost in the kitten's fur and face. Only the background is correctly exposed.

FILL-IN FLASH
Synchro sun or fill-in flash adds a controlled flash to brighten things up, especially eyes. It has no effect on the rest of the picture.

FLASH AND TIME
Many cameras have a 'slow speed synch' mode where the camera gives a long exposure in low light, but adds flash. It is very effective for shots like this disco scene where movement is combined with frozen detail.

THE BEST VIEWPOINT

ALTERING viewpoint is the only

ALTERING viewpoint is the only way to change the relative size and position of different parts of the scene – subject, foreground, background and surroundings. Different lenses from the same viewpoint simply vary the amount of scene covered, and switching lenses is just the same as blowing up a small part of a wide-angle view.

When people see something they want to photograph they tend to stay put, draw the camera up to eye level, and shoot almost without thinking. This method often produces acceptable but hardly imaginative pictures. Finding a superior or unusual viewpoint, on the other hand, allows a subject to be photographed with greater impact and interest, or present it in an unexpected manner.

With stationary objects such as buildings and landscapes, there's time to explore the composition from different viewpoints and an-

A DIFFERENT ANGLE

Everywhere you go there are viewpoints which are interesting because they are extreme. This photograph of St Mark's Square in Venice was taken from the top of the Campanile with a 300mm telephoto lens.

gles. From close by, a single structure can dominate the picture, whereas from further away other elements are naturally drawn into the scene, creating a different type of visual relationship. Similarly, you can try moving to the left and right, climb higher or sink down lower to see if this improves the shot. Small changes in viewpoint are worth trying, once the general camera position has been established. Moving around in this fashion can help conceal unwanted details or distracting colours, or include further foreground information to enhance the composition's depth.

Changes of viewpoint also affect how stationary subjects are lit. Assume the camera is first facing a frontally lit building.

Moving 90° to a new viewpoint shows an entirely fresh aspect to the structure, which is now lit from the side, revealing texture and creating plenty of interesting shadow and form. A third viewpoint some 180° from the original again alters the scene radically – the camera is now pointing towards the light source, so the visible face of the building is predominantly in shade.

VIEWPOINT AND SIZE

The exact place a picture is taken from fixes the relationship of elements in a scene. A close viewpoint exaggerates the relationship between near and far objects, giving greater prominence to the former regardless of its size. To

illustrate the importance of viewpoint selection, and its effect on composition, imagine a scene with a cottage in the foreground and mountains in the distance. In a shot taken at close quarters, the cottage looms large in the picture, dominating the background landscape. As the viewpoint changes by moving the camera away from the cottage, its relationship with the backdrop quickly alters. From fifty feet away, the cottage now looks quite a bit smaller, whereas the mountains are more or less the same size.

HIGH viewpoints attract the eye because they are unfamiliar – everyday life takes place with a mainly horizontal emphasis. Our eyes are displaced horizontally, and we are simply more accustomed to horizontal shifts of viewpoint. No-one casts a second glance at a building 500 feet long, but a building 500 feet high has

CLOSE VIEW MEANS WIDE VIEW
Shooting from a very close viewpoint (above) gives a feeling of urgency and action even if the subject is actually static. It can dramatize the image. Unless the subject is very small, a close view demands a wide-angle lens, which in turn means that a great expanse of background scene is included. This can make a very complicated composition, so the natural solution is to drop to a kneeling position, shifting the background emphasis to the sky. 20mm lens.

LONG SHOTS RELAX THE VIEWER
The photographer switched to a 70-210mm zoom tele lens at its maximum focal length for this alternative view of the same shot, below. The distant viewpoint changes the whole feel of the picture – you can tell it is not taken from an intimately close position, even if you know little about lenses. The background scale is totally altered by the use of the telephoto lens, and the buildings now make a good setting. The colours of the main subject look much brighter, too.

everyone craning their necks to see the top. Even standing on a chair changes an everyday domestic scene. Shooting down from a tall building gives a bird's eye view of great interest, as the scale of subjects we know well is altered. People are diminished in size, and other buildings appear less important. With a telephoto lens angled down, the sky and horizon also disappear from view, shaking us further out of our horizontal habits.

LOW viewpoints can also create visual drama. Pictures taken from ground level make subjects close to the camera look dominant and imposing. A worm's eye view of a traffic cone can make it look monumental, even though its only a couple of feet tall. People pictured from below take on a strength not apparent in an eye-level viewpoint.

When the camera is restricted to a fixed viewpoint, because of an obstruction or water hazard, a wide-angle enables you to include more of a subject without the need to move further away from it. This is very useful in confined spaces, but also enables subjects close to the camera to be included in the foreground. In landscapes this can produce a powerful impression of depth and distance.

TWIN-LENS COMPACTS

Dual lens and zoom compacts share with the SLR the ability to change focal length and this encourages you to alter your viewpoint too. Longer focal lengths, for instance, enable you to use a more distant camera position, but still obtain sufficient image magnification. That's especially important in portraits, as the perspective effect with short focal lengths used close to the subject is most unflattering due to distortion of features. Their medium telephoto 'portrait' lenses give the same image size but without the distortion.

COMPOSITION

COMPOSITION in photography differs from composition in painting because the photographer, unlike a painter starting with a blank canvas, has his 'canvas' (the viewfinder) full before the shot is taken. His skill lies in ordering these elements coherently, and deciding which to include and omit. Photographic composition is the structuring of graphic elements in an image, to express a visual statement and create a certain impression upon the viewer. This process can be deliberate, intuitive or even unwitting.

Form, pattern, texture, tone and colour are all parts of a composition, together with format, viewpoint and perspective. These elements can be arranged to create symmetry and harmony, to enhance a certain aspect of the image, or produce visual imbalance or discord. Initially the sheer number of compositional variables possible may seem perplexing, when all you want to do is take a picture. It's rare, however, for all these aspects to be present in any one shot. You'll soon start to develop an awareness of how they work and overlap, to develop your own photographic style.

POSITIONING ON THE THIRDS
Rules can work well – as all elements in this shot, placed roughly on 'thirds', go to show.

FRAMING

When composing a shot, do you fill the frame with one subject, or include less important subjects and surroundings? You need to decide whether you prefer a photograph of your subject on its own or if a stronger composition is obtained if you include some background details as well. Perhaps the background can be hinted at – unfocused elements may act as a frame to a sharper subject, and emphasize the feeling of depth.

The best place for the main subject is rarely slap in the middle of the frame – this position is too static, predictable and doesn't generate enough visual tension. Only place the subject centrally when you want to emphasize the formality or symmetry or the portrait – off-centre arrangements look better balanced and they allow you to relate the background to the principal subject. This type of composition encourages the viewer's eye to seek some other element to counterbalance the main off-centre point of interest.

In many shots a number of subjects interact, and their relative dominance and balance can only be resolved with experience. Equally, an important subject too close to the frame perimeter is usually regarded as visually disturbing or uncomfortable.

A frame within the photograph is a useful compositional device. Try shooting through a door or window onto a scene. This helps to draw the eye to the focal point of the picture. It provides cohesion to an image, and can also conceal unwanted details at the edges of the frame. Like other

GOLDEN RULES

Classical rules of composition can be referred to when composing, such as the Golden Mean (also called the Golden Section) or the Rule of Thirds.

The former (top diagram) states the ideal proportions of a rectangle are a ratio of 5:8; the vertical rectangle fitting inside this has the same ratio but is 5/8ths its size, and the smaller horizontal rectangle inside this is 5/8th of that. The space left is a square, and the dot shows one of the ideal Golden Section positions for a subject.

The Rule of Thirds (bottom) proposes a similar division of a 35mm frame, with its ratio of 2:3. Pairs of horizontal and vertical lines drawn through points a third of the way in from each corner create a grid. Where the lines intersect are supposed to be the optimum positions for the main subjects. However, the two rules clearly differ and in practice it seems better to find your own.

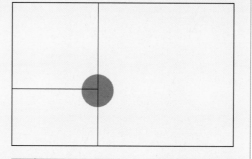

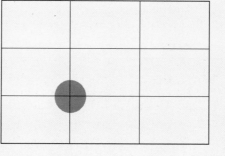

compositional gimmicks, the 'frame within a frame' composition should not be overused.

HORIZONS

The horizon frequently divides the photograph, especially in landscape studies. It is very important that this dominant feature is placed carefully. The natural tendency is to position the horizon across the centre of the frame, which gives an image stability, but little excitement. Of course, other options can be explored. Locating the horizon low in the picture allows the sky to dominate, and gives an impression of wide open spaces. This is a useful solution when a foreground is rather featureless. Conversely, lifting the horizon towards the top of frame gives an introspective and hemmed-in feel. The eyes first scan the lower part of the picture, then are drawn up to the horizon; this can introduce an element of surprise. Horizons can also be tilted to give a dynamic image, or omitted altogether with telephoto lenses, creating a composition in which orientation isn't always obvious. When a stretch of water is included in the scene, anything other than a level horizon looks like a mistake.

VISUAL WEIGHT

Identifying the most important element in a composition is important. Is it a single subject, or a number? Examine the various components of a scene, and determine which contribute and which detract from the visual message.

Certain elements possess a greater visual 'pull' than that due to size alone – the human face is probably the strongest example. When a picture contains just one face amongst a sea of other information, the face draws the initial attention regardless of its size. Words, numbers and other graphic symbols also draw in the viewer, especially when brightly coloured.

PURE COMPOSITION
Some photographs are almost entirely concerned with composition. Look at natural subjects, or man-made items, and see if you can find strong compositions by taking pictures so selective that they become abstract. Subjects which are flat rather than three-dimensional emphasize the photographer's rôle in creating a composition.

ELEMENTS

A number of basic compositional elements other than colour must be considered in any picture – tone, shape or form, line, texture, and pattern.

TONE – shading from white to black through greys – is present in colour pictures, but vital to monochrome composition. The quality of light falling upon the subject, its colour and properties of reflection all affect how it appears tonally. The function of tone is to convey form and shape, to give a three-dimensional appearance to subjects rendered on a flat surface. Tone sets the mood of a picture – a subject with predominantly pale tones is regarded as delicate, while mainly dark tones represent strength or drama. The tones of an image can be modified by the exposure and processing.

SHAPE helps the viewer identify the image portrayed in a picture. When the shape is presented against a plain, contrasting backdrop and backlit to reduce other information, the visual clue is at its heaviest – hence the appeal of the silhouette. Flowing shapes can lead the eye towards the focal point of the shot, but complex shapes demand careful choice of viewpoint, to avoid confusion.

LINE is closely related to shape, and is used to unify or structure a composition. A strong line can draw attention to a point of interest, carry the eye up to the horizon, or divide a picture into sections. Lead-in lines, such as those given by linear perspective, lead the eye through the picture, connecting the foreground and background in a dynamic way.

PATTERN occurs wherever shapes or lines are repeated, forming rhythms to attract the eye. It is mainly employed as a secondary compositional device, but can become the main subject of the

picture in certain graphic images. Patterns emerge in any lighting conditions, depending upon the viewpoint and the powers of observation possessed by the photographer. A row of railings lit from one side casts strong shadows which may create a double pattern.

Softer lighting can disclose sub-

tler patterns in natural forms, as in groups of fruit or pieces of bark on a tree. Tight framing with a telephoto or from close to a subject often removes distracting elements to reveal pattern.

TEXTURE conveys information about the surfaces of subjects, its three-dimensional quality being

greatly enhanced by strong side-lighting. A face can be made to look smooth and therefore young, or full of lines and blemishes and therefore older, simply by adjusting lighting direction. There are occasions when texture is irrelevant, as in a silhouette, but sometimes backlighting can reveal it strikingly alongside pure shapes.

TONE AND PATTERN

Tone, transitions from light to dark, gives objects rounded form and 'weight' in photographs (top left). Patterns and textures (bottom left), diminishing with depth, can also help the viewer judge scale and perspective. Close-up 'mystery object' pictures are often examples of texture used without tone.

COMPOSITIONS FROM A VIEW

Taking a scene (below), it may be possible to compose different shapes of picture by eye. Use your zoom lens to select the area you want, and trim the print later on. The long panoramic format is used by some disposable cameras and a few special compacts; in fact, it takes a wider view than shown here.

FORMAT

The shape of a picture has a strong influence on composition. Most formats are rectangular, and you need to decide whether the camera should be held horizontally or vertically.

HORIZONTAL or 'landscape' format – which in the case of 35mm has a ratio of 3:2 – seems natural for a number of reasons. First, because our vision is binocular. In addition the landscape usually conforms to this axis, with the horizon the centre of attention. Subjects are usually placed in the lower part of the frame, to provide visual stability. Most cameras are designed to operate comfortably when held horizontally, the vertical aspect being far less ergonomic. Panoramic formats elongate the horizontal ratio beyond 3:2.

VERTICAL or 'portrait' format is often used because many subjects are arranged vertically – the human figure and face, trees and certain buildings. Again, the main subject is often placed in the lower portion of the frame.

SQUARE format is used by 6 x 6cm roll-film models such as those from Hasselblad, Bronica and Mamiya. Because most subjects are longer in one plane than another, composing within the formality of a 1:1 ratio image only suits certain subjects. Architectural views or scenes where symmetry is paramount work best. The 6 x 6 format is often used because it allows easy cropping of the large rollfilm negative to either vertical or horizontal when printing.

When composing a picture, the unexpected often creates the most interesting image. Just because a landscape is long and low doesn't mean a horizontal format has to be used. It's often preferable to go against the grain and find alternative views of familiar subjects by using a surprising format shape.

A SENSE OF MOVEMENT

IF YOUR subjects suffer from appearing like a succession of frozen statues, you can improve your shots by introducing movement. Cameras, and films, are now able to cope with fast-moving subjects and can even create the appearance of motion when none is present. Various techniques and effects can be used to portray movement, ranging from stopping the action to letting it flow.

which the subject is likely to pass, or where action will reach a peak; the shutter is pressed an instant before the subject reaches the point of sharpest focus. This technique needs practice. You need to use a high shutter speed, such as 1/1000, or faster. To create the maximum freezing of a speeding subject, avoid those passing close to the camera and use a viewpoint head-on to the action.

FROZEN MOTION

To stop the fastest action requires a high shutter speed and possibly a high-speed film too. Capturing a brief moment in time renders a subject sharp and reveals details the eye cannot normally see because the movement is happening so quickly. To take this type of shot, it pays to choose a viewpoint a reasonable distance from the action, and use a telephoto to give the required subject magnification. The lens is pre-focused on a point

BLUR

Sometimes a frozen image lacks the sensation of movement, simply because our eyes never view this kind of reality. Flowing water is never seen as sharply frozen, but literally as a fluid and continuous movement. Different shutter speeds alter the way we recognize a subject. A car or train moving past our field of vision moves quite smoothly, and may tolerate only a little blurring and remain identifiable. A horse has a more complex

movement – the body moves up and down, and the legs move forwards and backwards to carry the horse forward. A lengthy exposure of this rhythmic motion may convey the feeling of motion far better than a sharper image.

PANNING

Between the high shutter speeds required to freeze motion, and the slower times necessary to induce blur, is a further technique – panning. Swing the camera to follow the movement of the subject across your field of vision, keeping the subject centred in the viewfinder. Press the release during the mid-point of this arc. Don't stand too close, or framing won't be easy, but move away and use a longer focal length lens. Stand with feet apart, so you can swing comfortably and freely. Pre-focus the lens. Select a slow shutter speed in the region 1/60 to 1/2. Frame the subject as it approaches, but avoid the temptation to re-focus. Track with the subject, turning your whole body, and release the shutter smoothly, keeping the camera moving in the same arc – don't stop as soon as the shutter is fired. Choose a background that will give impression of movement. Streaking of detail in the background and foreground, against a sharper subject, gives an impression of speed.

FROZEN OPTIONS
When action involves stances, expressions, gestures and peak moments, a fast shutter speed can freeze all the details which the eye misses. The happy toboggan rider, left, is an example of frozen motion used to advantage.

TOTAL BLUR
A combination of a randomly-moving subject, a slow shutter speed and panning leaves no part of this picture sharp, yet it remains clearly recognizable. This technique conveys a powerful impression of movement.

PANNED BLUR
Panning with the moving express train creates a blur from trees in the foreground but keeps the train sharp, in an unusual composition with a wide-angle lens which makes the scene look almost like a model railway.

FLASH AND BLUR
The fairground bumper car shot, below, uses a simple combination of a brief time exposure and on-camera flash, with the camera set to aperture priority automatic at a medium aperture setting. Shoot plenty of frames to be sure of getting the right effect.

TRACKING FROM A MOVING VEHICLE

TRACKING FROM A MOVING VEHICLE

The photographer shot from a car passenger window with a wide-angle lens to get the dramatic bike shot on the left; the motorcycle was only a couple of feet from his front element. A slow shutter speed will produce a powerfully streaked background, resembling a zoom effect, while a fast speed as used here can record the scene faithfully. A motor-drive is essential to allow quick reactions and provide a choice of final images. This is a dangerous way to take pictures unless you have two expert drivers, a road free from other users, and a safety harness.

TRACKING

Pictures taken from a moving vehicle of a subject travelling at a similar speed can also convey a vivid impression of movement. This technique is regularly used for dramatic shots of cars and motorcycles. A slow shutter speed can be used as the speed of the subject in relation to the camera is low or nil, and this allows the backdrop to blur against the sharp subject. The degree of blur varies depending on the shutter speed used, the velocity of the vehicles and the angle of the shot. When the picture is of one vehicle following another, blur increases towards the edges of the frame, as the background gets increasingly close to the camera.

CREATING MOTION

The camera can be moved during a lengthy exposure to create artificial motion in a static subject. Depending upon the plane of movement, the streaking effect will be parallel for lateral motion, curved for rotation of the camera, and radiating for moving the camera towards a subject. It works best with high contrast subjects.

With a zoom lens, alter the focal length during exposure by operating the zoom during a long shutter speed, with camera on a tripod. If you compose a shot of a stationary car and zoom during only part of a long exposure an impression of movement results. Zooming and slow-speed panning in combination can be particularly effective.

FLASH AND BLUR

The technique of mixing a burst of flash mixed with a slow shutter speed combines a sharp image with a degree of blurring – an experimental approach which can create dramatic effects, providing the subject is within flash range and ambient light levels are relatively low (at dusk or indoors).

SEQUENCE SHOOTING

An alternative approach is to suggest movement by creating a series of motor-drive images, or sequence which tells a story, analyzes movement, or divides an event into separate components. You can use an interval timer to record sequences which are too slow to be noticeable normally over a much longer period of time.

STROBE FLASH

Rapid pulses of flash from a suitable 'strobe' unit can capture a series of images on a single frame of film. This is rather like a very rapid multiple exposure, and worth trying with relatively simple movements initially.

PEAK OF THE ACTION

Capturing the decisive moment in a sporting event takes great skill and split-second timing – the chances are you won't record it by just machine-gunning pictures with a motor-drive. Study the sport, wait for the right moment and use your anticipation.

In certain sequences of movement, there is a point at which the action stops, or slows. When a tennis player, for example, pulls back the racquet to hit a shot, momentarily the racquet head is stationary.

A pole-vaulter hurtles forward and plants the pole, then rises up to clear the crossbar. At this point, there is relatively little movement. The action then increases as gravity returns the pole-vaulter to the ground. These brief moments can be frozen sharply with a slower shutter speed than when fast action is continuous, such as the racquet head travelling through the shot, or the pole-vaulter rising or descending.

Peak of the action shots can be taken with simple cameras. Press the shutter a fraction of a second before the action reaches its high 'static' point.

PERSPECTIVE

MULTIPLE CLUES TO PERSPECTIVE
This winter avenue of trees by Lee Frost has several primary perspective elements built-in – linear perspective, with the vanishing lines of the road; diminishing perspective, in the scale of the trees; tonal perspective, with dark tones at the foreground; and aerial perspective due to mist.

PHOTOGRAPHS reduce the three-dimensional real world to a flat surface of just two dimensions. A sense of depth is conveyed to the viewer by incorporating visual clues or illusions into the picture. The apparent perspective within the image can be varied by skilful composition. Changes of scale, converging lines, foreshortening of shapes, loss of contrast and shift of colour all help to convince us we are seeing objects at different distances in space.

To emphasize the sense of perspective, a viewpoint which reveals a range of different distances should be adopted. Depth can also be suggested by using differential focus – only part of the scene is sharply rendered, leaving the remainder defocused but visible. Flattened perspective can be used to produce a graphic effect.

LINEAR perspective is a powerful method of revealing depth, using lines which we know are parallel such as a railway track or the top and bottom of a building or wall. These lines appear to converge as they recede into the distance towards a vanishing point. If the lines travel all the way to the horizon and the view is not impeded, the effect is heightened. Compositions can use one vanishing point for optimum clarity, but many pictures of complex objects can feature two or more. A low, three-quarter viewpoint of a building, for example, has three – one horizontal point for each side of the building and a third point high above due to the convergence of its vertical sides. A low, close viewpoint exaggerates perspective, while a distant viewpoint lessens it.

DIMINISHING perspective is closely related to the linear variety. Equally sized objects such as a row of parking meters, a line of cars in a traffic jam or an avenue of trees appear progressively smaller the further they are from the camera position. There's an automatic assumption that the larger objects are placed in the foreground, and the smaller ones are higher in the frame closer to the horizon.

Differential focus can also emphasize the effect when a telephoto lens is used. The eye sees the zone of focus, and automatically regards one of the defocused areas as closer – a neat visual trick.

AERIAL perspective is produced by haze in the atmosphere. Objects at increasing distances from the camera are further reduced in contrast and lightened in tone. Backlighting emphasizes the impression of depth, especially when a UV filter is left off the lens. The effect is often witnessed when a telephoto lens is trained on a series of far-off hills, leaving out the immediate foreground. But wider focal lengths can also be used, as the sharp clear foreground carries more visual weight than distant hazy parts of the scene. Aerial perspective may also be observed in the relatively small spaces of interior scenes. Judicious use of lighting places darker tones in the foreground, blending into lighter areas produced by daylight through a distant window or door.

TONAL perspective operates on the principle that brilliantly lit tones advance, while darker areas recede. By this method, lightly col-

LENSES AND PERSPECTIVE

A common fallacy in photography is that switching lenses alters the perspective in a composition. If you're standing in the same spot the whole time, shooting a scene with several different optics, the perspective actually remains the same. Only the angle of view changes, as the picture sequence on focal length amply demonstrates on pages 20-21. Perspective only changes when a new viewpoint, nearer or further from the subject, is adopted. The effect produced by long focal length lenses, where everything seems to be piled on top of each other, is called telephoto compression. Taking a shot with a 50mm and a 500mm lens from the same position produces identical perspective, but the telephoto picture looks more compressed because this part of the scene is greatly enlarged – an effect the eye doesn't normally see. To alter perspective, change your working distance.

TELEPHOTO PERSPECTIVES
It is often thought that wide-angles 'give' perspective and long lenses don't. This is not true. They show different aspects of perspective. The compression given by a tele lens in the top shot of buildings is a flattened perspective, in which scale is shown very accurately, though the viewer sees it as exaggerated. The lower picture shows pure aerial perspective – this is more or less a perfect visual description of what the term means. The hills recede because each layer is lighter than the one in front of it.

oured objects placed against a darker backdrop appear to draw forward and create a sense of depth between the two elements. In dull light, for example, a burst of fill-in flash to lighten a person standing in the foreground makes the subject stand out sharply from the murky background. Colour choice also has an effect upon the way an image is perceived. As with light tones, warm colours also spring forward, and cool colours recede like dark tones.

CREATIVE COLOUR

AN APPRECIATION of colour is essential to effective communication in photography. Knowing the strength of different colours, what they each signify and how they interact is a key part of the medium's vocabulary.

Colour operates on several levels – visual, emotional and symbolic, and triggers a response faster than either shape or line.

If a colour needs to be described precisely, as in a computer art program, it can be broken into three separate components – hue, brightness and saturation.

HUE describes a colour's unique property, distinct from any other.

BRIGHTNESS expresses how light or dark the colour is.

SATURATION defines its purity. In photography, bright colours are said to be saturated, and mixed colours unsaturated.

PRIMARY AND SECONDARY

There are three 'additive' primary colours – red, green and blue. If you have three light sources in these colours, they can be mixed to make any other colour. In addition there are three complementary 'subtractive' primary colours – cyan (a greenish blue), magenta (a pinkish red) and yellow. If you have paint or ink in these colours, you can mix any other colour.

The additive and subtractive primaries are shown as a colour wheel on page 88. Each hue lies opposite its complementary colour; if you mix opposing colours, the result is grey. In colour photography, the brightest colours are subtractive primaries, which need only one emulsion layer to be reproduced, as films have layers of cyan, magenta and yellow dye images. The additive primaries use two emulsion layers – magenta and yellow to make red, for exam-

ple. They tend to be richer, with more variety of shades, but slightly darker. Secondary colours like purple, violet, blue-green and orange, which use three emulsion layers, can never be as brilliant.

Reds are dense, vibrant and powerful on most modern films. Yellows are light and may have a narrow range; they are not high on the film manufacturers' list of priorities. Blues tend to be dark, as people prefer a deep sky colour.

Green is the predominant colour in nature, and most films have a bright or yellowish foliage rendering rather than blue-green.

Violet is one of the most difficult colours to record accurately due to the dyes used in photographic materials, and many blue-violet flowers reflect high levels of infra-red which record as pink.

Orange is a mixture of red and yellow; when correctly exposed it is vibrant but very dark or light shades can be unpleasant on film.

SATURATED PRIMARIES
Slight under-exposure (above) saturates colours in a scene, so many photographers shooting on transparency set the film speed at one-third or a half stop under the recommended ISO rating. That means Kodachrome 64 is exposed at ISO 80, or Fujichrome Velvia (ISO 50) at ISO 64.

SINGLE COLOUR HARMONY
Colour harmony, right, is produced by using a limited range of shades of the same colour, or a restricted range of colours from the same sector of the colour wheel.

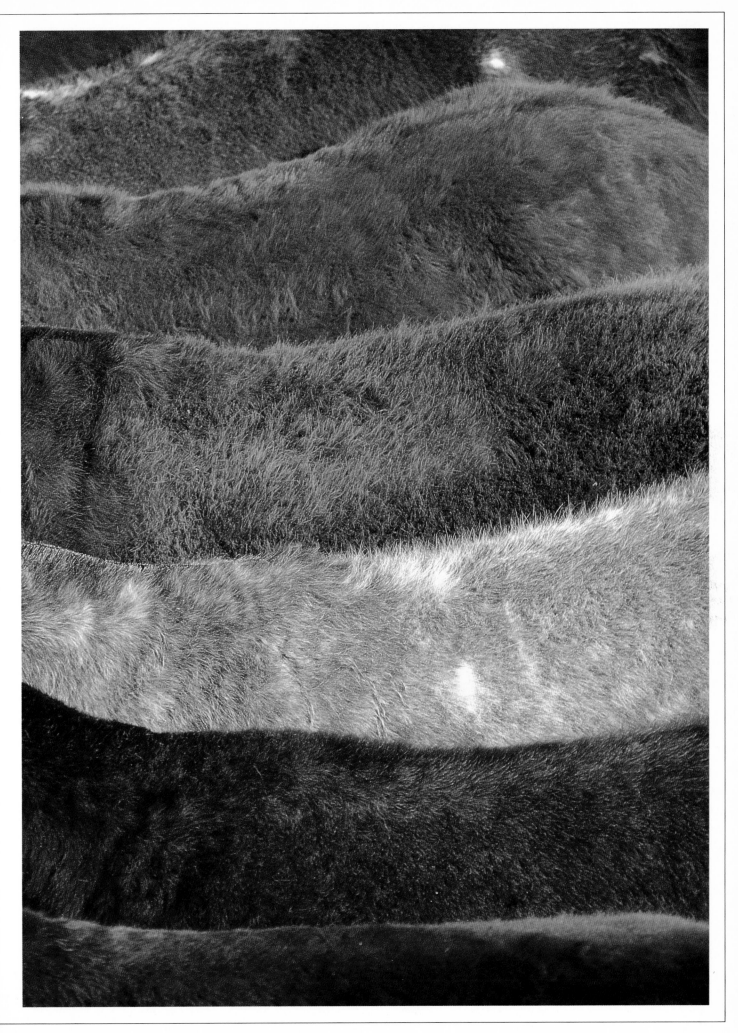

COMBINATIONS

Having grasped the basics of primary and secondary colour, we now turn to the real world – one in which colours occur in an infinite number of mixtures and juxtapositions. However, some basic guidelines can still be applied. Warm colours, such as yellow, orange and red appear to come forward, while cooler colours such as green, blue and violet recede.

If a photograph is composed of just two complementary hues of equal area, the warmer colour will always dominate a cooler partner. Even when the warm colour is relatively small, it has a visual weight out of all proportion to its size.

Orange, for example, has more impact when paired with its complementary blue, and yellow is especially vigorous when coupled with violet.

For this reason cooler colours like blue and green tend to be associated with backgrounds, creating colour harmony when appearing with smaller areas of warmer complementaries. Red and its complementary colour green share a similar luminosity, however, despite one being warm and the other cool. This is a most unstable pairing, as the edge between the colours produces an effect termed colour vibration.

Most photographs contain more than two colours, and these hues are often unsaturated. But an awareness of the colour wheel, which colours are strong and weak which combinations create discord or harmony enables a photographer to begin manipulating colour in composition.

BRILLIANT CONTRASTS
Pure colours clash and blend at the same time, and red jumps forward.

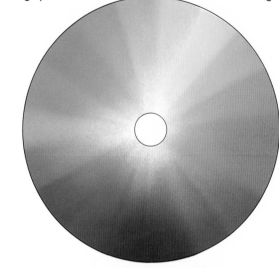

THE COLOUR WHEEL

The colour wheel maps out the primary colours so that they fall opposite their complementary colours – two opposites have maximum contrast, and if mixed, would make grey.

You can use the colour wheel to help pick opposite or adjacent colours, or sets of three, to create colour harmony or contrast. This wheel shows the colours at maximum brightness.

NEUTRALS

Unlike the colours on the circle described above, black, white and grey contain no hue, and are described as neutral. But they still play a significant part in photography. Colours look brighter next to these neutrals, or they act as a foil to each other. Mixing a colour with black or white produces the unsaturated hues we see every day.

White is a positive colour associated with cleanliness and purity, and conjures up images of fresh snow or weddings. White is also prone to colour casts, especially in shadow areas.

Black is often used as a backdrop or lead-in to other colours, or as a distinctive shape like a silhouette. Greys – between black and white – are common in nature and man-made environments. Elephants, whales, rocks, overcast skies, battleships and buildings all represent different shades of grey.

SOFT COLOURS
The landscape above gains by having only one dominant colour, with subtle light and shade.

NEUTRAL SETTINGS
A steel-grey sky provides a good backdrop to show off the sunlit colours of buildings, below.

BLACK AND WHITE

MOST photographs are taken in colour, with sales of negative film far outweighing transparency materials. Black and white accounts for a small percentage of the total market. Its followers maintain that it is a unique, challenging form of photographic expression, with flexibility and aesthetic qualities not available in any other media. Colour, they argue, obscures the true content of an image.

Photographers also shoot in black and white because it allows involvement in every stage of picture production, and greater control over the finished result. It is simpler to learn and understand than colour processing. There is little point in using normal mono films unless you wish to do your own processing and printing; Ilford XP2 film enables you to get black and white prints from a standard colour d & p service.

The art of black and white photography lies in the ability to observe coloured scenes and visualize them in shades of grey. An attractive landscape scene, a stunning sunset or unusual still-life may not always translate into an interesting monochrome print, especially if the colour component first attracted the eye. Those who have operated in both mediums concede that trying to shoot colour and monochrome simultaneously is virtually impossible – each demands a different way of seeing. Therefore it is better to concentrate on one film type at a time.

Consideration must also be given to the way panchromatic film responds to colour. Hues which contrast strongly to the eye may record similarly on the negative, and will therefore produce closely-associated tones in the print. Filters can be used to modify

a colour's rendition, the rule being that a filter lightens its own hue, and darkens opposing colours. A red filter, for example, will lighten a red rose and darken the green foliage surrounding it.

In addition to learning how colour subjects will appear in light and dark tones – in other words, contrast – the absence of colour also places greater emphasis on line, form and texture. Reducing colours to blacks, whites and greys makes shapes stronger, and suppresses distracting colour details. Simplicity is the keyword when building pictures in monochrome.

Colour may need much consideration when shooting in monochrome, but there's no need to evaluate light sources, or worry how different sources will affect film. Black and white materials also have the greatest tolerance to exposure error, and a print can

often be made from a poorly exposed negative. This is no excuse, of course, for slovenly technique.

MOOD AND DEPTH

One of the great strengths of monochrome is its ability to express mood. A typical finished print should contain a full range of tones from light through to dark, but limiting the tonal scale brings quite different effects. An image composed mainly of dark greys has a sombre, heavy effect – this is termed low key. Equally a picture exhibiting predominantly light tones of grey brings a bright, airy feel – this is high key.

The illusion of depth in a black and white image can be produced by the recession of tones, or careful use of shapes in composition. A range of hills will become progressively paler in tone the further

A FULL RANGE OF TONES
A good black and white print can display a great range of subtle grey shades as well as the extremes

POWERFUL PORTRAITURE
Monochrome is a first-class portrait medium which brings out character, particularly in male sitters

they are from the camera, creating an attractive series of grey shapes. A winding ribbon of road disappearing into the distance gives a similar effect, leading the eye from foreground to background.

Monochrome is also a fine medium for revealing pattern and texture in a subject. Strong sunshine from one side gives a directional light which reveals the form and shape of subjects it illuminates. Adjacent highlight and shadow areas, such as those seen in a ploughed field, roof tiles or many other subjects, can create strong patterns which are no longer present in overcast light.

Mood can be further controlled by careful adjustment of processing and printing. Normal development produces negatives of average contrast which print well on normal grades of paper. Shorter development times lower contrast, while longer times increase it. During enlargement, a print can be locally controlled in tone by 'dodging and burning' – the practice of shielding a portion of the print, or allowing extra light to fall upon it. Multigrade papers and filters allow local control of contrast too, so a whole palette of effects can be created beyond the camera exposure.

ENHANCING PRINTS

Because of the inevitability of small blemishes or dust spots, a black and white print usually requires some retouching when dry. Special dyes are available for this purpose, and are applied sparingly with a small sable brush. Careful spotting conceals these imperfections and tidies up the print's overall appearance.

Further enhancement of a black and white image is possible with toning and tinting. Sepia toning is a simple process which gives the print a nostalgic feel reminiscent of older photographs, but a range of other colours is also possible. Selenium and gold toning are both harder to control,

but produce subtle variable effects which also increase the permanence of the print to an archival level. Fine art photographers nearly always tone their prints for added black density and permanence.

Hand tinting of a finished print adds an element of colour and creates a most distinctive appearance. The best effects are seen when the colour is applied sparingly, though more garish treatments and strident colours also have their place.

SELECTIVE PRINTING
A straightforward print lacked character and contrast, and had too much distracting detail. Dodging tools (right) are held under the enlarger during printing to make some areas lighter; other areas are darkened by burning-in, the printer using his hands to control extra exposure locally. The result has been exaggerated here. A black border was finally printed, using a card mask, round the edge of the 10 x 8" print to hold in the subject-matter visually.

TONING PRINTS

Sepia toning (left) is a simple process you can carry out on any existing black and white print. There are many other toners available, including blue (below left) which is very well-suited to snow scenes and seascapes. Ilford's XP2 black and white film is designed to the be processed and printed by ordinary colour labs on colour paper, and if you take this type of film to a mini-lab, you can ask for sepia, blue or other colours of monochromatic print without using toners.

INSTANT MONO

Polaroid's 35mm black and white slide film, Polapan, produces rich tones (below) and can be processed in a couple of minutes, ready for projection.

USING STUDIO LIGHTS

THERE ARE two main advantages to using artificial lighting. It can be controlled in strength, direction and quality, and it is available at all times of day (and night). Before using your own lights, it is important to understand how light reacts when it meets a surface. Light is usually reflected but it may also be transmitted, absorbed, or refracted.

Light can be softened by passing it through a diffusing material which scatters the directions of the light rays. The quality of reflected light depends upon the nature of the surface it is bounced off. Specular reflection occurs with shiny surfaces, while a textured surface gives diffuse reflection. Coloured surfaces absorb some light and reflect other wavelengths, while black absorbs most light.

Lamps may be used bare, or modified by attachments (reflectors, umbrellas, large area 'window lights', barn doors, snoots and honeycombs) to diffuse or channel the light. A point source of light like the sun or a bare bulb gives harsh, contrasty illumina-

tion. Cloud cover over the sun, or a reflector or diffuser used with a bare bulb increases the apparent size of the source and softens the lighting.

Various types of diffuser can be positioned in front of the lamp and each employs a translucent material or screen. Reflectors are placed further away from the lamp, and light is bounced onto them and then onto the subject. This gives a greater spread of light but demands greater light intensity. Umbrellas are the most common reflector attachment, and can be covered in a variety of materials. Reflectors such as sheets of white card or mirrors can also be placed close to the subject itself.

Light from a bare bulb is omnidirectional. Channelling it into a specific area or beam limits the area of subject lit, like a spotlight. This can be achieved by various attachments which enclose the lamp and allow light to escape through a shaped aperture. Barn doors are adjustable on all four sides, while honeycombs and snoots give increasingly defined pools of light.

ONE LIGHT

To explore the techniques and versatility of using artificial lighting, a static or still life subject is initially preferable. This enables the effects of one light to be studied as it is moved to different positions. Later it shows how introducing reflectors or extra lamps reduces contrast and creates better lighting solutions. With experience you can then turn to live subjects, such as studio portraits.

First set up your still life subject containing various shapes and textures on a table with free space around it. An arrangement of flowers in a vase with a collection of assorted fruits provides a diverse selection of elements, and it helps that some of the petals are translucent. Erect a plain background some distance behind the subject. Now set up the camera on a tripod, and choose a viewpoint which gives the most pleasing composition against the backdrop.

The first light shone on the subject is the 'key' light – this produces the main highlights and shadows. Use a bare bulb giving a

hard type of illumination. Fix the light at a certain height on a stand and observe the subject as the light is moved. Take notice of how textures and shadows change with the light in different positions. A colleague to help with changing the light position is a big advantage.

With the light near the camera position, clear details are seen and shadows are minimized, but a subject lacks form. With a light at right angles to the camera, highlights and shadows are approximately equal, and form and texture are enhanced.

As the light moves behind the subject, it lies in shadow from the camera position and contrast is maximized. A low light hidden by the subject gives a rim-lit effect and the translucent flower petals glow with transmitted light.

SOFTER LIGHT

Establish the best place for the 'key' light – a three-quarter frontal position is often used. Now add an umbrella reflector to the lamp, or hold a sheet of translucent paper between the light and the subject. These methods increase the area of the light source to give a more diffuse light quality, softening shadows and lowering contrast. This effect should be clearly seen on the subject.

Adding a white card reflector on the far side of the subject to the light source bounces light back into the shadow areas and lowers the lighting ratio. A similar effect can be achieved by adding a second lamp to the set up. This should be about a quarter the power of the key light, and placed in the other three-quarter frontal position.

Increasing the output of the second lamp to half the key light gives further fill-in illumination. A second lamp can also be used to light the background, if there is sufficiently space behind the subject, normally mounted on a floor stand behind the sitter's chair.

A HOME STUDIO
Electronic flash, stands, diffusers, background and reflectors make up the basic home studio kit.

LIGHTING A STUDIO PORTRAIT

1 Working by room lighting, the shot is composed using a 100mm lens, ideal for a good head and shoulders in a normal sized room. Turn the sitter's body slightly to one side, to avoid a flat-on shape.

2 Set up the main light on the same side of the camera as the sitter is turned to, about three feet above the camera and to the side. The light should have a diffusing umbrella or soft-box about 42" (1 metre) across.

3 A large silver reflector has been placed just out of shot, very close to the sitter, on the side opposite the light. A white sheet or polystyrene insulation board will do fine. It lightens the dark shadows of the main light.

4 A small slave flash can be clipped into place above and behind the sitter, well out of shot. This provides a hair light which helps pick the face out from the background. Adjust it to be one f-stop brighter than the main light.

5 A background light can be placed behind the sitter's stool, aimed at the background paper or material. You can't do this if the sitter is too close to the backdrop. The background now looks cleaner and brighter. Light skimmed from the side shows creases!

6 For a final touch, the silver reflector has been replaced with gold, which gives a tanned look to skin tones. The hair light has a yellow filter, and the background light has a pale red filter, changing its colour in a subtle way.

LIGHTING EFFECTS

1 Spotlighting – using an optical spotlight or a bare flashtube with no reflector, pure hard light is produced which creates sharp shadows. Keep the light close to the camera for flattering results.

2 Coloured gel lighting – using coloured filters over all your flash heads does not mean losing all the realistic colours in your pictures. Yellow and blue filters, or red and green, will mix to produce white.

3 Under-lighting – often used as an effect in old horror movies, lighting coming from underneath the face is not always unflattering. It can look attractive, especially if reflected off a warm colour surface.

4 Back lighting – two lights aim towards the camera from behind the sitter, on either side. A lens hood is essential. Try to keep the bright light off the nose and eyes. A white reflector near the camera puts light into the face. You can allow hair to "burn out".

5 Silhouette lighting – use a white background, and one or two lights which should be behind the sitter, but lighting the backdrop only. Give enough exposure for a clean white with a pure black silhouette, or use a colour gel on the background.

6 Soft lighting – with two flash units in the same position as for back lighting, they are turned so no light strikes the sitter directly. Instead it is all reflected off two large white panels either side of the camera. A blue filtered flash lights the backdrop.

FLASH OR TUNGSTEN?

Flash tends to be the most popular of these two light sources. It provides a powerful, consistent, and above all, cool type of illumination. The brief burst of high intensity light freezes movement. By avoiding excess heat, subjects can be placed close to the lamps without discomfort, and accessories built around the light to modify its output.

Flash is rated at the same colour temperature as daylight, so needs no filtration with daylight films, and can be mixed with natural lighting. Flash lights are technically complex, however, and require a modelling lamp to enable the effect of the light output to be previewed. Cost is also much higher than simple tungsten lamps, and repairs must be handled by specialists.

A tungsten light gives off plenty of heat, and provides a continuous source of illumination of lower power. This means subjects can be deliberately blurred for effect, but fast action cannot be frozen. For static subjects, extra exposure can be given by keeping the shutter open for a longer time. The colour balance of tungsten requires tungsten film, or filtration with daylight type. Tungsten lights are technically very simple, and can be repaired easily.

TUNGSTEN STILL LIFE
Excellent results can be obtained using tungsten balanced film and tungsten lights, as long as the subject is static. Exposures may be several seconds. Photographed with photoflood lamps and Ektachrome 64T film using 24mm wide angle lens and offcuts of signmaker's Perspex.

DEVELOPING FILM

THE OBJECTIVE of film processing is to convert an accurately-exposed latent image into a negative suitable for enlargement, or a transparency for positive viewing. The processing sequence is a series of steps which, if followed correctly, always produces a predictable result. Colour films are developed to a stricter routine, feature a greater number of steps than monochrome and require higher temperatures. In black and white there is considerable scope for varying the processing procedure, depending upon how 'graphic' you want the final image to be.

In monochrome, the four main stages of processing are film development followed by stop bath, fixation, and lastly washing and drying. Development converts the exposed silver halide crystals, or invisible latent image, into visible black silver. This process is halted after a time by immersing the film in a stop bath – this neutralizes the developer and avoids contamination of the next solution. At this stage an image isn't apparent, as unexposed silver halides are still present in the emulsion. The fixing bath makes these water soluble, but doesn't affect the desired silver image.

Thorough washing in water removes any remaining halides or other chemicals. A final rinse with a small amount of wetting agent then prepares the film for drying. Hanging the film from one end on a line or in a special cabinet drains water away, and the wetting agent prevents drying marks. Drying should take place in a dust-free environment, and gentle heats speeds up the process. A small weight on the lower end of the film avoids curling.

DEVELOPERS

Film development is governed by four variables – developer type, agitation frequency, duration of development and the solution temperature. The latter is usually 20°C for all solutions, though variations are possible. Developer manufacturers publish a list of processing times and recommended agitation for various film/developer combinations. These should be strictly adhered to, until experience enables you to change the developer duration. Too short a time usually produces a thin negative, while extended development makes negatives dense, contrasty and hard to print. Agitation ensures fresh solution constantly

circulates to all parts of the film, ensuring even development.

Various types of developer are available, each giving slightly different negative characteristics. Developers can give fine grain, increase film speed, or enhance definition and contrast – but not all at the same time. Different developers have been created to boost one aspect of performance, and enable a photographer to tailor film development to final print use, whether artistic or realistic. Generally speaking, a manufacturer's recommended developer will produce a good tonal range at the exposure index of each film. The contrast level can be adjusted to suit the type of enlarger illumination being used – normal contrast for a condenser type, or higher contrast for a diffusor enlarger.

Fine-grain developers are popular, though some require the film speed to be down-rated. Acutance developers concentrate on creating higher contrast between high and low negative density, this enhanced definition producing crisp images. When an increase in film speed is required, a high energy developer may be employed. Universal developers can be used to economically process both film and printing papers, though it fails

to provide optimum quality with either.

Developers are supplied either as concentrated solutions, or in powder form. A measure of developer is used with a precise amount of water to prepare a stock solution of the correct temperature. Stock film developer can be retained and reused at increased processing times, though the trend is towards one-shot types which are discarded after single use. Developers should be properly stored to prevent air oxydizing the solution and making it less active.

COLOUR PROCESSING

Though following broadly similar principles, home processing of colour film can be more complex than monochrome – black and white film has a single emulsion layer, all colour films have three (each carrying a latent image). Precise times must be followed for each step, and solutions must be maintained at higher temperatures – up to 38°C. When a colour negative is developed, dyes are formed in place of the silver grains of the developed image, whereas with a colour transparency, an inverse or positive image must be created from the negative latent image before the dyes are produced during development. These two films therefore have completely different processing needs; slide film uses two development stages, the first creating a silver image which is then 'reversed' to produce the final colour picture..

Colour negatives are processed by kits of C41 chemistry, modern versions of which require only a few stages. During development the colour dyes created are the precise opposite of those appearing in the original scene (printing the negative reverses the colours once more, returning them to normal). A combined bleach/fixer (blix) solution makes the silver image soluble, and washing removes them, leaving just the coloured dyes. Finally a stabilizer

SAFETY IN THE DARKROOM

Because you will often need to be working with a combination of chemical liquids (some dangerous in themselves), water and electricity in a dimly lit or totally blacked out area, you should pay particular attention to safety.

● Separating your darkroom into a dry side and a wet side will help prevent many potential mishaps since electrical equipment should never be handled with wet hands.

● All chemicals, when not in use, should be in properly

sealed containers and out of reach of children. Most modern photo chemicals have clear hazard warnings and treatments marked should they accidentally get into your eyes, on your skin or be swallowed. Some do not – although this is illegal in Europe.

● You will often be working in dim lighting or darkness, so always keep the floor area free from clutter or wires, and develop the habit of putting your equipment, paper, trays, and so on in exactly the same position.

● Ventilation is important! Darkrooms need effective black out, but don't just seal round the door and windows. Install a proper light-proof ventilator grille or a Vent-Axia darkroom fan. Failing this, get into a routine of leaving the darkroom every half hour for a 'breather'.

● Luminous tags and stickers can't affect film and paper unless you place it right next to them, so put these on switches, pull cords, handles or the corners of benches. They help you keep your orientation in total darkness.

ACTION SEQUENCE – PROCESSING A ROLL OF FILM

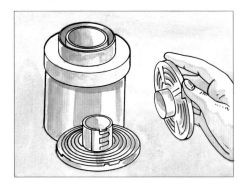

1 Load film in the dark or inside a light-tight changing bag! First examine the spiral to check it is totally dry and in good working order.

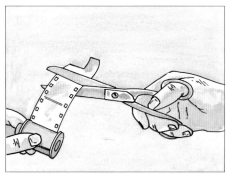

2 Cut off the film leader, making a straight end with rounded corners. Turn out the room light, or put everything in a changing bag.

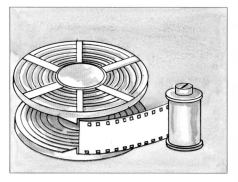

3 Feed the shaped end into the spiral reel entry, then use the reel's auto action to draw it out of the cassette smoothly into the reel.

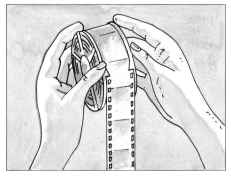

4 Beginners should use a reel like this. Alternating the two halves pulls the film through. Centre load reels are for experts!

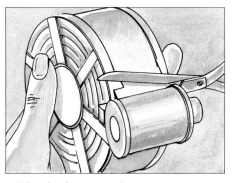

5 When loading is complete, use scissors to cut the film right at the cassette mouth. The processing cycle can now commence.

6 Put the loaded spiral and retaining clip (if supplied) on the centre column, then into the developing tank. Fit the tank lid.

7 Pour in developer at exact temperature, quickly; tap the tank on a worktop to dislodge bubbles. Fit watertight lid; invert for 5 seconds every 30 to agitate (or as dev instructions).

8 10 seconds before the dev time ends, pour out developer smoothly; pour in stop bath or water; agitate with twist rod 30 seconds; pour out stop bath; pour in fixer, agitate.

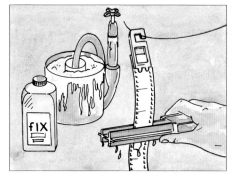

9 Rapid-fix for 2 minutes; return fixer to bottle. Wash in 10 changes of water for 2 minutes each, or running water for 20 minutes. Remove film, hang up, squeegee, let dry.

---

stops the dyes from fading. C41 kits can be used to process Ilford's chromogenic or dye-based XP2 black and white material.

The E6 process is designed for colour transparency films, and involves many steps. First a negative image is formed in black silver by a simple developer, then the film is washed. Now the reversal bath fogs unexposed areas of the film. The next step is the colour developer, which activates the colour couplers built into the emulsion layers. These help form positive images created by the reversal bath. After a conditioning bath, a blix loosens the silver halogens and these are removed by washing. As in C41 processing, a stabilizer is the final step in the E6 cycle. Kodachrome films do not have integral colour couplers in the emulsion: they are added during processing at Kodak's specialized laboratories.

MONOCHROME PRINTING

ONCE a black and white film has been processed and dried, prints can be produced from individual negatives. As with film and developers, a wide choice of printing papers is available, each type consisting of a thin emulsion layer attached to a base.

Traditional fibre-based papers produce the highest image quality, especially at the extremes of tonal range, but are more awkward to handle than resin-coated (RC) papers. Economic single weight fibre paper is often used for contact sheets and rough prints, while exhibition or display prints are made on double weight. Resin coated papers are less prone to damage and easier to wash and dry, but give a slightly inferior tonal range. RC paper processing requires less chemicals and is of shorter duration.

Other paper variables include image tone, which is usually neutral black for bromide materials. Some papers with a chlorobromide content exhibit a warmer, brownish colour. Surface finish is yet another variable – glossy, lustre, pearl and semi-matt are the main ones available. Glossy has a brilliant shine on RC papers, but is more diffused with fibre types. Lustre reveals a finely textured surface, while 'pearl' and 'velvet' are midway between the lustre and glossy. Semi-matt has a duller finish with least reflection.

The most significant paper variable is contrast, which usually spans from grades 0 to 5. Grade 2 is widely regarded as normal contrast, though papers can differ in the amount of contrast delivered. Grade 0 is the softest, and grade 5 is the hardest or most contrasty version. Printing papers are also available in variable-contrast form. Filters introduced into the light path between negative and paper control the contrast. This saves keeping stocks of each paper grade in various sheet sizes.

Matching a paper to an individual negative takes skill and experience – it also depends upon subjective taste and the end function of the print. Negatives of average quality usually print well on a normal grade of paper, a contrasty image falls better onto a softer grade, and low-contrast negatives may require a hard paper for a satisfactory result.

CONTACT SHEET
Making a contact proof of a sheet of negatives is a good practice, as the small positive images are easier to assess than negatives, and gives a clearer idea of how a picture will print up.

DODGING AND BURNING

Producing your own prints enables local control of exposure to be made. Parts of a print can be 'burned-in' or 'dodged' – this means giving extra or less exposure respectively. Burning-in is often accomplished by allowing further light to reach an area of the print through a hole made by hands, or cut in a piece of card. With the latter, several different shapes and sizes can be prepared, and held at various heights under the light source for different effects. Burning-in might be used to print in a light sky tone, for instance.

Dodging is the reverse procedure – a small piece of opaque material prevents light falling locally on the paper. Black card is often used, attached to thin wire so it can be controlled from beyond the print area. A dark face can be held back by dodging to produce a more pleasing tone.

Each technique demands the card or hands are moved around during exposure, to prevent a hard or noticeable edge appearing between the normal and modified parts of the print. With practice subtle or even dramatic effects can be achieved, which the viewer will perceive as exactly how the picture was taken.

BASIC METHOD

Standard monochrome printing mainly involves following a set procedure, though individual photographers always operate slightly differently. First the desired print size is established by setting the easel arms, if these are adjustable. Then any cropping of the negative is worked out once the image is projected onto the easel. Now the only adjustments necessary should be the lens aperture – this works best when stopped down a couple of aperture clicks from its maximum setting – or to the exposure time to correct print density. Avoid jogging the enlarger during the exposure, or walking around on a wooden floor, as even minor vibrations will ruin image sharpness.

The exposed sheet of paper should be totally submerged in the developer, which is kept at a constant 20°C, for the full recommended time – this varies according to the type of paper used. Too short a development time may give weak print tones, with dark greys where a rich black should appear. Keeping the print in the developer solution longer than the recommended time can eventually place a veil over highlight areas. Resist the temptation to pull the print out early, even though it looks too dark, because subdued safelighting gives a poor indicator of real print density. Process normally and wait until the print is viewed by stronger lighting after fixation before making adjustments to enlarger settings.

After the full development time has elapsed, the print should be carefully raised out of the solution with a print tong, allowed to drain off excess chemical, and then placed in the next tray – the stop bath, or plain water in an emergency. Submersion for half a minute is sufficient. Again raise the print, this time with a different tong to avoid contamination, drain the print and transfer it to the fixing bath. Again leave the print in the solution for the full time, though it can be lifted for inspection. A wash in water is the final stage of the wet side processing cycle.

With any darkroom procedure, it is important that the standard routine is mastered before any variations are practiced – otherwise it may be difficult to rectify early mistakes. As your experience grows, you can then modify techniques to suit your own requirements, enlarger type and materials used.

ACTION SEQUENCE – BLACK AND WHITE PRINTING

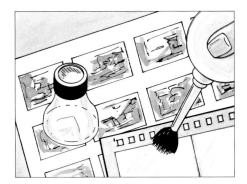

1 Select the negative to be printed with a magnifying loupe and a contact sheet, and blow all dust off it with a brush or air spray.

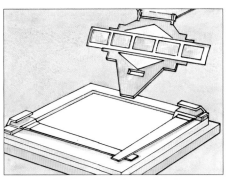

2 Put negative emulsion down in the carrier and slot into enlarger. Adjust easel to fit size of paper. Switch safelight on, room light off.

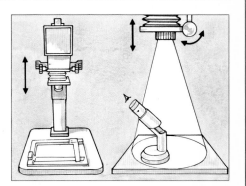

3 Turn enlarger on with lens at full aperture; raise or lower head to set size of image, use focusing (with a focus finder) for sharpness.

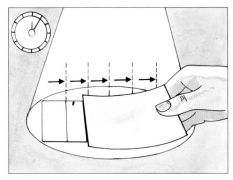

4 Cut some 2" wide strips of normal RC printing paper. Place one under a typical image area, and expose it in timed 5-second steps.

5 Place this 'test strip' in developer for the full time (1-2 mins); keep it immersed and moving. Move to stop bath, and then to fix solution.

6 After 30 seconds in fix, you can switch white light on (close your paper box!) to judge which step is the best, set time on timer.

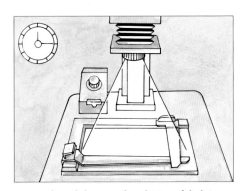

7 Wash and dry your hands! In safelighting, place a full sheet of paper in the easel. Expose for set time, and develop exactly as the strip.

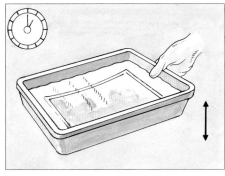

8 Develop the print, gently rocking the dish to agitate, using tongs to transfer it to the stop, fix and finally to a 5-minute running water wash.

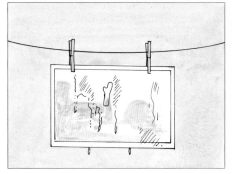

9 Squeegee excess water off and clip to a line to dry. Fibre-based papers require a 30 minute wash and special drying conditions.

TEST STRIP
Cut a full 10 x 8" sheet into five 2 x 8" strips. Use a black card to uncover 1" sections as you make repeated 5 second exposures – step 1 receives 5 seconds, step 8 gets 40. Pick the best exposure.

MAKING COLOUR PRINTS

PRINTS can be produced from colour negatives or transparencies. Producing a colour print requires accuracy in both exposure and filtration, so a colour enlarger provides illumination which can be varied by the use of filters. Most have a dichroic colour head built in enabling degrees of filtration to be dialled in, but simple models accept colour filters in a drawer.

The method of filtration most widely used is termed 'subtractive', and involves three primary colour filters – cyan, yellow and magenta. These alter light balance individually or in pairs, by subtracting colour from white light. Using all three together is not desirable as this blocks out all colours.

Like colour film, printing papers contain three emulsion layers, sensitive to red, blue and green light. These produce cyan, yellow and magenta image dyes respectively upon processing.

Because of variations in subject lighting, film response, types of enlarger, and printing paper, some adjustment of filtration is inevitable in almost every negative. The integral orange mask makes negatives difficult to interpret, so a contact sheet or series of enprints is advisable as a starting point.

DRUM PROCESSING
Unlike black and white papers, colour materials must be processed in total darkness, so an enclosed drum is used – not open trays. Once loaded, this enables most steps of the sequence to be conducted by normal room lighting. The processing cycle is similar to that used for films, and requires a precise approach to

timing, temperatures and agitation. Print drums can be agitated by hand on the wet bench, or placed on a cradle in a processor unit with a thermostatically controlled bath to keep solutions at the desired temperature. Operation of the drum is by a manual crank handle, or can be motorized. Some types are fully automatic.

TWO TESTS

Packs of paper are supplied with a recommended filter combination to correct any colour bias of that batch. This information should be dialled into the enlarger head, or built up in the filter drawer, as the initial step towards correct filtration. Separate test strips are required to establish the changes to filtration, and to find the correct exposure time. The test strip for exposure is made along the same lines as that for a monochrome print – see page 99.

Judging colour deficiencies is the trickier of the two tests. A colour chart showing how a correctly filtered and perfectly exposed print is affected by variations in filtration and exposure is handy for assessment and comparison. Colour balance is also influenced by subjective factors – you may wish to 'warm up' the colour of the original scene.

In subtractive printing, colour casts are corrected by increasing the same colour filter, or by reducing its complementary. The chart below lists the options possible for all colour casts.

Always view a test print with a consistent light source, such as a specially corrected or daylight fluorescent tube. If the test print looks slightly red, then cyan can be removed, or yellow and magenta added to the filter combination. An 05 alteration will give a slight change of colour, 15 and 30 unit changes give increasingly heavy shifts.

Altering the filter combination also has an effect upon print exposure, so any change requires a recalculation. When a filter is added, the original exposure time is multiplied by the filter factor. Removing a filter means the exposure time should be divided by its filter factor.

Clearly altering yellow has the least effect on exposure time, while changes to cyan and especially magenta has a significant effect.

COLOUR PRINTS FROM SLIDES

Printing from a colour transparency involves producing a positive image from a positive original. In some ways this is easier than working with negatives, as the projected image can be viewed on the baseboard, and the original slide can also be referred to. The processing procedure is broadly similar to that of the colour negative in that two tests are required to obtain correct exposure and filtration but, with positive papers, exposure and filtration techniques are the opposite of those for negatives. So further

exposure makes a print lighter, not darker, and colour casts are eliminated by reducing that colour in the filter combination.

A conventional masking frame which produces white borders with a negative original makes black borders with a transparency. A mask the same size as the image area can be used, and extra exposure given to the surround to make them white. When dodging and burning in techniques are used to locally affect a print, the reverse of negative techniques

apply. Dodging or shading part of the image makes it darker, while burning-in makes it lighter.

Reversal papers feature lower contrast than negative materials, to counterbalance the higher contrast of the original transparency. Conventional reversal papers form image dyes during development, whereas Cibachrome has colour dyes already built into the emulsion. This is termed the dye destruction process, and produces brilliant saturated colour similar to the original. Processing times are also shorter than with other reversal papers.

ACTION SEQUENCE – MAKING A COLOUR PRINT

1 Wearing rubber gloves, prepare the three processing solutions to the correct temperature. Warm the drum too, but keep the interior dry.

2 The enlarger procedure is the same as for monochrome, in total darkness. Load exposed paper into the drum emulsion side inwards.

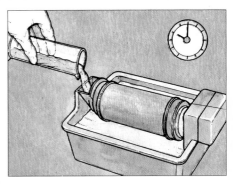

3 Pour developer into drum; start rotation. Watch time and temperature carefully. Drain developer early, to be empty when time is up.

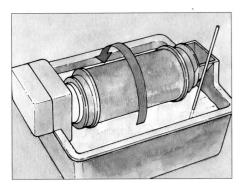

4 The bleach/fix (blix) is now poured into the drum and rotation starts. The recommended time is a minimum and the blix is re-usable.

5 Fill the drum with warm water for a short time, and then drain. The drum lid can then be removed, and the print carefully extracted.

6 Wash in an open tray. A continuous supply of water is best, or several changes so that fresh water reaches the print repeatedly.

7 When the recommended wash time is up, remove the print from the tray and carefully wipe or sponge off any excess water.

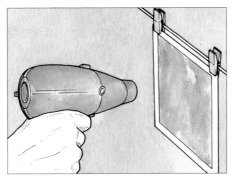

8 Dry in a dust free atmosphere, or speed up with a hairdryer. Wet prints tend to be blue or magenta, so judge the colour when dry.

9 Meanwhile the drum should be washed, cleaned and thoroughly dried, ready for the next print.

Normal	+20M needed	-20M	+20Y	-20Y	From neg

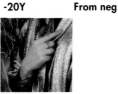

Normal	+20G needed	+20M	+20C	+20Y	From slide

FILTER ADJUSTMENTS

If your print from a negative shows a colour cast, you need to add filters to match the same colour as the cast. Casts in prints from colour slides are removed by using opposite filtration. Very strong casts are hard to judge but colour analyzers get you within 20 units automatically.

SELLING YOUR PICTURES

SOME photographers take pictures purely for enjoyment. Others try to meet their costs by selling the odd picture, and a few seek to make a career from the medium. To sell images of any kind, a photographer requires skill, preparation, research and the right outlook. The first requirement is basic technical competence. Picture buyers expect pin sharpness, correct exposure and careful composition as minimum criteria in every shot.

Slides should normally be colourful, while black and white prints ought to display a full range of tones and be spotted. Neat presentation of material helps too. Slides should be placed in transparent sleeves – never in boxes – and accompanied with a typed letter on a printed letterhead for a professional appearance. Return post and packaging is also advisable.

The next point is to ensure the pictures are relevant to the market being targeted. There's no point in sending off a portfolio of evocative monochrome prints to a publisher dealing exclusively in colour, or placing stunning pictures of steam trains before the art editor of a boat magazine. The area which interests you must be researched objectively and thoroughly, to avoid wasting everyone's time and effort. Reference material covering the freelance needs of publishers, picture agencies and other sources is contained in most libraries.

Sending pictures on a speculative basis is never 100% successful, so an individual must be prepared for rejection slips. The closer picture material is tailored to the market requirements, the fewer these will become. But if you do get turned down, have another go elsewhere.

GO FOR POPULAR SUBJECTS
If you want to sell through a picture library, your shots must be the kind of pictures which are easily asked for by name – a species of plant, a place, a person, an activity. Dramatic sunsets remain best-sellers.

BUSINESS ACUMEN

Skill as a photographer is insufficient to guarantee success in selling pictures. Business sense is also required, whether your intention is to sell a few images, or start a freelance operation. For the latter, an understanding bank manager and an efficient accountant need locating to help you start up and keep your finances in order. Tax authorities should also be informed of your plans, together with planning bodies if you intend to work from home.

Presentation is everything when dealing with new clients. The initial impression formed about you will stem from not just the standard of your pictures, but the accompanying paraphernalia. So it pays to have some stationary designed and printed – letterheads, compliments slips and business cards. A rubber stamp to mark transparencies or prints with your details also looks professional.

Whatever volume of pictures you send out, a systematic approach to logging them in and out is essential. You can keep records of transactions on a computer, or ordinary file system. Prints and slides also need to be labelled, then stored safely and efficiently, so a picture can be retrieved swiftly. There are several low-cost computer programs which will produce the very small labels you need for slide mounts.

Copyright applies to amateurs just as to professionals; unless you sell all rights, your heirs can benefit from sales of your work for 50 years after your death, so use a copyright stamp!

STOCK LIBRARY

Joining a picture library is a long term commitment. Photographers are usually asked to commit a good number of slides to the library for a period of years. Initial submissions vary but are often run to hundreds of pictures. It is expected that this body of work should be topped up at frequent intervals – perhaps 30 to 50 extra images each month.

Typically, libraries charge 50% of whatever fees accrue from sales of a photographer's pictures. That's because they duplicate slides several times over, market them widely in areas an individual often cannot tap, and handle all the paperwork and bill collecting. It can be a long time before money starts to trickle back to the photographer; a wait of eighteen months or two years is average.

Many different types of stock library exist, from specialist outfits dealing with one or a handful of subjects, to large agencies covering numerous or general themes. Some accept 35mm transparencies – others only deal in medium and large film formats. Research into the precise requirements of individual organisations pays dividends here.

POWER TO THE PEOPLE
Although it is easier to photograph places and things, the most saleable pictures you take will always be shots of people. You can photograph people at public events freely, as the photographer did above, but don't assume that any picture you take in the street can be sold. Court cases have proved otherwise, and model releases are necessary if your pictures show ordinary people as opposed to performers or participants in carnivals and parades. Professionals often hire models just to look like ordinary people in scenes.

OTHER MARKETS

Producers of calendars, postcards, posters and prints all seek pictures contributed by freelances. This area of the market differs from advertising or magazine photography, in that the images are intended to stand alone, or with minimal accompanying words. Again, research is essential to pinpoint a specific target, as the market is extremely diverse and forever changing or updating.

Posters are pictures of broad appeal produced at low cost on cheap paper – often pop stars or small animals for sticking on youngsters' bedroom walls. Specialist prints are a fairly recent development, and of high image and paper quality. These are intended to be hung in the home, office or restaurant to provide modern, fashionable decor or create a certain mood. Postcards and calendars cover a wide variety of subjects, and range from cheap and cheerful to high calibre products. You can even publish your own at moderate cost.

Magazines and books are another prime target, but once again the old adage of making submitted pictures relevant to the title applies. It pays to concentrate on one area, such as gardening, fishing, buildings, cars or even photography itself. Then you study the existing publications and the standard of pictures inside to establish a list of shots they might well use. Picture editors will also hold a submission of pictures for a while before reaching a decision whether to publish, so don't expect an answer by return of post! Many publishers pay a fixed fee for pictures, but don't be afraid to ask what it is. Keep an eye out for photographic competitions too – these are announced regularly in magazines, and the prizes of money, travel or equipment make them well worth entering. Study the winners of previous competitions to gauge the standards required.

CARE AND ATTENTION

THERE is more to photography than just pressing a shutter button. Photographic equipment must be looked after carefully if you want it to function efficiently and have a long working life. Film needs to be handled and stored correctly to achieve optimum results. Finished photographs need to be properly organized and stored.

MAINTENANCE

The best way to make sure your camera or lens has a long life is to use it carefully, within reason, and clean it regularly. All lenses should be fitted with a protective UV filter, and those not mounted on the camera should always be fitted with front and rear caps. Transporting camera equipment calls for a suitable bag or case to keep gear together and protect it from damage – the different types are covered on pages 42 and 43. A camera, just like any other piece of machinery, benefits from servicing. If it is used occasionally it could last for years without attention, but an annual service might be advisable for a frequently used camera.

Regular cleaning of cameras and lenses in a dust-free area is recommended. Where a camera has interchangeable components, these should be detached and laid out separately on a clean surface. The first step is to remove abrasive dust and fine particles with either a can of compressed air, a blower brush or miniature vacuum cleaner. A soft-textured brush can be used for delicate parts such as the shutter curtains and lens front element, though extreme care is necessary. Cotton buds can be used for crevices and round small controls on the camera exterior. When all dust and debris has been removed, surfaces can be wiped clean with a cloth. Don't forget to polish the internal battery contacts too.

Increasing automation makes DIY-checks of camera functions trickier, but some basic operations can often be tested. With the lens removed and the camera held up to the light with its back open, slow shutter speeds can be timed for accuracy. Start at the slowest speed and try each in turn – a visual check will ensure successive speeds are half the previous setting and can be made up to about 1/125. The mirror mechanism should be inspected, and the seat-

A CLEANING KIT
A cleaning kit is worth gathering to keep equipment in tip-top condition – this one comprises a vacuum brush which sucks dust away when you squeeze it, moist wipes, a special Canon lens cleaning cloth, cotton buds for removing 'crevice' dirt, lens tissues and a bottle of lens cleaner.

ing of the focusing screen. Metering accuracy is best checked by comparing readings with those of another camera or meter. Apertures should be checked for repeat accuracy; does ƒ8 always produce the same shape and size of hole? Slackness in focus, zoom or aperture ring mechanisms can develop over time, but can be tightened during servicing.

For long term storage, remove camera batteries and store these separately – a cell may leak and corrode the contacts inside a battery chamber. Also release camera shutter if cocked, and remove loaded film from the camera; if left in, this may permanently distort. Use cling wrap to protect equipment from dust. Include a dried sachet of silica gel to absorb moisture.

STORING PICTURES

Picture storage is important for three main reasons; to ensure photographs can be located efficiently and promptly, to keep them safe from damage, and to slow the processes of fading. Whatever volume of pictures you shoot now or have generated over the years, never leave photographs lying around loose or pushed carelessly

into a shoebox. Colour materials are most prone to gradual fading with time, as the dyes that make up the image are less stable than the silver used in the black and white process. A selection of archival or acid-free products can be bought to provide optimum protection of stored images.

Negatives are best kept by cutting them into strips of five or six images, and placing them in translucent filing bags or a sheet held in a ring binder. Transparencies are often returned from processing in plastic or card mounts. Each slide image retained after editing should be slipped into a clear sleeve or a file sheet. Though glass mounts offer higher protection, they can break and damage the slide, and should not be used for transparencies which are sent by post. Condensation may also become trapped between the glass and cause damage. Prints are best kept in a purpose-made album made from acid free paper products or plastics.

When suitably protected and labelled with information on the mount or print, these materials then require collective storage. Unedited slides can be kept inside the boxes they are sent in from the processing lab, with a label on

FILM HANDLING

Film kept for short periods at room temperature won't come to any harm, but in the longer term it's best to store materials in a refrigerator, especially those of higher speed ratings. Use film before the expiry date printed on carton.

Allow chilled film to return to normal temperatures for about three hours before loading it into the camera. When shooting outdoors or by a window, keep film as cool as possible, particularly during hot conditions. Avoid leaving film lying around in a car on

sunny days, as temperatures inside can soar. A low cost cool box and quantity of ice will stop transported film getting too hot. When humidity is high, pack film into a sealed container with some dried silica gel crystals.

Exposed film is equally vulnerable to damage through heat and moisture. Treat these rolls like unexposed film, and process promptly to avoid loss of contrast or colour casts appearing. Use a marking system to tell exposed film from unexposed – or wind the leader into the cassette.

ACTION SEQUENCE – CLEANING A CAMERA AND LENS

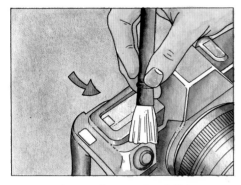

1 Using a large, soft artist's brush flick away dust from all the crevices and controls on the camera body – leave the lens ON.

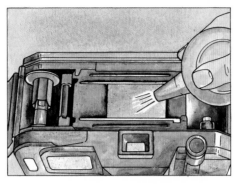

2 Make sure the camera isn't loaded! Open the back, and using a blower bulb – remove the brush part – blow all dust out of the inside.

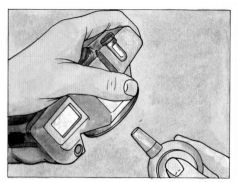

3 Remove the lens and place carefully aside. Hold the camera mount downwards, and gently blow a few times into it to dislodge dust.

4 Blow dust off the lens rear element. Re-fit the lens (do not use a brush on the lens rear, or inside the lens throat of the camera).

5 Remove lens cap. Use the soft brush to sweep dust away from the front element perimeter, then blow front element clean.

6 Use a lens-wipe ONLY if a fingerprint or splash actually marks the lens. Then use the wipe to clean any marks on the body.

top for identification, and finished slide shows can be kept in projector slide trays ready for projection. These methods prevent individual slides from being viewed quickly. Plastic sheets in a ring binder or suspension file drawer make it easier to view many pictures at once and select individually. Each sheet holds 20 to 24 35mm slides. When high volumes of picture material are involved, a filing and cross-referencing system is essential, for which a personal computer is ideal.

SLIDE AND NEGATIVE STORAGE
Ring binders and suspension files are ideal for film strips and mounted slides respectively. Prints can be kept in albums – use a quick-dry photo pen to write on the back, or the ink may smudge.

TROUBLESHOOTING

ACCIDENTS can happen in any complex process, and despite increasing automation, photography is no exception. Usually there is a simple reason for the mistake. A process of deduction should point towards a fault in one of three areas – camera handling, film stock, or processing.

The wrong camera settings or an incorrect accessory may have been used, a technique could need refining, or gremlins might have got into the camera or processing equipment. Errors in film manufacture sometimes occur, though infrequently. A more likely explanation is inadequate film storage, or even use of the wrong film stock. The rebate area gives the biggest clue to film faults. If the problem affects this part of the film, a processing error is probable. Data imprinted normally on the film edge indicates correct processing.

Below are the most common problems encountered, with explanations of how they can be avoided.

CAMERA SHAKE

Careless handling or using a shutter speed too slow for the lens fitted often results in slight movement of the camera at the precise moment of exposure. This is sufficient to knock the edge off picture sharpness, especially when enlarged. Shake also occurs when a tripod mounted camera is blown by wind or affected by vibration during a long exposure. Shake is prevented by ensuring the camera is stable when hand-held, and the shutter speed is fast enough for the focal length used. Shoot tripod pictures when the wind dies down, hang an outfit bag on the tripod to increase its mass, or use the mirror lock-up facility of an SLR if fitted.

CAMERA SHAKE
Don't jab the shutter release button carelessly – this is the result.

TOO CLOSE FOR THE MINIMUM DISTANCE
A 'focus free' camera will not give sharp images of small subjects.

HIGH CONTRAST EXPOSURE PROBLEMS
Light from a window fools the meter.

EXPOSURE ERROR

Over-exposure or under-exposure of an image is observed when an incorrect aperture or shutter speed is set on a manual camera, or if an automatic model fails to take a meter reading from the main subject. An indoor portrait of a person sat in front of a window leads to under-exposure, due to the brighter background; a subject placed in the window light with a dark room behind will be overexposed, as the opposite applies. Correct exposure is obtained by moving the meter close to the subject for a reading, then recomposing the shot.

INCORRECT FOCUS

Often occurs with subjects close to compact cameras, as the separate viewfinder system gives no information as to the lens focus position. Also seen with AF cameras when the focusing sensor is not placed on the main subject. Check that the subject is beyond the minimum focusing distance of the lens, and that the sensor is accurately placed. Focus lock can be employed with compositions where the sensor would miss the important part of the scene.

LIGHT LEAK

Unwanted exposure of film to light, also known as fogging. Caused by accidental opening of the camera back, loading film in bright sunlight, a faulty cassette or exposure to light before processing, creates random streaks or patches of light. These may ruin a handful of frames, or the entire film if the exposure was prolonged. Pictures taken before a new film has been fully wound to the correct position may also be affected. Prevent light leaks by loading film in the shade, and by never opening the camera back except to load and remove film, or for cleaning when empty.

DOUBLE EXPOSURE

Inadvertent double exposure (as in the example on the right) is caused by failure of the film advance mechanism or, in manual wind-on SLRs, accidental pressing of the film rewind lever. It may also occur when a film is partially or fully exposed, rewound, and then re-inserted into the camera. The first cause requires a camera repair, the second more careful handling, and the third greater attention with reloaded film. If a film is rewound when partially exposed, clearly mark the number of frames used immediately, as it is easy to forget.

BARREL DISTORTION

Vertical or horizontal lines in a composition can bend outwards when placed towards the frame edges, forming the shape of a barrel. This indicates a lens without fully resolved rectilinear correction. Pincushion distortion, when the lines bow inwards, is the opposite effect. Often seen with budget wide-angle or wide zoom optics. This can be prevented by keeping straight lines away from the frame edges.

VIGNETTE

When a fuzzy black image appears in all four corners of the frame, a lens hood too deep for the focal length has been fitted, or a combination of filters mounted on the front of the lens has protruded into the image area. The effect is usually seen with wide-angle focal lengths set to smaller apertures. Switching to the correct hood for a lens, or removing one of the filters, should prevent vignetting.

SCRATCHES

One or more horizontal lines running along part or the whole of the film length indicate unwanted small particles of debris. These can either enter the open camera

back, and rub against the soft emulsion as film is wound through, or they have been on to the squeegee that wiped the film dry after processing. Regular washing of processing equipment and a can of compressed air to clean the camera should remove the debris.

CRIMP MARK

This is a small kink or crimp mark in the film surface, caused by careless handling. Too much pressure has been exerted on the film surface, causing it to permanently buckle. It occurs more frequently with larger areas of emulsion during or after processing, such as clumsily handled roll film.

RED-EYE

A ghoulish reddening of the eyes caused by a low powered flashgun being fired from too close to the lens axis. In dim lighting conditions, light is reflected from the inner lens surfaces of the eye as the pupil is dilated. Often seen with compact flash portraits, which is why some up-market models now incorporate a pre-flash to close down the iris in the

eyes. It may also be prevented by diffusing the flash of a compact, or asking the subject to avert their gaze from the camera. Moving an accessory flash to a higher or wider position also helps, or using bounce flash.

FLASH CUT-OFF

When a part of the image area in a flash shot taken with an SLR is rendered black, this points towards incorrect flash synchronisation. Too fast a shutter speed has been set, resulting in one of the shutter blinds travelling across the frame when the flash fired. The shutter speed should be reset to permit the fully open blinds to coincide with the brief burst of flash – refer to the camera manual to find the maximum usable shutter speed.

FLASH EXPOSURE ERROR

Subjects close to the camera may be inside the minimum range of the flash, and receive too much light before the flash can quench the output. This results in a burned out or over-exposed image. Similarly, subjects beyond the maximum reach of the flash will

be too dark or under-exposed. To obtain correct exposure, position important elements or subjects of a composition within the near and far limits of the flash. If two subjects are equally important, place them at similar distances from the camera to avoid one being rendered lighter than the other.

FLASH SHADOWS

When a subject is placed too close to a light-toned backdrop, heavy shadows can occur with the hard light emitted by direct flash. Shadows can be prevented by placing the subject against a darker background, or by moving the flash so that the flash falls to one side. Bounce or diffused flash also softens shadows.

REFLECTIONS

A bright, distracting reflection in a window or shiny backdrop is often seen with pictures taken by direct flash. This can be avoided by shooting from a different angle so that the background is at an angle to the camera, by arranging the subject differently, or by employing bounce flash.

PROJECTS

THIS third and final section of the book takes the form of a series of photographic projects. We'll assume that you've already diligently read the two earlier sections, which means you should now be properly equipped, or at least have a clear idea of which items are needed. You'll also have a good grasp of key photographic techniques. What's needed now is an opportunity to put everything you've learned into practice.

Apart from being paid for their troubles, professional photographers enjoy one other significant advantage. They are given commissions by clients, which require subjects to be shot in certain ways. The enthusiast, on the other hand, has no such specific goals in mind, and takes pictures mainly for pleasure, not profit. This lack of single-mindedness is often a barrier to successful work.

The twelve projects assembled here, however, provide a diversity of subject material to cater for a whole range of tastes. Each major theme or subject is broken down and explored in some detail. Objectives are established first, then methods of how to achieve particular effects and images. Explanatory texts are accompanied by informative pictures and illustrations – it's just like having a personal tutor working alongside you.

Portraiture, for example, has always been popular with photographers. We show how to shoot a formal portrait in both available and studio lighting conditions, and how to tackle a tricky group portrait. Candid studies reveal people

behaving more naturally, and require a completely different, low-profile approach.

Children are obviously much photographed too; we reveal how to capture great results here also. Man's curiosity with all shapes and sizes of the human race is matched by one other subject, covered by the Animals project. Whether as domestic pets, in zoos and parks, or as wildlife in their natural habitats, animals provide a rich source of picture opportunities. Again, many different techniques are needed for each aspect.

Landscape is one of photography's enduring themes, and is tackled by just about everybody. But how many are satisfied with their results? In this project, you'll be shown when to shoot, why waiting for the right light is important, and how to frame the subject. Garden pictures are also encompassed, those you might visit and your own patch. A project on Travel describes at length how to make the most of your holidays, to avoid returning home with the usual snapshots. In stark contrast to the leisurely pace of the previous project, the aim of Action Photography is to convey the very essence of sporting effort.

Further projects include Architecture, Still life, Special Events and Night Photography, and the section is rounded off with a series of tricks and techniques which enable your camera to produce out-of-the-ordinary Creative Effects. Armed with these dozen themes, there's now no excuse for saying 'I don't know what to shoot'.

POSED PORTRAITS

EVERY photographer enjoys taking pictures of people, but producing a planned portrait requires both technical and social skills. A formal portrait differs from a candid shot because in it the subject (or group of people) is fully aware of the camera and often looking directly into the lens. This gives a formal portrait a quite different emphasis or feeling.

The photographer is supposed to be in charge of the portrait session, should have a particular effect in mind and direct the sitter (or individuals in a group) to adopt a particular pose or stance. He also advises on clothes, props, accessories and backgrounds.

When shooting a posed portrait, the camera should be set up in advance; loaded, with shutter, aperture and focus settings preset for the conditions, the right lens and filters already fitted. Then almost exclusive attention can be paid to the subject. Group shots are more demanding to take, as several people and their expres-

sions have to be right at the moment of exposure. With friends, relatives or complete strangers, any posed shot tests a photographer's ability to deal with people courteously, clearly and firmly.

INDIVIDUALS

There are a number of framing options when shooting a picture of a single sitter. A shot can show the full-length figure, standing, sitting, working or just relaxing in a relevant environment. Moving in closer for a three-quarter length shot limits the compositional choices, but you can still have a background scene, and some of the problems of posing legs and feet are avoided. At a closer distance you can compose a head and shoulders with only a vague hint of background, or even a full-face tightly cropped head excluding everything else. Of all four types, this last places most emphasis on the eyes and expression.

A formal portrait is often a

serious occasion, intended to show the subject in his or her best light. As a consequence some people can be quite nervous. Here the photographer should provide encouragement and give direction, without letting the technical aspects of camera control interfere.

By showing that the mechanics of picture-taking are running smoothly and unobtrusively, the photographer appears in command, even if panic is just below the surface. Be efficient and avoid dawdling, as a subject may be busy or have a short attention span. Ask a child to smile for too long, for instance, and the rigidity of the face or the boredom will be obvious in the picture.

There is no reason to copy High Street photographic studio styles, in any case. The best professionals don't put their subjects in front of canvas backgrounds, they take them into carefully-chosen outdoor locations, or an appropriate part of the sitter's own home. The most expensive pro-

fessional portraits are ones which look like fashion posters, magazine editorial shots, or a well-executed painting. The idea of a 'formal' portrait should certainly never imply a stuffy, posed-on-a-stool picture taken using studio flash and a potted plant. So the 'serious' occasion may only be serious because of the subject's own preconceived ideas; you may be able to suggest a much more interesting, relevant image, and turn the occasion into a partnership of ideas between photographer and sitter.

Involving the subject so they become an active participant stops the sitter feeling too self-conscious. Break the ice with apprehensive sitters by explaining the effect you are seeking in the portrait, demonstrating the pose wanted, even inviting the subject to look through the viewfinder while you yourself adopt the required stance. By these means, a rapport is built with your subject which places them at their ease.

The best way to build up

ENVIRONMENTAL OR STUDIO?
Posed portraits fall into two main categories. Environmental portraits put the subject in the right setting, at work or at home, or against a background associated with their hobby or sport. Studio portraits imitate a traditional painting, using drapes or a painted backdrop to provide a neutral setting. Sometimes, throwing a domestic or office background out of focus does this job.
Left is an environmental portrait of a potter, set up and posed carefully, lit with fill-in flash. On the right is a formal studio-type portrait taken in an ordinary room using two mains-powered portable flash heads and a graded colour backdrop. Before undertaking a portrait session, you must have a clear idea of which type of portrait your sitter wants.

experience as a portrait photographer is to limit the number of technical variables at the outset. That means using just one lens and taking pictures at a location you know and have tested before. The available light may be the only unknown quantity, but it creates natural-looking pictures and enables a photographer to concentrate on the important business of portraiture – capturing an image which makes a statement about the subject's personality.

Outdoors, harsh sunlight may make your subject squint and cast ugly shadows across the face. There are several ways to make a better shot here. You can turn the subject around so you are shooting into the light, though this leaves the face in shadow and the hair rim-lit; you can find a shadier spot if the sky is cloudless; or you can use a white reflector outside the frame area to bounce light back under the chin. Better light for portraits is provided by thin cloud cover, which gives a softer effect with attractive modelling of female features.

When window illumination is employed indoors, one or two lighting techniques can be used to advantage. Try placing sheets of tracing paper over the window to diffuse the light entering the room. This makes natural light even softer and most flattering for portraits. When the window is at an oblique angle to the face, use a large area reflector such as a sheet of white card to bounce light back into the shadow side. The closer this is placed to the subject, the greater the fill-in effect, but don't let it intrude inside the image area.

Tungsten lamps and portable or studio flash equipment enable portraits to be taken anywhere indoors. The lighting techniques already discussed apply here, with particular reference to bounce lighting, diffusion and reflectors. Effective pictures can be taken with just one light, providing it is sufficiently diffused.

Backgrounds are an important component of portraits, especially when the framing includes more than a tightly cropped head shot. A plain wall can be used, or seamless paper hung on a pole. This is available in nine-foot wide rolls in a wide range of colours, which should be chosen so that the backdrop complements the primary tone set by the portrait. Some amateur dealers stock half-width rolls which cost less, are easy to handle, and are fine for shots of one person. Other surfaces may also be used; fabrics like canvas or velvet, netting, painted brickwork and many other alternatives.

When the existing background is worth using, avoid distracting lines or shapes that fall behind the head – trees, telegraph poles, plants, mirrors, curtains and so on. With indoor shots keep a look out for unwanted details entering the frame edge, such as light fittings or power points.

Capturing the right skin tone is another critical aspect of portraiture. When taking a close-up shot of a very pale or dark-skinned subject by ambient light, be careful with metering to avoid exposure error. On the whole, people want to appear with a medium skin colour regardless of their race or natural colouring. Oriental sitters prefer a delicate white skin with a touch of pink, not a golden skin-tone; red-faced European farmers like to appear slightly healthy, not crimson; African and Asian subjects like to be able to see detail and a well modelled complexion.

Take a reading off a similarly lit grey card (average subject); for dark skin increase exposure by one stop, for red faces or moderately dark skin increase by half a stop. For very light skin, use normal exposure, except if the subject is a woman wanting to look glamorous or young – then, you should overexpose the film by a stop, so that the skin tones are very light indeed, and only the eyes and mouth really stand out.

SHOOTING IN THE SHADE
In bright sunlight look for a shady spot to take a portrait, as the softer illumination is more flattering. The light level here allowed a wide aperture, which also throws the background out of focus.

THE RIGHT EXPOSURE
This cheerful casual portrait of a roadside diner cook is slightly overexposed to give a bright skin tone and plenty of detail.

POSING AN INDIVIDUAL

When the subject looks towards the camera rather than occupying themselves in some other activity, the pose adopted is a vital ingredient in a formal portrait. There are two components involved – facial expression, and what to do with hands, arms and legs in wider framed shots.

The expression on the subject's face can usually be controlled by the photographer when a rapport has been built up. You can request a serious or friendly look, or pull a certain type of face yourself to show what's needed. Cracking jokes produces a more relaxed countenance. By now the sitter will have placed their trust in the person taking the shot, and assume they know which expressions are most suitable.

Three quite different tight head shots can be achieved by placing the subject face on to the camera, at a three-quarter angle or in profile. Only in the first two poses is it possible to look at the camera, while all three permit averted gazes. This can produce a less confrontational, sometimes intimate picture. The tighter the framing, the more powerful a picture can be.

With nothing to do except stare at the lens, people are suddenly aware of where they place their limbs, and stiffen up or become self-conscious. In a full length portrait, people asked to just stand there and look natural rarely do, so props are invaluable. Something simple to occupy the hands or arms is best, as the rest of the body then follows – a jacket can be hung over one shoulder for a casual appearance, or a chair provided to lean on. If props aren't obvious or appropriate, ask the subject to fold their arms or stand with arms akimbo. Formal portraits of people at work require less arrangement, as the subject already has a familiar task to do.

The seated figure requires careful posing. Low, comfortable armchairs hide the figure as the knees are raised, but this may suit some subjects. Higher seats ensure a clear view of the figure and don't allow the subject to slouch. Fitted armrests provide a natural place for the arms to lie along, or for an elbow to support the chin in a thoughtful pose. Always cut pictures above the knee, not just below, and never cut off arms!

GROUPS

Photographing a group of people is more challenging than shooting a portrait of an individual. Instead of capturing a single facet of personality, the objective is to capture a group's identity and the relationship between its members. That's not a simple task when there are several people to instruct – you'll need organizational ability and a sense of humour on top of the photographic and social skills already mentioned. You should stay aware of how individuals look, and the overall effect of the shot. Most of all a photographer needs to demonstrate that he is in charge and give clear commands, using tact and avoiding a dictatorial approach.

Your camera should be ready to take a shot before the group is in position. That means the film should be already loaded, the lens focused, and settings to give correct exposure dialled in. If you try to do any of these tasks after arranging a group, the composition will be disrupted and people will become restless. Photographers who regularly shoot groups keep a steady patter going to keep facial expressions relaxed and focus everyone's interest. Tell a few jokes, or ask questions which show you're interested in the sitter, to keep your session going and ensure attention doesn't wander.

A basic necessity of any group picture is to show each face clearly. That means ensuring that short people are not concealed by taller individuals, and that in side-lighting, a shadow cast by one person doesn't fall across another's head. This can be achieved by careful placement of the group, or by adopting a higher viewpoint so that everyone is looking up.

Once a reasonable composition has been formed, the next task is to make sure individual facial expressions are satisfactory. Watching several faces at the same time isn't easy, so photographers who regularly shoot groups always take

ARRANGING A GROUP
The rock band studio shot, above, needed careful arrangement. Note the asymmetrical triangle formed by the faces and echoed by the hands, and the use of a bench seat with sitting and standing poses. All the members of the group are in contact – supported by others – and all the faces are evenly lit.

several frames, just to make sure each member of the group is looking towards the camera, and that no-one is blinking, scratching their nose, or turning their head towards a distraction.

Groups should be composed according to their character or nature. For instance, it would be pointless to try to artistically arrange a crowd of apprentices at work! An arranged 'candid' shot would be more appropriate. For a formal record of company directors or club officials, however, a photographer can compose the shot to reveal the hierarchy or power structure. Clearly the boss should be the focal point, but resist positioning this person at the centre. Instead, place the boss ahead of the rest of the group, or stand the group on a staircase with the boss at the very top, or to one side.

If you're stuck for ideas, see if a centre of interest is available to hold a group together. For example, a baby is the obvious visual focus at a christening, but needn't be placed centrally in the shot. Instead of a formal row of people equidistant from the camera, position the mother and baby in front, and then cluster the others around. If there's no obvious focal point, introduce one; a bench, table or tree, anything that brings the group together.

The background to a group photograph should be relatively plain and not distract attention from the subject. Alternatively it can make a positive contribution to the image, giving clues to the group's identity. Pictures can be taken at logical places. You might shoot firemen at the fire station against a tender, arranged by the 'greasy pole' or, for an unusual

viewpoint, from the training tower looking down with the camera.

It's preferable to use available light where possible, especially with larger groups. Indoors the light levels may be low, but will contain more atmosphere than if flash is used. Don't be afraid to use a tripod when a slow film is loaded in the camera. People can keep still for a second or two, providing they are comfortable. When flash is employed, use more than one unit to even out the lighting, and ensure everyone's face is clearly lit. Studio flash modelling lamps let you check the lighting effect and ensure the shadow of one person isn't falling across another.

When the arrangement of a larger group is nearly complete, shoot a few 'grabbed' frames – these often have more appeal than the finished pose, with interaction between group members.

POSING A GROUP

With groups, there's greater scope for imagination in positioning people, and it's advisable to move away from traditional methods. A regimented row of people such as a wedding group or the tiered rows of a football team is a tired, predictable formula. When taking a shot of a family group, for example, a rigid arrangement is quite inappropriate. Adopt a more casual approach, so that the finished effect is informal even if it takes much careful arrangement.

Avoid sitting the whole family on the settee or a series of chairs facing forwards. Ask one of the children to sit on the floor, lie at an angle on an arm of the chair, or stand behind those sitting. The idea is to position individuals so that their faces are at different heights for greater visual interest. This effect is enhanced if you shoot from a viewpoint off to one side rather than smack in the middle. Gaps between family members make the composition look weak and the relationships cold, so it's better to draw people together into a tighter group. Ask one or both of the parents to place their arms round children to bond the group together.

EQUIPMENT

Individual portraits and group shots can be taken without recourse to specialist equipment, though a tripod is recommended at all times. Almost any compact or SLR can be used, as the shutter speed and aperture requirements are relatively straightforward. Because the subject is virtually static, a moderate shutter speed of 1/60 or 1/125 of a second will freeze any action. A wide aperture is only used when minimal depth of field is necessary to lift the sitter out of a distracting or cluttered backdrop. Nor is focusing a problem – a framed head and shoulders falls within the focusing range of all compact and SLR cameras.

A WIDE-ANGLE SETTING
The 40mm Distagon lens for the Hasselblad 6 x 6cm SLR is normally reserved for architectural work. Here, the photographer has used it to show the wealth of bric-a-brac surrounding 'Speedy' Allen, a Lincolnshire country house-clearance dealer. Distortion is avoided by keeping the subject as a small part of the shot.

Choice of focal length is important, however. Standard or short telephoto lenses are recommended, such as those in the range from 50-135mm for the 35mm format (or 75-200mm for medium format). These optics produce a better perspective for individual portraits – longer lenses also do, but the working distance between camera and sitter becomes impractical. Wide-angle optics used close to the subject to achieve the required image size tend to distort faces by magnifying whatever feature is closest to the camera – usually the nose! Wide-angles can be used for scene-setting portraits, where the environment carries a strong message about the subject.

As group shots are usually taken from greater camera to subject distances, lens choice can vary according to the space available. Usually a moderate wide-angle of 28mm or 35mm, standard lens or short telephoto suffices. Very confined areas may mean a powerful wide lens of 20mm or 24mm is needed; when using extreme wide-angles, avoid placing people right at the edge as distortion of their features may occur.

A burst of fill-in flash is a handy facility when shooting in sidelit or backlit sunny conditions, or in softer light when cloudy. Strong lighting from one side produces too much contrast, so a measure of flash reduces this ratio by illuminating the darker side of the face. When shooting into the light or if the light is overcast, flash adds a sparkle to the eyes and pumps life into an area of the scene otherwise dominated by shadow.

Filters inevitably play a part in portraiture. For shots of individuals a soft focus filter is useful to conceal skin blemishes, while a spot diffuser creates atmosphere by softening the frame edges. In cooler ambient light or shadow, a warm-up filter can be employed to avoid an over-blue appearance, returning skin to a healthier hue.

CHILDREN AND BABIES

ADULTS are often self-conscious in the presence of a camera, but children can act more naturally and without inhibition. A child's actions are spontaneous and unpredictable so, for successful photographs of children, the golden rule is to have your camera handy, keep film loaded and be prepared to shoot.

NEW-BORN BABY

A continuing record of a child's growth from birth onwards can be a fascinating and rewarding project. Newborn babies should be made comfortable on a bed or a rug, or cradled by a parent. Try to use natural light for a softer effect. If using flash, bounce the light rather than fire it directly into the baby's eyes. Direct flash from a compact camera tends to destroy the intimacy of the moment.

A new-born baby sleeps a lot and obtaining a facial expression, other than a yawn, may prove difficult. Try to get the baby to look up, and establish eye-contact with another adult. Use scale to create an interesting composition – the baby with a parent's large hand, perhaps, or baby on the back of a parent. Emphasize the small size and fragility of baby.

A slightly older baby can be photographed having a bath, or playing with its rattle. To make a more suitable viewpoint, bring the camera down from adult eye-level to low level to take shots. Avoid cluttered, distracting backdrops if possible – a plain bedspread is suitably neutral and is familiar to the baby too.

As the baby starts moving around exploring its environment., keep your camera rolling. Take shots of a selection of 'firsts' in the baby's range of experiences – the first time it sits up unaided, the first crawl on all fours, first trip round the settee, the baby's first Christmas. That first walk on faltering steps is a picture definitely not to be missed. Or take shots of the baby strapped in a chair inside

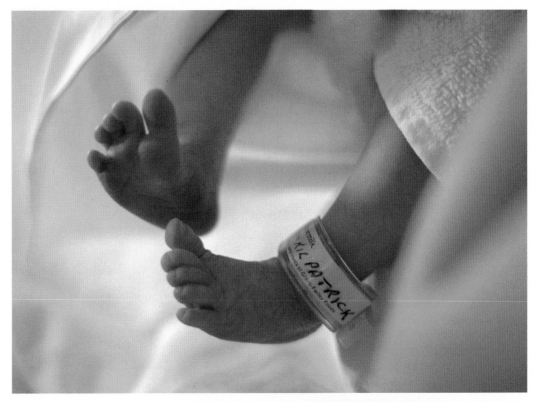

A RECORD FROM BIRTH
Many photographers today are able to record the moments immediately after birth, and their 'baby album' can start from the very beginning. Even if this is not possible, take pictures which tell the story. Tiny feet and hands (above) are difficult to photograph without a macro lens or the help of flash. Use bounced flash when photographing very young babies; not only is it much kinder to the far-from-perfect skin which many newborn babies display, it avoids distress to eyes only just getting used to the light. Natural light is always the best choice when there is enough, so use a fast film.
As baby grows up, the switch from supine to sitting position with a little support makes pictures much easier, and you can move away from the nursery environment. Under-ones respond happily to animals and people they know; at this age (right) baby is still small enough for mum to be a background and support. Avoid bright sun. This picture was taken in the open shade of a farmyard stall by light reflected from the sunlit concrete.

your car, perhaps asleep, or being wheeled along in a pushchair. Capture records of the habits they develop like sucking fingers or ruffling their hair.

TODDLERS

Children of this age are inquisitive, charming and fully aware of the camera. They're also able to respond to your promptings as you take further pictures recording the child's development, though it's best not to confuse them with too many instructions. Good picture opportunities occur when a small child is absorbed in a toy and unaware of your presence – use a telephoto lens to avoid distracting them. At this stage of growth, the head tends to be quite large in proportion to the rest of the body, so a longer working distance avoids further distortion and gives a more accurate perspective. Getting down to a low level always creates a more intimate or personal study.

Try photographing everyday situations. Toddlers dressing, playing, bathing and eating can make good subjects. Take pictures of toddlers interacting together, either with a brother or sister, or friends and children of a similar age. As well as the joy and laughter, don't forget the emotions of bad times too – moments of frustration, irritation, dispute and tears. Small children wrapped up against the elements in protective clothes make charming pictures.

SITUATIONS
There's no reason why every picture in your collection must be a head-on face shot. Babies outdoors on warm days are free from bulky clothing, and where a front view may not please everyone a rear view is usually amusing. Always look out for seasonal and outdoor activities (above) particularly if they will remind grown-ups of their own early experiences in the world. This shot was arranged, but it looks spontaneous. Children love climbing trees and walls; try a shot from the ground to capture a low-angle viewpoint. Be careful with exposure measurement when pointing the camera up, as a large expanse of bright sky may be involved. Visits to theme parks and leisure attractions can produce colourful shots, even if the subject gets a little lost (left). Load a fast film so that you can capture action, and avoid flash if possible – it spoils the atmosphere. Adults can get bored with the length of time children are prepared to stay on rides or in play areas, and the camera gives YOU something to do until they get tired out!

Further first-time opportunities now occur with that special quality – the first bike ride (with stabilizers), netting that first fish, kicking the first football, the first trip to the zoo, and so on. Try to catch the surprise in the child's face. Birthdays, picnics, and school sports days provide great potential for memorable pictures.

Try not to take all the photographs indoors. A trip to the shops, riding in a supermarket trolley, a ride by car or train all make a pleasant change. Don't put the camera away if it rains or snows. A most appealing shot is a small child's nose pressed up against a misty window.

Many young children are naturals and they enjoy 'performing' for the camera, but you may be asked to photograph a child who is camera-shy. These toddlers hide their faces behind protective arms and hands – the shyness usually get worse with coaxing. Bribery with sweets may get them to open up, but why not take the picture as it is? It makes as effective a record as that of a non-bashful child, and shows a genuine stage of development.

GROWING UP

Beyond infancy, many parents rely on the annual visit of the school photographer to keep up what started enthusiastically as a baby album. Because less time is spent with the kids, photography is relegated to weekend and holiday activity snaps, birthday and Christmas portraits.

If you are lucky enough to have photogenic children, they are natural models. You can set up action pictures, or positively theatrical set-pieces. Children enjoy showing off and dressing up alike. Record the new mountain bike, the latest pre-teen fashions, and the hobbies or sports they enjoy most. Your children's friends can be involved, as well, whether in team or group activities or as subjects on their own.

Teenagers tend to be self-conscious only when confronted by parents with a camera. It can be a better idea to let teenage children borrow the camera (or be given a suitable rugged compact or basic SLR) and shoot their own pictures. Photography is a well-established part of the curriculum in British and American schools for 14 to 17-year-olds, with examination passes counting towards college or university entrance for both fine arts and vocational degree courses.

THE ADVANTAGE OF ACTIVITIES

LIFE'S UNCERTAINTIES...
Don't ask for a big smile every shot. Top, some hesitation on being shown how to ride a donkey. Bottom, tired or shy or both – or just younger than the rest of the dance class.

Pictures of children just 'sitting there' don't work well because children hardly ever sit still – they like to be doing things.
For better pictures, try to arrange your photography to coincide with activities, or set up something to do for the picture. New toys, if they are photogenic rather than intrusive, always provide an opportunity.

Here are some suggestions for the baby album:
● Baby with mirror, puzzled at reflection.
● Baby at mothers breast – an intimate shot.
● Splashing about in the bath – mind the camera doesn't get wet.
● Proud grandparent with child – picture spans the generations.
● Child with family pet.

And for older children:
● Watering the garden with a hose or spray – but once again, watch the camera!
● Catch the action at the peak of swinging, or the movement on a slide.
● Feeding farm animals or riding a pony or donkey (horses are too big).
● At the swimming pool.
● At ballet or dancing class – this usually works well because dance practice halls are large and light, and dance leotards are colourful.
● Playing football.
● Playing a computer game – a difficult subject, as you need to capture the glow from the screen (shot from behind the TV set).

SUGGESTED EQUIPMENT

To photograph children you can use anything from a compact or an instant camera to an SLR. With the latter use a variety of lenses, from extreme wide-angle to good telephoto, for different effects. It's impossible to keep a camera round your neck permanently, but keep one handy, not hidden away in its case. Make sure you are familiar with your camera, and can operate it quickly and automatically.

Keep the camera ready for action, either on auto or with manual settings suitable for the lighting, or keep a flashgun ready. Pre-set the focus to a short distance with non-AF cameras.

Short focal length lenses used close to a child's face and head may distort features, so back off and use a longer lens if possible, or at least drop to knee level so that you are not looking down on the child's head. A camera with a date recording facility is handy to keep pictures in chronological order, but remember that this prints the date on the negative, spoiling shots for 'serious' uses. Most photo labs now date the back of their prints, so if you have your films processed quickly you will have a record of when the shots were taken.

Because growing children race around with boundless energy, you may need to use a fairly fast shutter speed to freeze action. Indoors this can mean using a wide aperture, which makes focusing critical even if it has the advantage of turning cluttered backgrounds into a more acceptable blur. A flash powerful enough for bounce shots is useful, as young children can move round a room so quickly that even, overall lighting is desirable. Slower shutter speeds to blur the subject can convey the energy of a child in motion, and capture the mood better than a frozen shot. Distracting backdrops can also be avoided by selecting a high or low viewpoint.

PERIOD PIECE PORTRAITURE

Professional photographers have introduced a style of child portraiture which, although sentimental, is great fun for children, parents and photographer alike. They will often use old-time locations, barnyards and forgotten corners to take portrait sitters back in time. Sometimes the photographic studio supplies the clothes, hats or props, but often the parents have heirloom clothes they want to use. Children enjoy dressing up, and television gives them a good idea of what all this is about, so 'being an actor' for a picture is not a difficult idea to grasp.

Here, the youngster is part of the scene, as a frame-filling close-up would not look right. Natural light is important, and flash spoils the effect completely, so he uses locations like a big old wooden barn with high doors open to let the light in. You can buy cobweb sprays from any photo studio or theatrical supplier, to make new windows look neglected, and with the help of some old planks or whitewashed bricks it's possible to make a Victorian corner in your garage. These pictures are more fantasy than a portrait – but they might be valuable one day if the little sitter becomes famous!

COVERING SPORTS EVENTS

STREETWISE ACTION
Many sports events take place against cluttered backdrops of crowds or television advertising slogans positioned at the best vantage-points by sponsors. The London Marathon is an accessible sports event, but most pictures look very static. The runners do not go particularly fast, they are often bunched together, viewpoint and visibility may be restricted and the city street backgrounds are far from ideal. The photographer overcame all these problems, and the poor light, by closing in on a single runner and using a slow shutter speed with pan. This gives a sense of movement, and turns the spectators and barrier into a vague blur.

THE OBJECTIVE of action pictures is to reveal the drama, excitement, skill and atmosphere of sporting endeavour. To achieve this often requires a comprehensive knowledge of a particular sporting subject, patience and timing. Equally important is the right type of equipment, a thorough command of the camera and an awareness of photographic techniques. Often it is the enthusiast for a particular sport who understands it best and shoots the most effective images.

Filling the frame with the subject is essential to successful sport pictures. Familiarity with a sport helps a photographer predict the direction of movement, or anticipate a significant piece of action. Each activity varies in its presentation – motor racing, for instance, is conducted at high speed over a wide area, but the competitors are almost totally concealed by a helmet, overalls and the car cockpit. Tennis action, on the other hand, is confined to the court area and punctuated by a rest after every two games. The efforts and expressions of the participants are fully on view. Some sports take place in a small area and are therefore easier to shoot – weightlifting and high jumping are good examples. The techniques for capturing each type of action are quite different.

When tackling an unfamiliar sport, it pays to acclimatize yourself to the nature of the action first, to avoid wasting time and film. Watch for the peak of the action, or moments of greatest significance. Prior to any sporting event, it pays to survey the location, work out the lighting orientation and pick out potential viewpoints. The finishing line isn't always the best place for racing – greater action often occurs at a bend or brow of a hill.

Film choice is also important. There's no guarantee of good lighting outdoors, the best action may occur in shade, or conditions can change dramatically during an

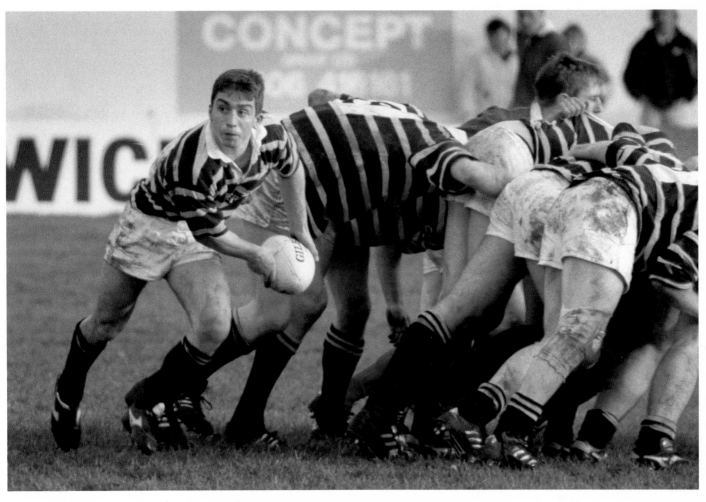

SHOOTING FROM THE SIDELINES
The action in a rugby match can move unpredictably and swiftly, so that any chosen position round the pitch will produce long shots, small groups of players, and dramatic close-ups.

event. Stopping action demands high shutter speeds, so it's sensible to carry choice of film speeds such as ISO 100 and ISO 400. You should aim for the highest quality image, bearing in mind the likely shutter/aperture combination. In duller light or indoors, faster or tungsten-balanced emulsions may be needed. Panning and blurring techniques require lower shutter speeds. See the table on page 61 for guidance.

Exposure metering is tricky when a moving subject passes from lighter to darker conditions or moves against a variably lit background. Rather than trying to meter continuously, take a general reading at reasonable intervals and set this manually on the camera. When subject movement is erratic, it pays to pre-focus longer lenses and press the shutter just before optimum sharpness is reached. This requires a good sense of timing.

TEAM SPORTS

These take place over a large area of ground, and contain much variety of action. Team sports can be difficult to understand and predict for those who don't know the complex rules. An intimate knowledge of the patterns and rhythms of play is a great advantage, so that the ball can be included in shot along with the participants. People in the UK now avidly watch American Football live or on TV, but few know exactly what's happening. Americans and British soccer have a similar relationship.

Rugby typifies the problems of shooting team sports. The action moves quickly from one part of the pitch to another – it can occur just a few inches from the touchline, then suddenly sweep some 200 or so feet away. Shooting at less important games gives you free reign of the pitch perimeter. Energetic types sometimes follow events by running up and down one touchline with the action, while others settle for a static central touchline position. The only problem is that most of the action may then take place closer to the opposite touchline. An alternative is to move to one end of the field, behind the goal posts. This is where the best moments occur in soccer.

Telephotos of 300mm or 400mm are suitable for following distant action, so the techniques of follow-focus should be practised. Shorter lenses such as a versatile 70-210mm tele-zoom, 50mm standard lens or 35mm wide-angle have their uses as the players move closer. Baseball follows a more predictable pattern, so long lenses can be trained on the batter's plate or the bases. However, it often takes place at night under floodlights, so colour balance of film needs attention and fast film speeds are called for.

Cricket is unique among team sports as the main action is centred on a small strip at the centre of a large circular pitch. A match, however, lasts for many hours, so patience is of the essence – there are long periods when little happens, then suddenly a catch is taken or the stumps are hit. A powerful telephoto of around 300mm will frame a group of fielders around the batsmen, while a 600mm will shoot a full-length figure in vertical format.

WATER SPORTS

Increasing interest is being shown in water-based activities, and they certainly make excellent subjects for photography. Identifying the optimum camera position is difficult to forecast, as action takes place over a wide area and movement can be very rapid. Water also introduces certain technical problems. Reflections from the surface can easily mislead automatic exposure meters. An incident light meter or spot meter will give more accurate results, or you can meter off a similar subject away from the reflections.

Pictures are usually taken from dry land or in a boat. With windsurfing it is possible to shoot from in the water itself, which brings various photographic constraints. With a friend or colleague on a windsurfer, pictures taken with a waterproofed camera on the water surface have much dynamism, especially as it passes close by. This should not be tried with strangers, or when there are other craft circulating.

Canoeing (right) brings fine picture opportunities – the action can be closely approached. From a low level, a canoeist splashing through choppy water or negotiating a slalom gate works well, while higher vantage points such as looking down from a bridge produce more graphic effects. In sailing, boats are larger and the action is relatively leisurely. Large areas of multicoloured sail record beautifully on film when backlit.

Water skiing and powerboats are exciting, high-speed subjects, but must be photographed from safe distances. The best action occurs with jumps or markers in skiing, and at the turns of a course for powerboats. Panning a powerboat making a straight run gives a terrific impression of movement. If you talk your way into the towing boat of a water-skier, refocusing is not necessary as the rope stays a constant length.

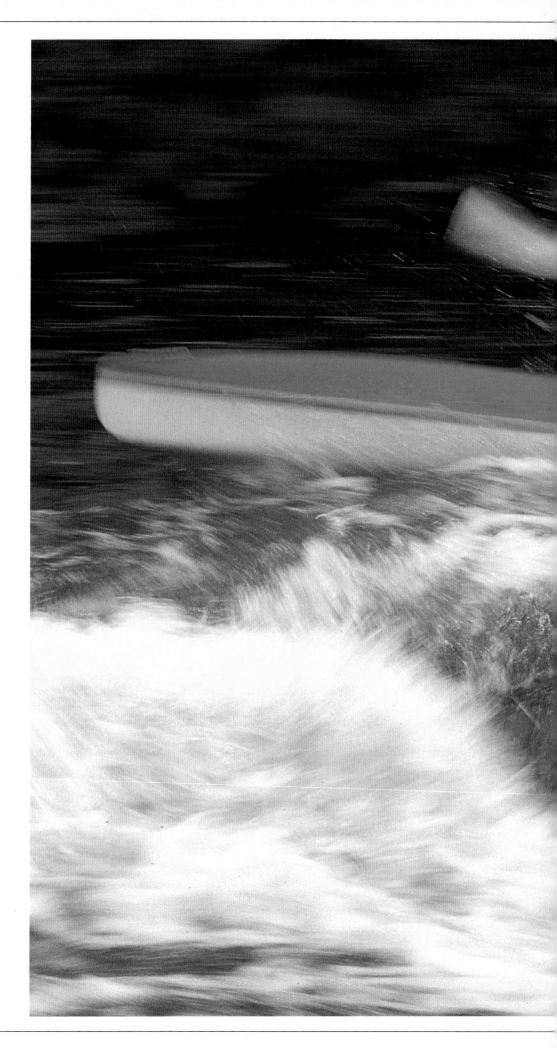

INDIVIDUAL SPORTS

Here attention focuses on the movement of single competitors as they reach the peak of the action, sweep around a bend or cross the finishing line. Expressions of triumph and elation, or agony and despair can be captured when the individual's face is visible. A golfer missing a short putt reveals an aspect completely different from an athletics competitor exhilarated by reaching the finishing line ahead of rivals.

Alternatively, moments of explosive action should be pinpointed – the pole-vaulter stretching every sinew to rise above the bar, a tennis player diving to reach a volley, or the instant of release by a shot putter or javelin thrower. This technique is also best used when the face of the competitor is masked, such as in horse-racing, or car and motorcycle competition. Bends or jumps are the ideal locations for motorized sports, as the action is more pronounced. Lenses can also be prefocused, and slower shutter speeds employed as the vehicle is travelling towards the camera or at an angle, rather than across the field of view.

Research into the person being photographed can pay off – whether they are right or left-handed, or the way they execute a certain manoeuvre. This helps a photographer choose a suitable viewpoint and camera angle. It is vital not to disrupt the concentration of players and competitors with noisy equipment, firing the shutter at a critical time, or using flash. This applies especially to sports where there are periods of silence, such as when a golfer is about to make a stroke.

WINTER SPORTS

Shooting fast action winter sports brings the same problems as other rapid sports, plus the added ingredients of unfavourable terrain and demanding conditions. Snow and

AN ANGLE ON ACTION
Some viewpoints have a graphic advantage – this discus thrower was taken with a long lens from almost directly above.

ice reflect light to a high degree, so metering must be carefully tackled. It's advisable to give more light to film than the meter indicates – one to one and a half stops is advisable, plus exposure bracketing if circumstances permit. A tip is to take a meter reading from the skin tone of your hand, providing the same light is falling upon the subject.

With downhill skiing or bob-sleigh, the action occurs in a instant, so the photographer needs to anticipate the moment of exposure. Professionals say they press the shutter a fraction of a second before they see the competitor hurtle into view – it's all down to timing and instinct. An 85C filter removes a blue cast in shots taken on sunny days in open shade, lit by sky-light reflected from snow.

Both cameras and people need protection from the adverse climate. Batteries operate inefficiently in extreme cold, so keep them warm by shielding the camera under clothing when possible, or by using a remote battery pack wired to the camera. Always carry spares too. Photographers also work best when warm, so appropriate clothing is essential.

CLIMBING AND CAVING

Commitment and expertise are vital in these sports, in order to reach the locations for photography... and survive. In each case it is paramount to keep equipment to an absolute minimum. No-one in their right mind takes a long telephoto up a mountain. Caving is one of the few sports where flash is essential, and the 'painting with light' technique is often used with the camera on a tripod. Protection of camera and lens is a high priority, to ensure proper functioning in terrible conditions.

INDOOR SPORTS

For the photographer, indoor sport is beset by problems, but is well worth the challenge. The usual difficulties in capturing fast action are compounded by low light levels and unpredictable light sources. At least indoor sports are limited in area. A prior visit to the venue often helps, as viewpoints and backgrounds can be worked out and lighting assessed. High and low vantage points create out-of-the-ordinary pictures.

Illumination levels and lamp types vary greatly. Yellowish lamps may be sodium vapour, whereas green may be mercury discharge lamps. If the light is warmer than daylight, use tungsten film or daylight film with a correction filter. Flash can be used at some events; check with the authorities, but be sure not to put the competitors off.

Take along both medium and high speed films to cover all eventualities. Lighting colour temperature makes no difference to black and white films. If light levels are too low, film can be pushed (uprated in its ISO speed) and processed accordingly, though ultra-fast film types are now available up to ISO 3200.

Lens choice is important; prime lenses of $f2$ or even faster, between 28mm and 135mm, allow higher shutter speed and greater depth of field. Fast longer telephotos are available, such as 180mm $f2.5$ or 300mm $f2.8$. Choose your viewpoint to suit the focal lengths in your outfit.

Movement in several directions, such as an arm moving in one direction and a leg the other, calls for a higher shutter speed. If movement is in one direction only, slower speeds can be used with panning. Much of the action in basketball, for instance, occurs around the hoop at each end of the court. A player can be caught at the top of a scoring leap to reduce the amount of movement and therefore the shutter speed.

Boxing is best pictured with a long lens from a high position away from the ring. At the ringside you cannot see the mat, and are looking up into a black void punctuated by harsh floodlights. Punches are very fast and need high speeds plus anticipation. Swimming poses particular difficulties as competitors spend much of the time under water or concealed by splashes.

When photographing sports involving physical exertion and where the body is partially exposed, such as in boxing or basketball, it is worth waiting for the players to break into a sweat. This makes the body, arms and face glisten. The technique is especially valuable for dark-skinned competitors shot in poor illumination, as the body is rim-lit with the source behind the subject, or frontal light is reflected back into the lens.

FLASH AND FLOODLIGHT
Electronic flash freezes action – floodlights add the shadows.

PREPARATION

The action photographer needs to be totally familiar with camera controls and lens operation. The only way to familiarize oneself with equipment is to practice – film loading, swapping lenses, and the direction controls turn when changing shutter speed and aperture. Focusing on a moving subject takes some getting used to, as does turning the zoom to keep the subject filling the viewfinder. Eventually, however, you will operate the camera naturally and automatically, without even looking at the various controls.

The other point about cameras concerns shutter timing – it takes a few milliseconds for the eye to see the action, the brain to react, the finger to press the button and the camera shutter to operate. All this time the subject has been moving, so anticipation of the action before it reaches a peak is an important skill to develop.

With longer events you can be waiting hours in poor weather for the right incident or expression. Warm clothing and a flask of hot drink will keep you comfortable and alert, but steer clear of alcohol as it dulls reflexes.

EQUIPMENT

It's vital to carry the bare minimum of equipment for maximum manoeuvrability. A motor-driven SLR is the ideal camera. SLRs feature a wide range of shutter speeds, provide accurate viewing of the image and allow a wide choice of lenses, including fast aperture versions, to be fitted.

Long fixed-focal-length lenses are essential when action occurs some distance away; fast 300mm and 600mm telephotos are commonplace among pros, but cost a small fortune. Long zooms of slower speed are more affordable, but demand faster film or excellent light conditions. Shorter zooms around 70-210mm help when action moves nearer the camera; 24mm to 35mm wide-angles are useful as scene setters.

Use a pair of SLR camera bodies, switching them when a film is used up, and reloading during intervals. Matching bodies saves thinking about differences in control layout between models.

Supporting a heavy telephoto by hand is impractical in sports like cricket, which last for hours. A tripod is used with the lens trained on the action.

PRESS PASSES

A common assumption among prospective sports photographers is that professionals are at a considerable advantage thanks to the press passes they are allocated. At larger sporting events these permits allow access to restricted areas. Sometimes there is a small benefit to be gained, but excellent pictures can also be shot from positions open to the general public. With a powerful telephoto lens, an amateur can obtain pictures from the terraces that will rival anything from the trackside. In certain major sports such as tennis, cycling or cross-country running, the action occurs close to spectators anyway, so a pass is of little consequence.

ANIMALS AND PETS

DOMESTIC pets, zoo animals and wildlife are all types of animal photography but they demand three widely different picture-taking techniques. A pet provides a readily accessible subject which may even (on good days) obey your commands. Lions on the veldt, on the other hand, are far from accessible or accommodating. The skills required for photography at the zoo fall somewhere between these two extremes – try photographing baby animals sticking closely to their mother. These are particularly appealing.

PETS

Photographing pets requires similar techniques to those used for children rather than wildlife photography. Domestic animals may be tame but they are unlikely to keep still, or produce expressions on demand, so a flexible and alert approach is needed. This may take more time than first envisaged.

Some knowledge of the particular animal's behaviour helps – when it is liable to be sleepy or hungry, where its haunts are, whether it responds to coaxing.

You will find your own pet more predictable than someone else's so it's advisable to spend time watching and getting to know an unfamiliar pet, and letting it get used to your presence. You could search around for good locations during this familiarization time, bearing in mind the colour of the main subject.

Dogs can often get overexcited if they realise they're the centre of attention. In this case, take the dog for a walk to burn off some excess energy before shooting commences. A dog can look fleetingly alert in response to its name or noises made by its owner or the photographer. You might try taking a formal portrait of a stationary dog indoors, and an unposed action shot outside. When the dog is running around use the panning technique. If you are able to allow the dog to swim set a high shutter speed to catch the water droplets sent flying when it shakes itself dry afterwards. Try to fill the frame as much as possible, and keep a close eye on the background – the less confusing this is, the better.

In a close-up portrait, focus on the dog's eyes and shiny nose – these are usually the centre of interest, but check that there is sufficient depth of field to render the whole head sharply.

When taking pictures of a puppy, place it with its mother to show their size difference. Pets photograph well with a child or adult owner; your portrait should aim to catch the relationship between the two. With adults, ask them to sit by the dog to make respective sizes similar.

Cats are often harder to control than dogs, but may be more photogenic. Shoot them where you find them, curled up in a chair, on a window sill or on top of a wall, in a tree or lying in a sunny spot. Cats are natural climbers; with a telephoto or zoom lens, use foliage to frame the cat for an attractive composition.

Cats also respond better to food, and head for warmth, so they can be enticed to a certain place by a titbit or a fire.

It's important to keep the cat's face in focus – with long haired varieties this is the animal's only sharply defined feature. When photographing a black cat wait for the light to strike it from the side to bring out details of its fur and whiskers; in ambient light open up by a couple of stops over the metered reading for correct exposure.

Kittens are very attractive and easily cajoled into action with toys or balls of wool. Get a friend to manipulate the toys while you concentrate on expressions. Pre-focus the lens and wait until the animal appears sharply in the SLR viewfinder. It pays to get right down to ground level with the camera. An alternative is to shoot a kitten curled up with its mother, or playing with brothers and sisters.

To take pictures of small mammals like rabbits, mice, gerbils, hamsters and guinea pigs you need some activity, and feeding often looks interesting. You can either photograph the animal in its cage or hutch, or place them on a covered tabletop indoors. Rabbits and guinea pigs stay quite still for long periods. Gerbils, hamsters and mice will stay still if placed on a wire mesh, but once they do move they're very quick, which may prevent refocusing.

The small scale of most mammals requires the use of a telephoto or zoom, rather than a standard lens, to provide a good image size in the viewfinder and give a comfortable working distance. You might include the owner's hand to show how small the

CLOSE-UP WORK
Most lenses do not focus close enough to take a picture of a mouse as clearly as this. A +2 dioptre close-up lens solves the problem with most subjects. Birds, and anything likely to attack your lens with beak or claw, are better photographed using a zoom lens with a macro facility, so you can stay a few feet away.

A LOW VIEWPOINT
Pets are often photographed from eye-level looking down, so different viewpoints give your pictures a fresher look. Cats are natural climbers, so the photographer aimed his camera up to capture this cat sunning itself on top of a wall.

pet is, or place a mouse or hamster on a child's head or shoulder for an amusing shot.

Birds are confined within the small area of a cage, so large degrees of movement are prevented. A cage with a glass front is good as obstruction is minimal, or with a wire cage hold the camera right up to the wires to throw the mesh out of focus. When using flash, look out for mirrors reflecting the light back at the camera, and hold the flash close to the wires to avoid casting shadows.

Goldfish and tropical fish make colourful pets, but the low light levels they're kept in may make flash necessary. You will need to experiment as flash passes through water and air differently. Keep the camera tight up to the glass surface to avoid reflections, and turn the room light off when focusing has been set. If possible, poke the lens through a hole in a large sheet of black card, and erect a similar uniform surface at the back of the tank, perhaps painted blue to contrast with brightly coloured fish.

ZOOS

Zoos enable you to photograph 'wild' animals without having to incur vast travelling expenses. The animals may be better groomed than they would be in the wild, and they will not be startled by people.

When shooting at the zoo, you can either show the animals in captivity by clearly showing the restraining element, or attempt the illusion of more natural surroundings. Each animal is restricted in movement by a pen or cage, but wire mesh, iron bars or glass can 'disappear' with a little ingenuity. SLR users will find a telephoto lens used at its maximum aperture not only provides good magnification; it concentrates attention on the subject because of shallow depth-of-field – obstructions in the foreground and distracting background details are

SHOOTING THROUGH GLASS
Smaller monkeys, mammals and most reptiles are often seen through glass from the inside of the zoo house, even if they also have a netting enclosure outdoors. By shooting into the light from the inside and allowing extra exposure, the photographer ensured that the distracting netting behind the monkeys disappeared.

SPOT METERING
Animal fur can be very dark, as anyone who has photographed a black dog will know. Details such as eyes disappear entirely unless there is enough light and the exposure is corrected to show detail in what would normally be a dense shadow area. The photographer switched to spot metering mode on a

Minolta 9000 AF SLR used with a 300mm *f*2.8 Apo telephoto lens for the shot above. Positioning the spot metering circle over the gorilla's face ensured plenty of detail. A subject like this would be almost impossible to shoot in backlight (see above) but the absence of netting round a walled and trenched enclosure gave an unimpeded view.

rendered out of focus and therefore reduced in importance.

For animals behind glass screens, avoid standing back with a compact and firing the flash straight onto the glass, as reflections will invariably spoil the picture. Move close up to the glass surface, even pressing the camera onto the glass if it's clean. SLR owners can bounce flash output, or shoot obliquely.

As with domestic pets, taking pictures at a zoo demands patience as animals alternate between rest and activity. They are usually most alert around feeding times. Concentrate on focusing on the animals' eyes as this is the main point of interest. The panning technique might be used to capture the essence of a smaller animal hurtling about once it wakes up.

An animal with its offspring makes a good picture. For example, a monkey with a baby riding piggyback is a perennially amusing subject. The zoo's information officer may be able to help with details of when youngsters are due to be born, or available to photograph.

WILDLIFE

Photographing animals in the wild ranges from small birds in the garden all the way up to elephants in the bush or whales in the ocean. Whatever the scale of the subject, the main problem is getting close enough to create an image of reasonable size in the camera viewfinder. With any wildlife picture the subject's behaviour determines the photographic technique employed. With rarer species a fleeting glimpse may be the only opportunity to take pictures, so lighting and framing sometimes have to be accepted as they are.

Birds are a popular subject as they are common, active and less secretive than other animals. Pictures can be taken by a bird table or bird bath in a garden, or from a temporary or specially constructed hide or blind. For the former, the

A NATURAL SETTING
Although a truly natural background is never possible in a zoo, the use of a very long telephoto lens (in this case a 500mm mirror lens) can help exclude extraneous or out-of-place details. Try to set the subject against an area of dark shadow or foliage. Avoid the zoo walls (see the gorilla, left) which immediately give away the nature of the setting. Elevated viewpoints can help if the ground has been prepared to imitate natural habitat, but in most zoos ordinary grass or even concrete removes this opportunity. Use wide apertures to throw details out of focus, and be careful to exclude signs, feeding bowls or scraps of zoo food, and spectators.

camera can be placed quite close to the perch, and operated remotely by a bulb release or infrared mechanism. Flash can even be employed at close quarters without frightening birds – perhaps they think it's lightning.

Photographing rare birds from a concealing hide calls for patience and perseverance, not to mention a licence in most countries. It is an offence in Britain to photograph some birds which you may consider everyday visitors to your garden. All birds of prey (raptors) are subject to restrictions of this kind.

A hide is only effective if birds accept it as part of their surroundings, and you are advised only to erect hides if you are an experienced natural historian and have the necessary licence in your pocket. The hide is either moved closer to the subject each day or gradually erected on the same spot. But if there is any indication that the birds are being disturbed, work must stop or the hide withdrawn. Arrival and departure from the hide requires caution and timing, as this normally occurs when the birds are absent from the scene.

It is much easier to visit reserves where public hides have been erected, and photography is permitted. Many otherwise prohibited species can be photographed with the co-operation of those who breed and conserve them. You can visit a falconry centre and see birds of prey at close quarters, photograph them in flight, and learn how to handle them yourself. This does not alter the fact that in Britain you cannot 'stalk' wild birds of prey to photograph them.

Regulations and licences only apply to purposeful photography, visiting a location in order to find and photograph a species. If you happen to see the bird or animal you are entirely free to pick up your camera and photograph it. What you are not allowed to do is to follow it when it moves away,

or return to the spot with more equipment. The moment you set out with the intention of photographing a protected species, you require a licence, and in some cases no licences are granted or available (there is, in effect, a total ban on approaching birds on the nest, nestlings, and litters of young).

STALKING

Animals in the wild are usually approached by stalking them on foot, though obviously this is not a technique recommended for dangerous species. Most safari holiday and wildlife centre resident staff will teach fieldcraft and stalking methods.

Stalking demands stealth, and this means camouflaging both equipment and yourself, especially exposed fair skin. Advance towards the subject from downwind and avoid wearing scented products, as these will be quickly detected by an animal's heightened sense of smell. Travelling on foot also necessitates carrying the minimal amount of cameras, lenses and film. Movement over terrain should be as silent and unobtrusive as possible.

Baby animals are always well protected by their parents, and should not be approached too closely. You'll need a powerful telephoto to obtain reasonable magnification of young cats, elephants and so on. Large animals become aroused and even dangerous if they think their young are being threatened.

Fast shutter speeds of at least 1/500 of a second are recommended, both to stop camera shake with long telephotos and to freeze any movement in the subject. This usually means shooting at the widest aperture the lens will permit, which also gives minimal depth of field so focusing is also critical. The wide aperture will also not show any concealing foliage the photographer employs close to the lens.

PHOTO ACTIVITY HOLIDAYS
Amateur photographers, above, on a photographic weekend including an afternoon at the Scottish Academy of Falconry, photographing hawks being flown. The Landrover has a platform and a ladder to the roof to act as an elevated viewpoint.

EYE CONTACT
While birds in flight defeat the fastest reflexes (human and single lens alike) close-ups are possible with the help of handlers. The eye and beak are best captured side-on, except in the case of owls.

EQUIPMENT

Compacts are best used for pet photographs, and certain zoo shots. Automated exposure, flash and focus control make them ideal for 'candid' pictures around the home, and when a closer view of an animal is available at the zoo. Their speed of use makes them ideal for grab shots of animals on their own, or interacting with their owners or people visiting the zoo. Dual lens or zoom models which offer a short telephoto focal length can also be used to magnify animals further away across ditches and moats, but the lack of control over the aperture setting is a major disadvantage when confronted by bars or mesh.

The SLR permits aperture and shutter settings to be adjusted, gives a wider choice of focal lengths and can focus selectively, so its flexibility and portability marks it out as a more suitable instrument. Longer telephotos can pick out and frame animals in the distance. Flash may be used as a main light or fill-in, and can be bounced or removed from the hot-shoe with a synchronising cable. Polarizing filters can be used to remove reflections from glass enclosures, or an FL-D can be used when shooting in fluorescent light with daylight film.

For wildlife photography powerful telephotos are the norm, which once again points to the 35mm SLR. Medium format equipment is too expensive and unwieldy when you consider the priority is for travelling unobtrusively and shooting quickly. One of the new breed of SLRs with a quieter shutter, motor-wind and autofocus operation, such as the Canon EOS 100, Minolta Dynax 7xi or Nikon F4 can be of considerable help when stalking a timid wild animal. The alternative is a manual-wind, manual-focus camera with a deliberately quiet action and optional mirror lock-up for tripod shots, such as the Olympus OM4 Ti.

INTERACTION WITH PEOPLE
Theme parks and dolphinariums often put visitors in close contact with animals. There is no point in trying to get a natural picture – so look, instead, for the shot which shows people and animals together.

SHOOTING IN SAFARI PARKS

Safari parks have been created both in the country of the animal's origin, for the purposes of protection, and in other countries to enable people to see wildlife species in a less restrictive environment. In Africa, parks are viewed from hired vehicles; as the terrain is rough a 4WD jeep, truck or Landrover is a typical means of transport. These keep the occupants from harm and allow reasonably close proximity to dangerous or timid animals. Photographs can be taken through windows, or from a roof hatch which gives all-round visibility.

In Europe and America, private cars are used to travel across parks on well made tarmac roads. Strict laws usually insist that car windows are kept tightly closed as animals may pose a danger. Where these restrictions don't apply,

keep a sharp lookout when a window is opened to take a picture. When shooting through glass, choose a side window preferably, as the oblique front and rear windscreens can create distortions. It's also easier to get the lens right up to a side window.

Make sure windows are clean before entering the park to reduce loss of definition to a minimum. Mask off white lettering by lens front element with black tape to avoid reflections. Shoot at the widest aperture holding the lens as close to the glass as possible. With heavier lenses, use a monopod for support. It pays to observe animal behaviour for a while before shooting. Use a standard or wide-angle lens to place the animal in its setting. Telephotos give tighter framed shots; sometimes you can fill the frame with just a head.

STILL LIFE

STILL LIFE photography is often ignored because it may seem less exciting than action shots, inanimate compared to portraiture, and more confined in scale than the broad landscape. It is, however, a subject which can reveal a photographer at his most creative. Successful pictures depend entirely upon the imagination, originality, deftness and artistic sensitivity of the creator. In still life, pressing the shutter is often the culmination of a lengthy process of careful picture building and refinement.

A still life image can take many forms. It does not have to resemble an artist's still life composition, as photographers call all pictures of objects taken in the studio 'still life'. It may be a simple arrangement of elements as found in nature, lit by available light. It may be created on a tabletop or in a studio environment, and made to appear either natural or artificial. Daylight coming through a window may provide the illumination; for greater control use tungsten photo lamps or electronic flash.

Shooting a still life image does not necessarily require a daunting array of expensive equipment. A tripod-mounted 35mm SLR and 50mm standard lens can be employed to record a fisherman's catch in a basket on the quayside, for example. The composition may be tightly framed, or include trawlers setting the scene in the background. A different kind of still life image can be produced with specialized equipment in a studio, where larger format cameras, a selection of surfaces and backgrounds, light tables, professional studio flash and various lighting accessories enable a vast range of effects to be created.

It may benefit a still life novice to commence dabbling in the subject by discovering subjects outside; this will help you gain compositional proficiency. Then you might graduate to working on a tabletop indoors, using illumination by a window to learn basic

FOUND SUBJECTS OUT OF DOORS
Still life doesn't have to be in a studio, or arranged. Accidental still-life compositions abound; the photographer's task is to crop them down to a composition.

lighting effects. With more experience pictures can then be tackled in a home studio, which simultaneously examines aesthetic and technical skills.

OUTDOORS

Pebbles, plants, petals, feathers, eggs, leaves, wood – the raw materials of still life abound in nature, and locating them is relatively easy. Composing them in a satisfying manner inside the regulated border of a picture frame is the hard part. At its most confined, an outdoor still life study may overlap with a close-up image such as a flower detail, while at the other extreme will include a

much larger subject area, such as the quayside scene described earlier. Many still life pictures employ subjects which are sufficiently small in scale to fit onto a tabletop.

Simplicity is often the best approach when first composing still lifes, which means starting with just one major element or perhaps a small group. A still life can express many things – order, harmony, mood or atmosphere, a sense of balance or a nostalgic feel. Certainly your picture should contain an overall theme. This might be achieved by selecting related or opposing colours, contrasting textures or a design that concentrates on shape or form.

You might spot an interesting abstract image formed by scraps of rusted metal, by bark peeling off a tree, or vegetation growing around a discarded locomotive wheel. How the subject looks is more important than what it actually is, so try compositions from various angles and distances, even if the subject will then be unrecognizable. Strong sidelighting emphasizes texture and relief, as crisp shadows are produced. Coarser textures are still obvious even when the illumination is more diffused, so harsh sunlight is not a prerequisite when searching for texture.

Repetition of a shape across an area creates pattern – this can be a stack of logs viewed from one end, the balustrades of a staircase, tracks left in sand by a bird, animal or human, or on a larger scale waves in the sea. A pattern works best when it includes a large number of similar elements, and implies that these continue beyond the frame. Telephotos are useful for seeing pattern, as the lens isolates sections of close or distant scenes.

Still lifes of plants and flowers shot outside are often more convincing than studio shots, though they may be affected by wind. Avoid shooting in very breezy or blustery conditions if you want a sharp image. Anchoring or steadying devices placed out of shot, such as a clothes peg, or masking tape, may be used. Wait for the right light. Insects such as bees or ladybirds on the plant give a sense of scale to the picture.

WINDOW LIGHT

Natural light is free but changeable and limited in intensity. It can produce atmospheric indoor still lifes when suitably diffused. A net curtain or tracing paper over a window softens the light falling on a tabletop set, which can then be further controlled by reflectors. A north-facing window gives the most diffused light as no direct sun can shine through, though it may be reflected off other buildings. Avoid overdoing the diffusion, as light that produces no shadow makes a subject look flat.

Shooting a still life indoors limits the size of subjects; choose something which can be comfortably handled and propped on a tabletop. Lighting effects are more easily controlled with smaller objects. You might opt for a single subject, such as an item of jewellery, a piece of fruit, a glass decanter or a kitchen utensil. Alternatively small groups of related or contrasting objects and props may be used, such as foreign coins and notes, or a collection of decorative pottery. Another possi-

CREATIVE IDEAS AT HOME
The photographer painted both the pear and the background paper, and set up his 35mm still life by window-light with white card reflectors. He used Fujichrome 50 film and a Tamron 90mm ƒ2.5 Macro lens, designed specifically for high sharpness at close distances and easy focusing in natural light.

bility is to aim for a graphic or abstract image using objects you have found or made. The only limitations to subject matter are those set by your imagination and ability to improvise.

The choice of background is as important as the main subject. In a conventional photograph the background is often large in area, but in a still life it can be quite limited. When the camera is above the subject and looks down at an angle, the backdrop becomes relatively small, so a variety of surfaces and materials can be employed. Try painting your own.

When the set is on a small scale, the background can be chosen to set off a subject. The finish of polished metals is shown off by natural surfaces such as slate, for example. Other subjects may work better on paper, velvet, vinyl or canvas. Different patterns and colours increase the number of possible permutations. Don't be afraid to use the unexpected; it will often make the difference between ordinary and outstanding images.

STUDIO

Creating a still life picture in a studio environment enables a photographer to fully control subject and background arrangement, camera placement and, most important, the lighting. Lighting quality is critical to the success of a still life image, even if it is one of the later aspects to grapple with.

The most important thing about any studio is the ability to black it out, like a darkroom, so that the light quality can be judged precisely.

Artificial illumination in the form of tungsten lamps or studio flash liberates a photographer from working within daylight hours. Light direction, quality and intensity are also infinitely more flexible. This means lighting can be tailored to specific subjects to bring out its character. The area to be lit and depth of field may also be closely governed.

Shiny or reflective subjects such as polished metal and glazed ceramics require different treatment from textured objects such as an old book, a wooden utensil or a loaf of bread and cheese. An item made of glass can be lit from various directions, bringing out different facets of the container, and its contents. When a composition includes a mixture of surfaces or materials, the lighting should be biased towards the dominant subject, or introduced with a certain effect in mind.

One lamp and a selection of reflectors and diffusing materials is all you need to start lighting still lifes. A background that complements the main subject should also be chosen. In addition to ready-made backgrounds in solid or graded colours, a black and neutral grey paper background can be lit with a coloured filter to change its hue when more than one lamp is employed. This technique (called 'chroma-zoning') can produce saturated colours or delicate pastels by changing the power of the coloured light.

TOTAL CONTROL IN THE STUDIO
This highly polished brass carriage clock has surfaces which reflect whatever surrounds it. Trying to photograph a subject like this outdoors, or in a normal room, results in many unwanted reflections. The solution is to work in a studio, which means blacking out the windows and using artifical tungsten or flash light. Here the clock has been to ten minutes past two – a time often used by professionals photographing clocks or watches – and lit the clock without any direct light. All the lights were aimed at sheets of white card or through large white diffusors, all round the clock. More white surfaces were added until no reflections except white could be seen in the brass. At the base of the clock, you can see how the burgundy velvet and the key are both reflected. A shot like this may take an hour to set up, and five minutes to photograph.

SIMPLE LIGHTING

When first using artificial lighting its a good idea to begin with one main light source. This simple approach allows you to watch the lighting direction and see how it affects objects in a still life composition. As the light is moved around, be aware of highlights and shadows. Side or low lighting can bring out texture, while hot spots on shiny objects are best dealt with by diffusing the light source. Sometimes texture can be revealed by a slight repositioning of the object. Five principal light directions are used in still lifes:

FRONT LIGHTING With the main light placed near the camera, frontal lighting emphasizes colour but produces little shadow. Moving the light further to one side further accentuates form and shape, but forms shadows too. These can be filled in by reflectors placed to the sides and rear of the set.

SIDE LIGHTING This dramatically reveals form and texture, making the still life more three-dimensional. When a collection of objects is used, it's important to use a reflector opposite the light to make sure subjects furthest from it aren't shaded. Another idea is to place darker items near the light, and lighter ones closer to the reflector to even up the tonal balance.

BACK LIGHTING can be an effective form of lighting for translucent subjects such as glass, though care should be taken to avoid flare. Opaque items are rendered as a silhouette, or rim-lit. Evenness of the background is essential, so the light source should be placed well behind the set and thoroughly diffused. A sheet of opal Perspex or layers of thick tracing paper should do the trick.

TOP LIGHTING Lighting a subject from above creates obvious highlight and shadow, though the lat-

LIGHTING FROM BEHIND
A translucent subject can be lit entirely from behind if placed on a glass sheet.

ter is often filled-in naturally if the subject is standing on a light-toned surface. This type of light direction permits a seamless background to fade into darkness if light and subject are both carefully positioned.

BASE LIGHTING This is an unusual but highly effective lighting direction for certain subjects. Glassware and its contents can look most enticing when illuminated from beneath, but solid subjects tend to appear silhouetted as

in back lighting. A reflector placed horizontally over the set directs light back onto the subject and creates fill-in – this gives added form to translucent shapes and throws light into the shadow area of opaque objects too.

SEAMLESS BACKDROPS

A seamless or 'scoop' background can be simply constructed when the set is of limited size. The background material needs to be flexible, like paper, and is laid under the subject position and then raised so that it disappears out of the top of the frame. On a tabletop this can be achieved by placing a large object behind the paper and draping it over, taping it on a wall or onto a supporting horizontal pole.

A seamless backdrop is especially useful when the still life is artificially lit. A diffuse light source placed above the subject picks out the subject from the background. If the lighting is carefully positioned, the subject is light at the top and darker at the base, while the backdrop is the reverse due to light fall-off along the sloping surface.

PROFESSIONAL OR AMATEUR?
Still life photography is bread-and-butter work for professionals, while many amateurs feel it will be too complex to tackle. The picture above shows the quality of a standard 4 x 5" professional studio shot of fruit taken using high-powered studio flash. The creative amateur, however, may find more scope on the kitchen table – and produce graphic results. The peppers, left, were set up using low-cost tungsten photoflood bulbs and a 35mm camera. A sheet of black Perspex and a black fabric in the background were the only props. With a tripod, a standard lens and one or two lights, any SLR owner can tackle this kind of set-up.

STILL LIFE WITH MOVEMENT
Another very simple black-background shot, left, shows how electronic flash can be used to freeze movement in a still life set-up. This is the kind of experiment which needs a helping hand. Professionals have assistants – amateur still life photographers need them, too. If you want to try shots with water or splashing drinks, be sure to keep it well away from both the camera and your electronic flash units. The black background is a good starting point for simple compositions.

TRADITIONAL GROUPS
Sunlight penetrating your attic or basement may provide chance groupings of cobwebby, dusty objects which make a good still life. If you can't find these shots, make your own. The black and white picture below was put together by a group of amateurs at a photo workshop. The bricks are thin tiles stuck on wood, the window frame is propped in place, the base is some old planks, the cobwebs are from a spray can, and the light is from flash units.

EQUIPMENT

The SLR, either in 35mm or 120 format, is the camera to use for still lifes. Compacts don't give enough manual control, and technical cameras (as shown in the light tent photograph below) are beyond the budget of most enthusiasts. It's a different matter for the professional, of course – here the 4 x 5" monorail will be favoured.

Still lifes can be shot at the closer end of the focusing range of normal lenses. A 50mm standard, short telephoto or tele-zoom is recommended. Useful filters include warm-up, soft focus, and an 80A or 80B if tungsten lights are used with daylight film.

Tungsten lighting is ideal for your first experimental still life work. Two heads with stands will cost less than a single dedicated camera-top flashgun, and the over-run photoflood bulbs (No 1, 275w or No 2, 500w) each last for two or three hours.

A tripod should always be employed to allow the use of slow film for fine grain and maximum sharpness.

Flash or tungsten multi-lamp set-ups need careful positioning and individual control. A typical lighting system will include the main light, fill-in, rim lighting if the subject is opaque, and separate lighting for the background. Flash systems will require a flash meter to provide the aperture read-out. Added to the lamps should be a variety of diffuser attachments and reflectors, and a selection of working surfaces and backgrounds.

Many bits and pieces such as small mirrors, clamps for holding things in place, scissors, knives, other tools and cleaning materials can be bought as you need them. Spray-can products add surface sheen, 'water' droplets, 'instant ice', cobwebs or floating smoke on demand. Glycerine drops are often substituted for water, as it maintains a better shape and doesn't evaporate.

LANDSCAPES

PHOTOGRAPHING landscapes – countryside, seascapes and gardens – may not appear to be technically demanding. The subject is mainly static except on a windy day or when it includes flowing water, and there are few variables a photographer can introduce to affect the scene. There are, however, many ways of improving landscape photographs by taking just a little extra care.

The secret of successful images lies in the creative interpretation and composition of whatever elements are present, and this usually demands a considered and methodical approach. A tripod is essential for serious work; it allows the use of high-quality, slow-speed films, a small aperture for greater depth of field, and makes careful and detailed assessment of the viewfinder contents easier.

TIME OF DAY

Landscapes change with the weather, the time of day and the seasons. There is no such thing as a best time to take pictures, because much depends upon the mood or effect sought. A sense of timing and an appreciation of natural light will help you more

LANDSCAPE WITH ATMOSPHERE

These two very different landscape shots, above and below, have one thing in common – the use of photographically created colour to give a mood as well as dramatic impact to the view. Painters rarely aim for effects like these. They are unique to photography.

The top picture was taken on a very fast, grainy tungsten-balanced Scotch 640T film, which gives a strong blue cast to the twilight composition of the coastline near Lynton (Valley of the Rocks) in North Devon, England.

The Lake District view below uses a graduated colour filter to reveal the shaft of sunlight and clouds, at the same time adding colour. Both pictures use a traditional horizontal composition.

than anything else. Rather than taking a scene as first observed, the successful landscape photographer waits for the right light.

When arriving at a promising location, it's worth considering what the same scene would look like at different times of the day. At dawn, mist may lie across the land; then low sunlight produces shadows that are no longer apparent around noon. In the afternoon the light changes again as the sun dips, and the day is crowned by a vivid sunset, followed by gentler colours at dusk. Cloud cover would change the scene considerably, with directionless light softening form and texture. Clearly your visit may not occur at the optimum time, so it could be worth returning when the light is more favourable.

Sun early or late in the day is a favourite light of landscape photographers, especially for flatter terrain, as it gives modelling and brings out texture. Low-angled sun also enables a location to be shot with different treatments, depending on the orientation of the camera. Pictures can be taken into the light, at angles to it, or with the sun coming over the shoulder.

Though the landscape is static,

speed of thought and rapid camera operation is sometimes essential. On stormy or windy days, a few minutes can vastly change the weight and balance of the sky and landscape. Dark hills may appear more distant than brightly sunlit slopes, giving a strong impression of depth. A heavy sky above a sunlit landscape can create fleeting drama. In clearer weather, a dazzling red sky may also be glimpsed between dawn and sunrise. All these effects can last just seconds. At sunrise and sunset, the sun appears to move faster compared to the middle hours of the day, and different effects occur quickly.

FRAMING

As with any composition, framing a landscape involves balancing various components. Many scenes contain one dominant element which by virtue of its colour, shape or tone attracts immediate attention. This might be a river shimmering in the late afternoon sun, or a solitary rock silhouetted on the horizon. This main point of interest should be placed in the frame so that it relates easily to the other, secondary elements of the composition. Usually an off-centre position works best. Placing the main item centrally is unimaginative; at the frame edge, unsettling.

When more than one major element is included, the composition must reconcile these different points of interest. This approach can produce a more dynamic composition. You may seek to form a relationship between the larger elements of a scene like mountains or a winding river and some smaller details like grass, flowers, or a rock. In this case two points of interest should be established, with one in the foreground and one in the background to give depth. Wide-angle lenses are best for this style, as a broad zone of sharpness is given, and foreground elements are given great emphasis.

VERTICAL ELEMENTS

Many mountain landscapes fit well into a vertical 35mm or 8 x 10" print shape. In pictures like this Welsh mountain view, sunshine is not essential; an overcast day may reveal more natural colours. The foreground elements, often rocks, vegetation or a river, demand a vertical composition. Wide-angle lenses are not always the best choice. Mountains look better with lenses of 50 to 100mm.

Telephotos produce a magnified view of a smaller area of the scene, and create foreshortening; the classic shot here is a series of hills receding further into haze. With long focal lengths it's possible to compose in a graphic or even abstract way, creating a two-dimensional picture of minimal depth. Nor does the horizon need to be included.

Rather than shooting lazily through the open window of a parked car, a photographer should attempt to find a viewpoint that gives the best sense of scale and perspective. This may entail plenty of walking or hill-climbing whilst loaded down by a camera bag and tripod, but can pay enormous dividends in improved pictures. Don't settle for the obvious

viewpoint or the 'picture postcard' view, use some shoe-leather to explore other possibilities and depart from the beaten track. Higher vantage points often open up panoramic sweeps of a scene rarely spotted from a road. If some foreground interest can be included, the composition will automatically convey a strong feeling of scale and depth.

GARDEN PHOTOGRAPHY

C hoosing a garden as a subject reduces the vast scale of the landscape to more manageable proportions. Your own personal patch is easier to record than public or show gardens, as it can be viewed at any time, from any angle and throughout the seasons.

The best light for pictures is usually sunshine veiled by thin cloud in mid-morning or mid-afternoon. Sidelight in these conditions creates plenty of colour and form without the harsh shadows of the sun in a clear sky. Bright light just after a shower or rain is another good time, as the moisture brings out the best in the greenery. Choose the orientation of your shots with care, because sunlight coming from

behind you flattens the picture as shadows are minimized.

As your garden is available for pictures all year round, why not take a picture of the planting and growing sequence every month, from the same spot? When visiting a formal garden it pays to be there very early, or on a weekday, to avoid people. Take a walk round first to work out the best viewpoints and lighting angles. Each area looks quite different in the early morning compared to late afternoon. When a building is included as a backdrop to a garden, watch for leaning-out verticals if the camera is tilted down to capture the foreground. A lower viewpoint is usually the best answer.

EQUIPMENT

Landscape pictures can be taken with a typical hand-held compact, but the SLR gives more control over camera settings. Interchangeable lenses bring greater optical versatility.

Some compact models now have useful 28mm wide-angle lenses fitted, or take panoramic format shots, but generally auto exposure and autofocus help very little with distant scenes. Integral automatic meters can be easily confused into under-exposure by areas of bright sky, so an exposure lock, backlight button or spot metering facility helps. Infinity focus buttons are also of limited benefit, as control over depth of field is what is really wanted, and you may prefer to focus deliberately on the middle distance and re-compose the scene with the focus locked. This works fine on a bright day, but if the light is poor you have to understand the exposure program in your camera. Many compacts shoot at fairly wide apertures most of the time and don't give much depth of field despite their semi-wide-angle lenses.

An SLR with manual control of focus, shutter speed and aperture is the ideal landscape camera, and it helps if the built-in meter can switch to spot readings or something more selective than an average or 'intelligent' pattern.

Partial or spot metering allows the important part of a scene to be pinpointed and accurately exposed. Many serious landscape photographers use a separate meter fitted with an incident light diffuser – the incident light reading measures the light falling on the subject, not the light reflected off it, and can therefore reproduce tones and colours with precision. A sturdy but portable tripod and a selection of filters should also be carried. For colour work these often comprise a polarizer to saturate blue sky, various graduated colours to balance a brighter sky against the landscape, and warm-up filters.

A choice of lenses from wide-angle to telephoto allows scenes to be interpreted in many different ways. Fast maximum apertures are not so critical with landscapes, as a tripod steadies the camera and differential focusing is seldom employed. Focal lengths of 17-24mm place extra emphasis on foreground interest and provide dramatic perspective, but less powerful wide-angles of 28mm or 35mm are also useful. Telephotos of moderate power in the range 70-200mm give extra 'weight' to views in mountain and hill country, but higher magnifications produced by 300mm or 500mm lenses can be used to isolate portions of a scene in a graphic manner, excluding the sky entirely.

THE LANDSCAPE OUTFIT
Walking shoes and a map are just as essential as your camera kit!

GETTING THE FOREGROUND IN PROPORTION

The sunflower fields near Arles in the extreme south of France are a favourite subject for landscape painters (Van Gogh was here) and photographers alike. They look like an ideal subject, but most people end up with very dull pictures. There are several reasons for this. Sunflowers face the rising sun, and they are well lit during the morning, but after noon the sun is usually behind the flower. You must be there at the right time. The fields are flat, stretching as far as the eye can see, and there are no easy elevated viewpoints unless you climb a tree. The flowers are at eye-level, so walking into the field is pointless. The solution, above, is to use a wide-angle lens which allows you to alter the scale of the foreground by moving closer, without changing the distant overall view. The normal view from the road with a 17mm wide-angle lens is very plain – just a stretch of sunflowers (top left). If you go really close, it's possible to make a single flower or a couple of flowers entirely fill the frame, their leaves obscuring the rest of the field completely. In the top right-hand picture you can see bees on the seed-heads, and the lens was only six inches from the flower, but the great depth of field of the wide-angle means that the distant flowers are still sharp.

The best compromise is probably the lower picture, with a natural progression in size of four nearby flowers, and the field stretching sharply to the horizon.

HOLIDAYS AND TRAVEL

MOST PEOPLE take holiday snaps when they travel to remind themselves of the good times they had. These snapshots, however, are personal souvenirs, and only have meaning for a small group of people. To return home with pictures that have a wider relevance, and which capture the atmosphere or mood of places visited, takes greater effort. Travel shots can mean many things – landscapes, portraiture, architecture, action.

Before setting off, a little research into the spot you are visiting pays dividends. Books, brochures and maps contain useful information, or you could speak to travel agents or people who have already travelled there. Take pictures *en route* too, especially interesting aerial views through the jet's windows. With either a compact or an SLR, it pays to hold the camera as close to the window as possible, to prevent imperfections or dirt affecting the shot.

TIME AND PLACE

When you arrive in a foreign country, check out the local postcards to see what the sights look like and make sure nothing is missing from your itinerary. Walk around for a while to soak up the atmosphere before firing off any shots; this gives you a chance to settle in and look for suitable locations and viewpoints. After a while you'll tune in to the feel of a place, and can look beyond the obvious pictures.

By all means take pictures of scenery and buildings, but also look out for details that make the place unusual – the produce on sale in the market and goods in shops, street signs, unusual modes of transport, and the quality of light itself. Although holidays are supposed to be relaxing, the unavoidable truth is that the best time for taking pictures is often early or late in the day, when the

lighting gives more character.

The appearance of a location can change dramatically in the course of a day, so be prepared to return to a location when it is better lit if necessary. A busy thoroughfare will be much quieter around dawn or during siesta time, for instance; take a series of shots to show how its character alters. You certainly don't need perpetual bright sunshine. Mist, storms, clouds and other weather conditions create atmospheric images too.

VIEWPOINT

The reason we travel is to see new sights, or visit famous places made familiar by countless postcards. Covering new ground automatically sharpens the senses, and it is important to keep this mood going for picture-taking. Better weather also encourages you to try new camera angles, explore other

viewpoint possibilities and experiment with techniques. Look up and down as well as scanning at normal eye-level, and seek out unusual vantage points such as balconies or roofs of buildings. It's worth using plenty of film, rather than skimping, as these opportunities don't come every day of the week.

Even with famous landmarks, there's always a fresh way to look at a scene, so don't just accept the conventional viewpoint. Rather than photograph the pyramids during harsh daytime sunlight, try a silhouette at dusk, with a camel and handler in the foreground to make a more interesting shape. Shoot the Golden Gate with a wide-angle from a car travelling across, rather than the obvious picture from high on the north hill with the city of San Francisco behind the bridge. Always search for novel methods of capturing an otherwise clichéd image.

PEOPLE

Travel is not just about place; it's equally about the people who inhabit the region. Locals and other tourists alike make good pictures, especially when interacting. A face full of character, a curious mode of headgear or colour of dress can say just as much about a culture as any scenic picture. Many people are perfectly happy to be photographed if approached, and will even happily pose when asked. Language is no barrier if you smile and make hand signals. Children are especially curious about visitors, but don't be surprised if a certain small fee is demanded for their 'co-operation'.

But when abroad, you should be aware how different cultures react to the presence of a camera. In certain countries taking a picture of a local person is considered highly discourteous or even downright intrusive (a Muslim woman, for instance). You can overstep the mark even on the regular tourist beat, as the author can personally testify when he tried to take a shot of a market trader asleep on his bench in Tunisia. It is up to the traveller to make himself aware of local considerations, and behave responsibly.

THE RIGHT TIME
To catch the best time for set-piece subjects like the floating market at Damnien Saduak (left) in Thailand, you must go with the crowds – but get to the front, and take a wide-angle like the 20mm lens used here. A standard lens may force you to stand back, so that crowds get in the way.

A DIFFERENT VIEW
Don't always go for the familiar tourist image. Try photojournalistic styles instead. In Hong Kong, the photographer switched to the 135mm setting of a 28-135mm zoom to pick out the vertical side of a tower block (right). Long telephotos can also pick out subjects over the heads of crowds.

THE BEACH

Pictures taken at the beach or at an interesting holiday location tend to suffer from one recurring fault: the light from about ten in the morning until around three or four in the afternoon, the time when most tourists are up and about, is too harsh and lacking in character. It's advisable to shoot pictorial views at other times.

You can employ these hours constructively, however, to research locations to be shot early or late in the day, or to capture amusing candids of people relaxing or trying water sports. If your camera is waterproof, paddle out and look back at the beach, or take a ride on a boat or pedalo and catch people doing the same thing. Exposures must be accurately controlled around beach areas, as sand and especially water reflect light strongly, and can easily fool the camera's TTL meter.

The most memorable shots from mountain locations or beachside holidays are often sunsets. These can be more vivid than anything seen back home. To avoid bland compositions, use a wider lens and position yourself to place something in the frame to add an interesting outline or shape. You can use boats, trees or (best of all) people to add a human interest. The other option is to use a telephoto to increase the size of the sun – here a tripod is essential to avoid camera shake. Bracket generously to give a variety of effects.

LOCAL COLOUR
Above: where photographing ordinary citizens (however colourful) is difficult, visit tourist attractions and shows. The standard of dress may be higher – and authentic – with no photographic restrictions.

AN ELEVATED VIEW
Below: cliff tops often give a good view of the entire beach. A telephoto lens makes a tight composition, and the high mid-day sun does not spoil the pattern of activity on this stretch of sand.

CITIES

In contrast to the peace and tranquillity of a rural location, cities are places of noise, excitement and bustling life. You can shoot pictures of architectural merit in older cities, or capture the bold size and shape of buildings in newer conurbations. In each case, you'll want to seek out details and take broader views.

For the shot that sums up the city, finding the optimum vantage point is critical. This may take some research, but is well worthwhile. At street level the view of the city centre is often obstructed by other buildings or assorted urban paraphernalia such as aerials, lamp-posts or telegraph cables.

One solution is to travel a distance out from the centre, to find a higher level of ground, bridge, multi-storey car park or other tall building. If you can gain access to this, there should be a clearer view of the city. A zoom lens will provide various framing options. Lighting quality and direction will also have to be considered.

Photographing individual or groups of architectural features is easier. Viewpoint and orientation are still important. A highly textured facade, for instance, will look at its best when lit from the side.

Often the best time to shoot a city is at dusk or night, when neon lights and other sources light up, giving a fresh appearance to a scene that may look quite mundane during the day.

Interiors of churches, museums, hotels and villas provide good subjects for days of poor weather. Though there may be enough light outside, the insides of buildings are often poorly lit. The other problem is squeezing everything into the frame, so a good wide-angle is essential; a 28mm or 24mm focal length is ideal. Smaller rooms can be filled-in with portable flash, but cathedrals are too large for this technique. Use a tripod instead, if this is permitted. It's hard to avoid converging verticals from low viewpoints, so try a higher position or emphasize the convergence by tilting the camera steeply.

NIGHT-TIME MAGIC
Cities can be transformed at night by office and street lighting and the streaks made by road traffic. Find a good viewpoint, and try to shoot at dusk, when the light is fading, rather than after dark when the sky will be completely black. This picture shows Hong Kong's Causeway Bay, Wanchi and Central district, from North Point. The photographer used a 6 x 6cm SLR and wide-angle lens. The hills behind the city are clearly picked out against the evening sky, and there is enough light reflected in the water to see all the boats clearly.

UNDERWATER

Shooting underwater pictures is like visiting another world, bringing exotic shapes and colours but also some unique problems to solve. Three types of camera may be used in a watery environment; compacts safely submersible to a few metres, regular cameras placed in waterproof housings, or specially sealed models such as the 35mm format rangefinder-focusing Nikonos complete with its own lenses and flash system.

Water bends or refracts light more than air, so objects appear larger and closer than they actually are. To compensate, underwater lenses have a shorter focal length than those for the equivalent angle of view on land. A standard lens on 35mm format is around 35mm, while the 28mm focal length is a moderate wide-angle.

In addition, light intensity reduces with depth, and water becomes progressively blue-green. Red filtration is used to offset the latter, though this too absorbs valuable light. Satisfactory pictures can be taken in water up to about 10 feet down, but at 20 feet poor light and heavy colour bias prevent normal photography.

A frequently used ambient-light technique here is to shoot upwards, to improve contrast and silhouette a subject against the lighter backdrop. Waiting for low tides also brings subjects closer to the surface. Scale is another visual problem, as there is nothing familiar to gauge the size of subjects. Asking a fellow diver to appear somewhere in shot can provide a solution.

When there is insufficient illumination, the underwater photographer removes the filters from lenses and resorts to flash – this method is mainly intended for subjects near the lens as light output falls off rapidly. One benefit is that flash freezes any motion. It's a good idea to separate the flash unit from the lens axis, so that particles in the water do not bounce the light straight back and create a misty effect – an overhead flash position looks most natural. With a translucent cover over the flashtube, slight diffusion gives softer light for subjects close to the lens.

SILHOUETTED AGAINST THE SURFACE
At the depths where many colourful and interesting subjects are found, the light is poor underwater. One solution, used above, is to light a foreground subject with flash while aiming the camera up towards the surface. No flash reaches the diver above, so a dramatic silhouette is created. This shot was taken at a depth of 20 metres in the Red Sea. The photographer uses a Pentax LX SLR with an underwater housing, and Nikonos III, IV and V underwater viewfinder cameras.

OFF-SEASON AND BUSINESS TRAVEL
Not all travel involves high season holidays or premium destinations, and you may still want to take your camera kit on business trips, or take a low-season break when the weather is unpredictable. Faster films, a tripod, flash and a good guide-book are essential on this kind of trip. Look for atmospheric shots. Cologne, above, is a German city many photographers visit off-season for the biennial photo trade fair 'photokina'. Trips like this can be a good time to concentrate on documentary or reportage-style black and white shots.

EQUIPMENT

Travelling poses one special problem when selecting equipment. You need to take a versatile outfit to cater for various picture opportunities, but not one so heavy that it compromises portability. A compact is easiest to carry, and dual lens or zoom versions provide a useful choice of focal lengths. Integral flash makes the camera more flexible. Durable compacts with added protection against the elements make excellent travelling companions.

Clearly zooms fit the bill for the SLR user, as one lens offers a range of focal lengths in a handy package. A useful kit can be made of just two lenses, a 28-70mm and a 70-210mm. Add two camera bodies, a flashgun and a 2x converter for the tele-zoom to give a 400mm lens and this covers most possibilities. For low light pictures, however, prime lenses feature faster maximum apertures. A tripod enables slow speed films to be used for optimum quality. One or two filters should find their way into the outfit bag too; a polarizer to saturate colour or cut out reflections, and an 81A to warm up colours on dull days are almost essential.

When visiting a very hot country, cameras and film should be kept as cool as possible. When a hire car is used, invest in a cheap cool box to store film in, and keep small packets of dried silica gel with cameras and lenses if humidity is high.

Conversely in cold climates, battery performance is badly affected, so a manual SLR that can operate its shutter without battery power is an intelligent choice. In extreme cases, the lubricating oils used in cameras can be replaced with 'winterized' versions which don't get stiff at sub-zero temperatures. Many electronic cameras are designed for use over a wide temperature range, and this procedure really only applies to traditional mechanical models. Film also needs careful use, as it can become brittle when very cold.

Salt-water spray, sand and dust don't mix well with photographic equipment. Keep each item in a plastic bag whenever possible, and clean regularly with a blower brush or cloth.

PICTURES AT NIGHT

SCENES which look bland or unpromising during the cold light of day can often be transformed come nightfall. The appearance of individual buildings, streets and whole cities changes as available light diminishes and artificial light sources are switched on. Though neon signs and floodlighting appear bright to the eye, light levels are rather low and camera exposures can run into many seconds or even minutes, especially when smaller apertures are set. For this reason, taking pictures at night demands the use of a tripod, cable release and B setting or equivalent on a camera.

TIMING

The reality is that shooting at the dead of night isn't always the optimum time for night photography. Buildings, funfairs and overall views of cities can benefit when there is still a little light left in the sky at the end of the day, by twilight or at dusk. The onset of dawn mixed with artificial lights gives a quite different feel – if you can rise early enough to capture it. These times prevent the subject being set against an inky, featureless backdrop and losing their characteristic shapes. Lighting effects change rapidly at twilight and dawn, so it's advisable to arrive at the location early and set the camera up ready for action.

Conversely, for pictures of the stars or moon, any residual daylight is a disadvantage. The moon is a useful element in night photography, as it is quite bright and shows up well. It can be shot normally or added quite simply to moonless shots by double exposure or slide duplicating. Pictures of star-tracks can be taken if the exposure is of sufficient duration. The combination of the earth's rotation and long exposure creates light streaks in the shapes of arcs.

A visit to an area festooned with colourful neon signs can produce vivid night pictures. The best places for this type of image are the commercial or entertainment centres of larger cities. Las Vegas, for example, 'lights up' at night. Another excellent time for night shots is immediately after rain, when reflections from wet pavements and cars heighten and multiply the vivid colours of neon signs. Because of the increased reflection, wet conditions bounce light into darker corners.

COLOUR BALANCE

Shooting nights scenes on black and white film carries one significant advantage – there is no need to resolve the colour of various sources of artificial illumination present in streets, shops and cities at night. With colour negative in the camera, some correction can be made at the printing stage. Those working with colour transparency, however, must consider the different colours and effects generated by a variety of light sources, as strong colour casts can appear on film.

On daylight film, the light from domestic tungsten bulbs creates a warm orange colour. Similarly, sodium street lights appear yellow, mercury vapour lights are a blueygreen, and fluorescent lights a cold green. Though some of these sources emit a narrow or discontinuous spectrum, filtration can be used on the lens to record the light more naturally. This assumes, of course, that a realistic effect is wanted, which is not always the case, especially as there is often a mixture of sources in broader scenes, with no single light dominating. Here full correction is impossible. Warm casts are often acceptable even though technically incorrect, though each picture presents a subjective case. Tungsten film will emphasize the blueness of a dusk sky. To compound the problem further, lengthy exposures can also produce strange colour casts of their own.

NIGHT EXPOSURE

Of greater practical relevance to the photographer shooting night scenes is the intensity of light, and its distribution. Night shots are often characterized by bright points or zones of bright light created by the source, areas of deep shadow and few middle tones in between. This gives predominantly low light levels as well as an uneven distribution of light. Long exposures are the only solution, but there is little that the photographer can do about the high contrast some scenes present.

One option is to use the conditions to create highly dramatic pictures, either letting the light source overexpose and bring in

8.50PM, LIVERPOOL
Sunset in northern latitudes falls later than it does in the Mediterranean or Florida. Shortly before 9.00pm in early or late summer, the floodlighting on the Royal Liver Building begins to show the makings of a good picture. Now is the time to set up the tripod and wait.

9.20PM, BALANCED LIGHT
As the light in the sky falls to below the brightness of the floodlit areas, the best time for dusk photography may last from a few minutes to an hour. This picture would lose all its subtle colour and atmosphere if taken in total darkness.

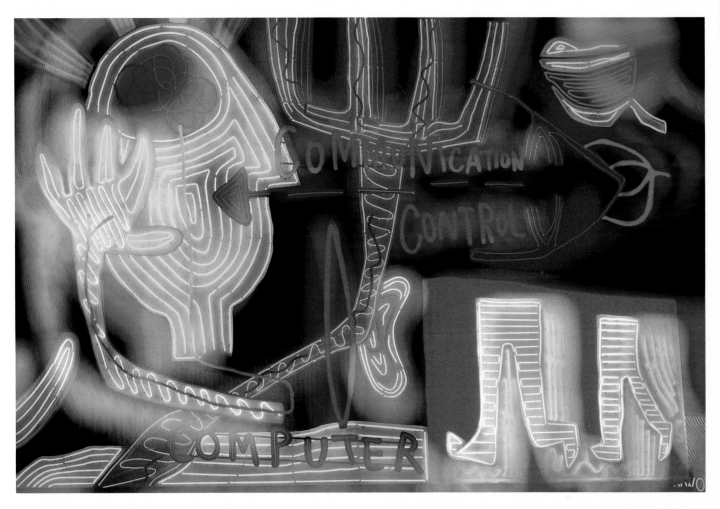

SIGNS OF THE TIMES
Neon signs in night-time streets are easy to photograph even without a tripod, which may not be a desirable thing to carry in a busy area like Tokyo's Shibuya (above). A double exposure gives the unusual effect.

FUN OF THE FAIR
A time exposure, with tripod, is needed for fairground pictures (below). The close viewpoint sets the wheel against a dusk sky, and includes the lit-up booth.

shadow detail, or expose for the lighting and let the darker areas run into inky blackness. Again the two techniques are open to much subjective interpretation.

Exposing most film for one second or longer times takes it beyond the parameters it was designed for, and results in reciprocity law failure, which means that the film acts as if it was of a slower ISO rating, so increased exposure must be given to compensate. Manufacturers issue data with some films, but more often you must write for a technical leaflet.

A typical Kodak film will give correct exposure when set at its official ISO rating and used with shutter speeds between one second and 1/10,000. Times longer

SETTINGS

The following table, based on the "Kodak Professional Data Guide" gives a starting point for various difficult-to-meter night scenes with ISO 100 film, though it is must be emphasized that bracketing of exposures is strongly recommended:

Brightly lit street	1/30 at $f2$
Neon signs	1/30 at $f4$
Subject lit by street lights	1/4 at $f2$
Floodlit buildings	1s at $f4$
Traffic streaks	20s at $f16$
Fairs, amusements	1/15 at $f2$
Firework displays	1/30 at $f2.8$
Floodlit sports	1/30 at $f2.8$
Full moon landscape	30s at $f2$
Full moon on snow	15s at $f2$
Skyline just after sundown	1/60 at $f4$
Same 10 mins later	1/30 at $f4$
City skyline with lights	4s at $f2.8$

than one second may need an extra half-stop (opening up to between $f5.6$ and $f8$, but giving the time the metering suggests for $f8$). Times longer than 10 seconds may need an extra stop, and longer than 20 seconds, an extra two stops.

Although extra time exposure can be given, the longer the exposure you give, the worse the problem gets, so it is always better to open up the aperture.

SPECIAL EFFECTS

Shooting at night may introduce certain technical limitations to photography, but it also opens up many creative possibilities. Because the general ambient level is low, brighter moving subjects record as a streak of light on film for as long as the shutter remains open. This effect is best seen in the headlights or tail-lamps of traffic captured by an elevated camera by a busy motorway or highway, or

in the swathes of colour produced by revolving fairground rides. Here choosing the right viewpoint is the key to effective pictures.

A favourite accessory of the night photographer is the starburst filter. This simple attachment transforms each point of light into a four, six or eight-point star and brings a hint of diffusion. When a scene includes many light sources, the effect can be rather dramatic. Other filters such as diffractors or multiple image types can be used instead, or used in combination with a starburst for an over-the-top treatment.

Unusual images can be created with plainer night scenes by various camera techniques. Zooming the lens during a lengthy exposure produces streaks of light exploding from the centre, while defocusing the lens part way through an exposure produces a very subtle effect. Some experimentation is needed to ensure success with these techniques, and bracketing

FLOODLIT BUILDINGS
Although the colour of floodlighting is hard to predict, it provides some of the best night shots in cities. Choose your location and time of evening carefully. In this shot, the photographer used the dolphin statue near London's Tower Bridge as a foreground silhouette, and gave enough exposure for full detail in the stonework, allowing the visible floodlights to burn out. He used a wide-angle lens on a 6 x 4.5cm rollfilm SLR.

of exposures is again suggested.

Another option is to mix light sources during a long exposure, by adding some flash from a portable gun to the existing artificial illumination. You might add some light to foreground detail in front of a floodlit church, for instance. If the exposure is many seconds long, you can 'paint' with light, or use several flashes.

FIREWORK DISPLAYS

Various celebrations give you the chance to shoot fireworks. As with all night shots, the first essential is a sturdy tripod as exposures can last for several seconds. An SLR is the obvious camera choice – greater control over exposure and focusing than typical compacts. Watch the opening display to obtain some idea of framing and positioning, then set up the camera with the lens set to an aperture of ƒ8.

Most SLRs have a B setting, where the shutter remains open for as long as the release is pressed. There are no rigid rules for exposure, as each firework display differs in light intensity, but general guidelines can be given. A good idea is to 'bracket' exposures, by taking pictures of different duration. Try a couple of seconds first for a single firework, then four, eight and sixteen seconds to include two or more displays. Use a locking cable release and press it carefully to avoid vibrations. Slow or medium speed colour films of ISO50-100 can be used, to ensure optimum image quality. Loading up with monochrome film seems ill-suited to such a colourful subject.

As a finishing touch, use a portable flash to add light to the faces and figures of people watching the display if they are included in the composition. Alternatively if the display takes place near a lake, position the camera a little higher if possible so that the heads of the crowd will be silhouetted against bright reflections in the water.

ARCHITECTURE

BUILDINGS are static objects even in the worst weather conditions, barring hurricanes and earthquakes, and as such pose no restrictions on exposure times. They offer great scope for creative photography at all times of year, 24 hours a day, as part of a view, in their own right, or as sources of close-ups. You may wish to shoot a building in isolation or pick out a detail, show it in context among surrounding structures, or capture a general urban scene.

Buildings can be recorded in a number of styles. The first is a formal architectural record approach, keeping the sides of the building strictly parallel and in proportion through choice of viewpoint. Closely associated with this style is the environmental record shot, the difference being that people can be included and you have more freedom in use of perspective. A third style is the artistic interpretation which produces a more graphic picture. For example, a skyscraper might be shot with its converging verticals emphasized by a low viewpoint and a wide-angle lens.

A WIDE VIEW
An extreme wide-angle (above) may be needed to include the full height of ceilings and columns. Deliberate converging verticals are not a fault – nor is the inclusion of moving figures.

Interiors of buildings may also be explored for picture opportunities; the whole scene can be recorded, or just a portion of it selected. In some cases it may also be possible to introduce a degree of illumination to create an altogether new angle of a familiar place.

LENS AND VIEWPOINT

Whereas shooting landscapes offers an almost unlimited choice of viewpoint, finding a satisfactory position to take pictures of a particular building can be a problem. Other structures can restrict your movement or access; trees, lights and street furniture are sometimes inconveniently in the way. This can mean a shot has to be taken from a viewpoint close to the subject with a wide-angle lens.

It's often better, when possible, to move back and shoot from a slightly greater camera to subject distance and with a longer focal length lens. An elevated viewpoint is nearly always desirable to reduce the dominance of the foreground and keep verticals parallel, so you might try gaining access to a building opposite the subject. Researching alternative views close to a building can be done quite quickly by walking around it, while those from some distance take more time to locate. An idea here is to enter the subject building itself, and look out for suitable vantage points. Another alternative is to seek out buildings adjacent to parks, rivers or stretches of water, which afford a clearer view and greater choice of camera position.

TELEPHOTO DETAILS
Many architectural features are relatively small and inaccessible. A telephoto lens is ideal for recording these. Many zooms are not suitable because they render parallel straight lines as curves towards the edges of the frame. In this shot a zoom does the job perfectly.

When a viewpoint is available at a distance, its essential to select the foreground area carefully. Large areas of featureless concrete or tarmac should be avoided; you can add interest to the shot by including a colourful flower bed, paving design or anything to lead the eye towards the main subject. Depth will be enhanced if this element is defocused, as the eye naturally progresses to the sharpest part of the picture.

TIME AND LIGHT

Lighting quality is another aspect of architectural photography which must be considered simultaneously with viewpoint. When shooting the exterior of any building or capturing an urban scene, it's important to choose a suitable time. Lighting conditions vary gradually throughout the day, and then change dramatically as night begins. When high structures are adjacent to the building you are photographing you may find that it is in shadow for part of the day.

Choosing the type of light to suit your subject is often a matter of personal taste, but certain guidelines can be suggested. Strong sidelight works well with structures featuring plenty of form and texture, often older buildings. The glass façade of a modern office block is often best shot in shadow, with bright sunlight

falling on the buildings opposite – these reflect in the surface. Diffused sunlight might be used where the structure is very complex, giving a clearer rendition than when the sun is in a bright sky. Overcast weather or the mid-day sun are rarely employed, as the former gives little or no shadow, and the latter no lighting character. Dawn and dusk can reveal shapes in silhouette. Sunset light on white or light stone is a particularly attractive effect.

In an urban scene one side of a street is often in shadow during sunshine, while early and late in the day the entire street level may be in shadow with just the tops of buildings illuminated by the low sun. When the whole street scene is being photographed, it is often better to wait for the street to be totally shaded, as exposure calculations are easier and the film can record this level of contrast.

At night, buildings and street scenes take on a totally different appearance. Distracting details are concealed and mundane-looking areas transformed into areas of interest. Street lights and floodlighting pick out facades of buildings, or highlight features such as fountains and statues. Use long exposures to record passing cars as light trails, which look best if several vehicles move fully through the frame while the shutter remains open.

INSIDE OUT
A view from a well-lit interior looking towards a garden area (above) can be particularly effective. The photographer used a wide-angle lens on a 6 x 7cm rollfilm camera.

THE IMPACT OF CURVES
This black and white study below enhances the curves of the subject with the curved geometry of a 30mm fisheye lens. Camera and lens were budget-priced Russian professional rollfilm equipment.

PEOPLE IN THE PICTURE

People can be included in shot by using a fairly fast shutter speed to freeze their movement, or they can be made to disappear if the shutter opening time is long enough. An exposure of 20 seconds, for instance, will not record a person walking across the front of a building, whereas if they stop at one point for a few seconds they will appear as a ghostly blur.

If the intention is to record people in shot, choose a time when lots of activity is occurring – rush hour or lunchtime. Pictures may be taken from street level, but obstructions can be created by the very people you are attempting to shoot. A busier impression is often given from a slightly higher viewpoint, such as a first floor window or low roof.

INTERIORS

Restricted viewpoint and subdued lighting make shooting interiors technically demanding. A wide-angle lens can be used to increase the area of an interior shown, but this may make details quite small and insignificant, giving an effect unlike that seen by the eye which scans a room one part at a time. This applies especially to decorated ceilings, which appear odd if composed in isolation with a steeply angled camera. Including part of an adjacent wall orients the viewer of the image.

When shooting interiors the eye also adapts to low light levels, but for photography a tripod is normally required, especially if a small aperture is used to give increased depth of field. Windows can cause problems by increasing local contrast during daytime. At other times artificial light illuminates the area. Using available light effectively captures the atmosphere of an interior, but mixed light sources can sometimes be difficult to handle in terms of film response and colour balance. For example, when daylight film is used fluorescent lamps give a cold green light, and tungsten lights produce a warm yellow/orange.

DISTANT, PERSPECTIVE, AND IMPACT
Your viewpoint and use or avoidance of deliberate converging verticals can have a great impact of the apparent scale and form of a building. Both the pictures on this page were taken using a special architectural camera, the Plaubel 670W, a lightweight folding rollfilm viewfinder model with a permanent wide-angle lens. The top picture is the closest possible viewpoint, with steep convergence (not slight accidental lack of parallel walls!), a polarizing filter, and the roof of the church tower entirely missing. The distant view in softer lighting, bottom, emphasises only the tower and the roofs, omitting the nave of the church and concentrating on its setting, with no polarizer.

USE NEGATIVE FILM FOR INTERIORS
In mixed interior lighting, where there is no possibility of lighting the subject with flash because of its size or nature, colour negative film is a better choice than colour slide. The award-winning swimming pool in a converted cruck barn (right) was photographed for the architects on negative film and hand-printed to ensure detail and balanced colours in the water, tiling, roof, beams and windows.

Long exposure durations should take into account film reciprocity failure.

One way around this problem is to introduce extra illumination to the interior, either to balance the existing light or to replace it. Some interiors are dark in certain places only, but generally the larger the internal space, the more difficult it is to add lighting. Flash can be employed to balance with a naturally lit interior, studio units being the best option as the modelling lamp allows the light quality and direction to be observed. Then it is simply a question of balancing light intensity between the two sources.

'Painting with light' with a portable flashgun is a popular method of lighting a murky interior. Here the camera shutter is left open while a series of manual flashes are fired in different parts of the scene. This experimental technique demands the photographer remain obscured from the camera view, by hiding behind walls, columns and natural obstructions.

EQUIPMENT

Camera choice depends upon the style of architectural shot required. Formal studies are best tackled with a camera fitted with a 'rising front' lens to avoid converging verticals. A number of 35mm and medium format SLRs accept shift or perspective control lenses for this purpose, and all large format cameras have some degree of 'camera movements' in-built. With a larger film format, greater detail and definition are available in the finished picture, all other factors being equal. A grid etched onto the ground glass focusing screen is a useful accessory for accurate framing and true verticals.

When a less formal or graphic picture is desired, a compact or 35mm SLR can deliver excellent results. A good wide-angle is handy when the photographer is limited to a close viewpoint, or for capturing interiors. Short to medium power telephotos are often needed for distant viewpoints or to isolate decorative or structural detail of building. Focal lengths beyond 200mm are rarely used, except to visually compress distant buildings together.

Filters are very useful, enhancing both lighting and colours. A polarizing filter is essential for colour work, deepening sky tone and making a light-coloured building stand out against it. This filter can also be used to control reflections in glass surfaces. Various colour or neutral graduates are also handy to reduce the intensity of a bright sky, or emphasize its hue. Yellow, orange or red filters progressively dramatize a sunlit scene shot in black and white.

CONVERGING VERTICALS

Tilting a camera upwards to include the top of a tall building in frame automatically makes its parallel sides converge. Though this appears normal to the eye, in a picture it can look like an accident. Image distortion of this nature is not suitable in architectural shots unless it's very deliberate.

Converging verticals can be avoided by using the correct technique. You can adopt a higher viewpoint approximately half the height of the subject building, so that the camera is level when pointing it. Or you can move further away and use a longer lens. In this case extra foreground is included, which can be treated as part of a composition or cropped out if a printing stage is included. Mild convergence of an original image can also be corrected at the printing stage, by slightly tilting the enlarger head and baseboard in opposite directions.

Other methods include fitting a 'shift' or perspective control lens available for a select number of 35mm SLRs. The two pictures above were taken with a normal 28mm wide-angle lens (top) and with the Olympus Zuiko 28mm PC lens (bottom). A similar facility is available on 4 x 5" technical cameras, which allows the lens standard to be considerably adjusted in relation to the film position. In each case the film remains vertical, which is the key to avoiding converging verticals.

CANDIDS

A **CANDID** picture is the opposite of a formal, arranged portrait. Usually it is any shot where the subject is unposed or unaware of the camera. There are exceptions, though, such as when the subject has noticed the photographer, but is too preoccupied with some other activity to look at the camera. In candid pictures, the subject rarely gazes directly towards the lens. Compared with a formal portrait there is little directing of the subject but, as a consequence of this method of shooting, people's gestures and expressions are more natural and revealing. This enables intimate, humorous and spontaneous images to be recorded.

Candid shots are sometimes taken by stealth or concealment, and you often need quick reactions. At first it's easier to try candids with people you know, though pictures of strangers or people at work can be equally rewarding once the techniques are

known. In each of these situations, permanently carrying the camera breeds familiarity, and people will soon forget it's there. Shots can then be taken when the subject's attention is diverted. The same applies to children, who will otherwise play up if they know a lens is pointed at them.

There are six main techniques for shooting candids:

HAND-HOLD the camera and wander around looking for potential subjects. Use a zoom or telephoto lens of around 200mm maximum focal length, and shoot at 1/250 sec on fast film. Be decisive and use quick reactions when shooting to avoid being spotted.

TRIPOD MOUNT the camera, with a telephoto, pointing at a place where people congregate – a bench or newspaper kiosk – and see what happens. Once the shot is framed there's no need to look

through the viewfinder. Look away or chat to a friend while taking shots with a cable release – people won't realize they're being photographed if you are not looking through the camera. You can use longer lenses and slower film, as there is no risk of camera shake.

CONCEAL YOURSELF in a position, such as behind an obstruction, with a powerful telephoto, or from an elevated viewpoint – a window, roof or balcony. People won't notice you in the distance, and rarely look upwards, so you are free to shoot at will.

PHOTOGRAPH A CROWD of people who are diverted by some other activity. This method is often used when spectators are engrossed in a sporting event, for example. The photographer can even stand right up close and shoot with a wide-angle lens without being noticed.

QUIET OBSERVATION
Candids with a longer lens – a telephoto around 100-135mm, or zoom – can be taken patiently, composing the shot from a position where you are not observed but can wait for the right expression and pose. The photographer took the study above looking through shrubbery, which adds foreground framing, while the artist's attention was firmly on her work.

CLOSE QUARTERS
Candids in news or magazine style are better taken from a position of involvement – so close that the subjects do not think you are taking pictures (right). This picture was taken while the Austrian farmer was sitting talking very close to the photographer, who used a 50mm standard lens.

Move close and openly use an extreme wide-angle lens on an SLR to include people in the foreground of a scene. They assume they are excluded from the composition, but they are actually positioned towards the frame edge because of the broad angle of view.

Shoot from the hip with a pre-focused lens, or keep the camera low and use its ground glass screen to guide composition. Additionally right-angle finders can be fitted to the eyepiece, or a mirror attachment onto the lens to permit 90° shooting. You can pretend to be fiddling with the controls or cleaning your camera, but really be taking pictures, providing direct eye contact with the subject is avoided.

GOING PUBLIC

When taking pictures of complete strangers or working in public places, it pays to be as inconspicuous as possible. You should carry the minimum of equipment, and store it in an ordinary bag, not a recognizable photo holdall or case. Your clothes should blend in too,

Black and White
Monochrome is ideal for street photography, concentrating attention on expressions.

Interaction
Right: look for humour and happiness, emotion and expression in your candids.

BE PREPARED!

Candid photography revolves around two techniques – keeping a low profile to remain unobtrusive, and being ready to shoot at all times. For the latter aspect, anticipation and a sense of composition is needed, while all camera controls should be familiar to the photographer, and preset. Lighting conditions can be assessed early, and the appropriate combination of aperture and shutter speed dialled in. Alternatively an automatic exposure mode can be used if the illumination is predictable and even.

Autofocusing is a useful facility, except when working at a distance and there is a chance of something passing between the camera and subject to temporarily obstruct the view. If this is the case, switch to manual operation. When a precise subject distance cannot be predicted, set the lens to the hyperfocal distance to give optimum depth of field.

Other points to watch for are the number of frames left on a roll of film. Unless you prevent it, Murphy's Law dictates that the best candid scene will occur just after you've taken picture number 36, and are swapping films.

so don't wear a suit to a rock festival, or jeans at a funeral. These two factors help you avoid disturbing potential subjects.

It is important to shoot quickly and without fuss. Don't spend too much time focusing on the subject, as the raised camera may be noticed. Instead pre-focus the camera by aiming the lens at an object the same distance away, then swing the camera back to the main subject when you're ready.

Use of longer telephotos is recommended if you find working close to strangers unnerving. This may require a tripod to support heavier lenses, so set up in an inconspicuous place. The long focal length gives shallow depth of field which isolates your subject from the surroundings. When shooting normally, one eye looks through the viewfinder and the other is closed, but it may pay to keep both eyes open – the one not looking through the lens can check whether any people are about to walk across the field of view and spoil the shot.

Candid groups are an interesting topic. Five people sitting on a park bench may never have seen each other before, but are united by the camera composition. The viewfinder frame has the potential to bring disparate elements together, giving great scope for humour, irony, social comment and human observation.

AT WORK

A rich and varied source of candid opportunities is provided by people working. A head shot often reveals the job done – the blackened features of a coalminer, the rustic charm of a shepherd out in the open, or a computer operator with the VDU screen reflected in spectacles. Sometimes the hands are a more important element than the eyes or a face; a craftsman in close up, for instance. Other possibilities include a window cleaner, watchmaker, musician, artist, surgeon or car

mechanic. The frame can be restricted to the hands only, or include a face but leave it out of focus or darker in the background.

It's a good idea to start at your own workplace. The people and environment are familiar, and you know the nature of work going on. Or you can aim for a more graphic image such as a steel erector balancing high on a girder, or window cleaners in a cradle on the side of an office block.

Indoor lighting in offices is often by fluorescent tube. Use a CC30M magenta filter to avoid casts on daylight-balanced colour film. If shooting under tungsten light, use an 80A blue filter (or tungsten film). The light source makes no difference when using black and white film, a favourite for the reportage-type image.

EQUIPMENT

SLR technology is the answer to many candid needs. The principal tool for distant pictures is the long telephoto lens. A 400mm optic fitted to a 35mm SLR gives a high magnification of a subject. A full length figure fills the horizontal frame at around 120 feet. Used at 60 feet it provides a tightly-framed upper torso, while someone standing 25-30 feet from the camera creates a head and shoulders composition.

In strong light with ISO 100 film loaded in the camera, a typical $f5.6$ maximum aperture will give a shutter speed of around 1/250 of a second. This is below the recommended speed for shake-free hand-holding, though experienced photographers may be able to cope. In duller light or to avoid shake, a faster ISO 400 film or some method of support is recommended. Use a tripod or monopod, or lean on a handy wall or post if available.

Candid shots are easier to shoot at close quarters when the camera is smaller, simple to use and operates unobtrusively. SLRs vary enormously in the noise they gen-

RESPONSES

Shooting candids in public places is usually a safe activity, but if you do it often enough, someone somewhere is bound to notice that their picture is being taken. Subject responses can range from being flattered or embarrassed through to anger or even violence, depending upon the culture or society you are working in. In tourist areas cameras are common, so a subject won't notice one being pointed at them if you work quickly. Certain people peddling their wares on the streets shy away from attention, because they're operating on the fringe of the law, so choose your subjects with a degree of common sense. A few words are often sufficient to defuse any situation, providing you speak the same language. In foreign countries or unfamiliar places, it pays to be more wary as an innocent candid shot can provoke a hostile reaction. Above: gipsy children may spot the camera and play up to it, but adult travellers usually keep well clear.

erate when the shutter is released and the instant-return mirror snaps back into place. Some new cameras are especially quiet in this area. Automatic models also wind-on film and cock the shutter immediately after firing, which can be a nuisance as this makes more noise than the shot itself. Cameras with between-the-lens leaf shutters, such as compacts and some (rather conspicuous) medium format models, are usually quieter. With shots taken at a

considerable distance, noise is less of a problem, so the motor-driven SLR is fine.

Shooting candids with black and white or colour negative is often preferable, as these films have greater exposure latitude, and can be cropped during printing to correct framing errors. New technology emulsions of ISO 400 offer excellent speed and good quality, while even faster emulsions up to ISO 3200 are now available for low light photography.

SPECIAL EVENTS

EVER SINCE hand-held photography became possible, the camera has been carried wherever man ventured. It has travelled to the bottom of deep mines and seas, to the tops of mountains and even to the moon. On an everyday level, it can also be used to capture meaningful moments in public life, like trips to the theatre, concerts, a wedding or a march. Here's how to take effective pictures at a wide variety of events.

WEDDINGS

An official wedding photographer has the onerous task of recording the entire wedding in a formal, traditional and comprehensive way, but other photographers – friends and relatives – can operate more informally. This often results in pictures which more accurately capture the atmosphere of the occasion.

If the photographer knows the bride well, it may be possible to take some shots of her preparations in the morning. As she is bound to be nervous, don't direct pictures or use flash as this will only put extra pressure on her. Adopt a low profile and stay in the background. With a medium telephoto lens and fast film, there should be some revealing moments as the mother tends to details of the dress, or as the bridesmaids arrange flowers. Alternatively the equally jumpy groom might be the pre-wedding subject.

Arrive at the wedding venue early and have a good look around to assess picture angles and lighting. Pictures can be taken of guests greeting each other. As the bride reaches the location, a professional may be taking tightly-framed shots of her getting out of the car. You should not interfere with his work, but reaction shots of the guests would be worthwhile at this moment.

During the ceremony, informal photographs are often frowned upon, especially with flash. But there may be opportunities later to capture the couple as they walk down the aisle or pass through the church doors. Again this is the prime time for the official photographer so you can busy yourself taking candid shots of the couple, family, friends and groups. People preoccupied with the main event make great studies in concentration.

The reception is a time when informal photography is more acceptable, and there are several significant moments to be captured. First there's the cutting of the cake, and the meal. Then the bride's father may make some serious points, the groom's speech is quite brief and the best man does his level best to embarrass his newly-married friend. Look for revealing pictures which are more than just a record of the day.

Shooting with zoom lenses allows different framing to be made from one viewpoint. Colour negative film of medium to high speed is recommended as it is more tolerant to exposure errors, and lots of prints can be cheaply made. Image quality is perfectly acceptable up to 10 x 8".

STAGE SHOWS

Shooting pictures during live shows at the theatre or at a concert can demand quite different techniques, depending upon the nature of the show. When there is a play or formal concert in progress don't take pictures with a noisy camera or use flash. Alternatively, at a loud rock concert, no-one would notice a camera shutter clicking above the noise.

For these reasons, shooting live performances which are studied and quiet demands a stealthy approach. It is almost impossible to take pictures as a member of the audience, so an alternative has to be found. You may be able to persuade the management to let you shoot from a concealed position high up on a balcony or terrace, or let you come along during a rehearsal. But even at these times, your activities should be as silent and unobtrusive as possible.

If you can wrap the camera in a sound-deadening material while still providing a hole for the lens and access to the main controls, do so. Lighting effects are relatively constant during a perform-

FORMAL WEDDING GROUPS
Friends may ask you produce wedding pictures and set up groups if no professional can be engaged. This shot was taken by a well-known professional who has photographed many society and royal weddings, but he doesn't make a fuss or dominate the day. He finds a good background, like this, and mainly uses 35mm cameras. The bride should be on the groom's left hand side, her veil lifted after the wedding; the best man balances the group rather than standing by the groom; the bridesmaids and page boys are arranged in a random order of height, 'held in' by taller girls at the ends of the line. It looks simple but it takes know-how to arrange this quickly.

ance so metering is simple, though the low levels will demand the use of fast tungsten colour film. Monochrome users needn't worry about colour balance, of course.

At modern rock concerts, the light-show is often as impressive as the music, if not more so, and flash is unnecessary as it will almost certainly make the light-show less effective on film.

Security precautions at major concerts normally prevent changing your location freely during the concert, and thronging the aisles near the stage is often frowned upon by 'bouncers', so good pictures of top artists are very much a matter of luck, unless you know the organizers very well. Cameras are often banned. At smaller concerts, with lesser stars, these problems are reduced, but the pictures don't sell as well.

If you can't get a good low viewpoint, shoot from further back and use film of at least ISO 400. Even faster film speed ensures the shutter speed will prevent shake and give a reasonable aperture. A standard lens should give a good shot of the whole set, while a telephoto or zoom can be used to pick out individual musicians.

PUSHING IT AT CONCERTS
It is increasingly difficult to gain access to concerts with a camera – despite the number of flashes fired in vain by the audience at a stage too far away to be reached by any of the flash light. If you can get into the 'pit' with a camera, you will need a fast medium telephoto lens such as an 85mm *f*1.8, 100mm *f*2 or 135mm *f*2, and some film which can be push-processed for extra sensitivity. A tungsten-light balanced ISO 160 Ektachrome was used to shoot by the stage spotlighting at a concert, right. This produces much more realistic results than flash.

THEATRICAL RECORDS
If you are asked to photograph a chorus or curtain-call by an amateur operatic or theatrical group, use colour negative film, as the photographer did for the group below. Although the stage spots and footlights were incorrectly balanced for the daylight film, he made his own prints using a Durst enlarger and processor, and corrected the colour in the enlarger.

PARADES

Organized events such as pageantry, carnivals or marches all require careful planning on the part of the photographer. Knowledge of when the event is to take place, and the route it will cover, is essential so that viewpoints can be 'staked out', obstructions avoided and the correct focal lengths chosen. Lighting conditions have to be reacted to on the day, but even here it is possible to predict where and when the subject will be in shade or sunlight.

An elevated viewpoint is a good choice when the procession is composed of a large number of people. Climb too high and the frontal aspect is lost, however, and people begin to look like a pattern of dots. From a suitably low roof or balcony a clear view is virtually guaranteed, and different lenses can be used from the same spot to give framing options. The disadvantage of the high vantage point is that you only have access to the procession for a few moments; if you try to follow on afterwards, your movements may be limited by the crowd.

If you decide to stay in one position, take plenty of equipment and set it all up beforehand. You may have one or two cameras attached to tripods, plus a hand-held option. Don't lock the tripod head up rigidly; allow the pan facility to move smoothly as you follow the subject. A wide-angle lens will set the scene, and a telephoto or zoom can pick out important elements or individuals. As time for pictures is limited, take quick but controlled images.

Shooting from street level has other advantages. First, it gives greater manoeuvrability, though it also carries the continuous risk of obstruction. A greater variety of shots are possible from eye-level. The key shots of the approaching event can be complemented by other details and supplementary views, while various crowd reactions can also be taken. Turning

CLOSING IN ON CARNIVAL COLOUR

The annual Venice Carnival, visited by thousands of photo enthusiasts, is often so crowded you can't move. The answer is to locate a really colourful costume and move in for a frame-filling close-up. The photographer used a 28-135mm zoom to make quick composition easy.

through 180° and 360° during the height of an event like this produces linked but widely differing images.

As you will be moving from one vantage point to another, a lighter and more portable outfit is essential. Carry the minimum of lenses and two loaded camera bodies as this will save valuable time reloading film as you don't want to miss an important moment.

Stick to manual focus if possible, as you will be placed well ahead of the procession – an AF camera may track back and forth if someone walks briefly in front of the lens.

AIR SHOWS

Taking pictures of modern or elderly aircraft in flight brings certain camera techniques into play. The first is the need to obtain accurate exposure. When the camera is pointed upwards, many shots suffer from under-exposure as the brighter sky surrounding the subject fools the camera meter into giving insufficient light.

There are several ways around this problem. If the camera has a narrow angle spotmeter, this will place the metering cell on the important part of the scene – the aircraft – though accuracy is critical. Another method is to meter from a similar toned subject at ground level, such as another aeroplane, though any surface will do. To avoid exposure errors, make

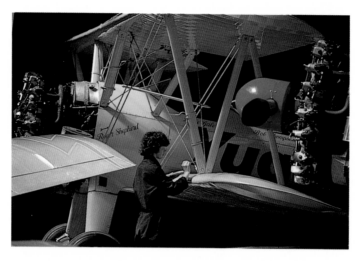

GROUND-LEVEL COLOUR
At air shows don't neglect picture opportunities with ground-based subjects. Access to hangars is often granted on open days, and these can be full of interesting material. This young lady putting the finishing touches to an elderly bi-plane turned out to have a vested interest in its air worthiness – she's an aerobatics performer and stands on its wings for a hobby!

sure its orientation corresponds to the subject, and move close so that the sky plays no part in the reading. With medium speed film loaded, set the camera to manual exposure using a fast shutter speed and appropriate aperture.

Aircraft in flight appear to be travelling comparatively slowly, but your panning techniques need to be spot on; speeds of 100-300mph are common. Position yourself so that the movement is across your field of view, rather than at an angle to it. Usually several passes are made along the same line, so the first can be used to frame the aircraft accurately. A telezoom is ideal for this purpose. The fast shutter speed removes the possibility of camera shake, while even wide apertures should provide ample depth of field.

LONG SHOTS AND CLOSE UPS

The British love a pancake race, a horse fair or one of many other unusual customs and traditions that spans the generations. These are less structured than processions, and easy access makes them excellent subjects. Britain has a vast number of large and smaller events, ranged throughout the year and in all parts of the country. A photographer might attempt to make a historical point, look for comic moments or

characters, or take shots which convey the eccentricity of the event.

This Morris Dancing troupe was photographed on a changeable Spring day in Derbyshire. First an establishing shot was taken, then a similar shot of the entire group airborne! The framing became increasingly tighter to reveal individual personalities. Finally, details of the unusual headgear and footwear added variety to the theme.

CREATIVE EFFECTS

MANY photographer's ambitions do not extend beyond shooting conventional photographs, but the medium is also capable of a wide range of special effects for those who wish to experiment further. Unusual images can be produced in-camera, during processing or at the printing stage, and by manipulating existing material. Often the only limitations to creative work are those of the imagination. Combining one or more effects can produce the most extraordinary results.

PICTURES OFF TV

Selection of shutter speed is critical when taking pictures off a television screen. The image repeatedly scans with a cycle lasting about 1/25 of a second, so using a shutter speed of 1/30 of a second or faster on the camera will result in a dark band covering part of the image. A speed of 1/15 of a second gives acceptable results, while slower speeds tend to show image blur when movement occurs on the screen.

Pictures are best taken in a darkened room to eliminate reflections, and the camera should be tripod mounted and square on to the TV set. Metering is usually accurate providing the screen image is tightly framed. Set the colour on the set slightly warmer to offset the small blue cast otherwise produced with daylight film. Use a video recorder to freeze frames and take pictures from these. Considerable enlargement of the film will reveal the lines or pattern that produces the TV image.

REMOTE CONTROL

Using a remote control device enables the camera to be placed in unusual, inaccessible or dangerous positions. Various mechanical, electrical, infrared or radio types are available. It is the precise positioning of the camera which creates interesting images. For

POLAROID TRANSFER
A creative effect unique to Polaroid's peel-apart instant films is 'image transfer'. Normally, the print film is removed from the camera as a sandwich of two layers with a developer solution between them. It takes 30 seconds for the image to form and migrate to the receiver sheet. If you peel them apart early and press the image-forming side on to watercolour paper or any absorbent medium, the image will transfer to this instead with changes in texture and colour.

TRIGGERED FROM THE SIDELINES
To secure this worm's eye view of a horse jumping over a fence, the photographer first of all fitted an infrared remote trigger and a motor-drive to a Minolta X-700 manual focus SLR. The camera was put in a polythene bag, with a 16mm full frame fish-eye lens through a hole, and buried in a few inches of leaf mould as close to the fence as possible.

instance, it would be impossible for a photographer to shoot pictures from the bonnet of a speeding racing car, from the wing of a hang-glider or from the top of a boat's mast while it sails. But the camera can be fixed in position beforehand, and fired remotely once under way. It is also possible to place a camera on a small tripod low by a hurdle at a sporting event, providing permission has been gained.

On an everyday level, a monopod can be used to raise the camera to an elevated position not normally attainable. A long cable or pneumatic release taped to the leg can be triggered by the photographer holding the monopod. Alternatively a harness or clamp can be employed to attach an SLR or compact to a bicycle or motorbike. A low viewpoint of the road gives a dramatic impression of speed with the latter. Wide-angle lenses and fast film ensure good depth of field and subject coverage. Safety of participants and equipment is a top priority whenever the camera is used remotely.

SANDWICH

Two transparencies can be combined to create a single image by the sandwich technique. Overexposed or 'thin' slides are preferable, as two correctly exposed slides of normal density will appear too dark when placed together. The best pictures to use are those which are simple in composition, so that the effect of the sandwich avoids confusion. Try to choose one main image as the focus of attention, and use the second slide to add colour, shape or texture, otherwise two strong pictures will compete.

The attraction of sandwiches is that they can be simply produced from existing pictures, without the need for complex darkroom processes. The two slides are held together by a short length of double-sided tape along one edge, making sure this is well clear of the image area. A light-box helps to position one on top of the other accurately. The sandwich can then be placed in a normal card mount, though a glass type is recommended for projection purposes as this squeezes the two images together for optimum focusing.

COMBINED IN A MOUNT
Two or more slides can be combined by sandwiching together in a glass slide mount. The dramatic picture above has silhouette images sandwiched with a picture of out-of-focus colours. Sandwiches can be projected directly, but must be copied on to a new single piece of film to have prints made or enter for competitions.

SANDWICH OR DUPE?

With a slide copier, there are two ways of combining a pair of images – sandwich, and double exposure. When two slides are sandwiched together and copied, the dark parts of one slide appear over the lighter areas of the other. Sandwiching works well for putting textures on top of light-toned scenes. When two slides are double-exposed on to one frame, the light parts of each slide record in the dark areas of the other. This is ideal for ghost-figures, superimposed sun and moon, combined portraits and filling a silhouette shape with an image.

SLIDE DUPLICATION

A slide copier is normally employed to make exact reproductions of original images, but an element of creativity can also be introduced. With a simple zoom copier a picture may be enhanced by cropping, changing colour by using filters, or altering density. More sophisticated devices with integral flash units can also adjust contrast and give automated exposure. With both types, two images can be combined on the same piece of film.

When combining images, it is important to ensure one picture has a uniform dark area – a night shot or a blue sky, perhaps. Detail in a lighter part of the second image will record in the darker area of the first. The technique is easiest with a camera featuring a multi-exposure facility.

SLIDE COPIER FANTASY
The surreal sunset, left, was created using a slide copier and several original images

LOOK, NO CAMERA
A photogram (below) is easily made with black and white paper processed in a home darkroom, a light source, and suitable objects.

INSTANT BACKGROUNDS
For small still life shots, you can make your own front-projection set using a slide projector, white screen, tungsten lights and tungsten-balanced film. In the two shots above, the glass ornament is positioned on a glass sheet, and two different backgrounds projected behind it.

BACKDROP PROJECTION

Projecting an image onto a subject or background is a method of creating unusual picture combinations. Professional equipment is available at great expense, but the same effects can also be produced economically with a slide projector at home. A transparency is placed in a projector and shone onto a model or face, or can be used to change the backdrop as the subject remains constant.

If the projected image is along a similar axis to the tripod mounted camera lens, a shadow is cast on the backdrop. The way to prevent this is to position the projector at an angle, so that the shadow misses the backdrop or the projection beam falls only on the background. Also placing the subject well forward of the background helps. Matching lighting styles produces a convincing image. Use tungsten film in the camera and floodlamps to match the colour balance.

PHOTOGRAM

It's possible to produce images in the darkroom without a negative or slide in the enlarger, by placing objects directly on the printing paper surface. As the paper is light sensitive, the part shielded by the object when white light is turned on is unexposed and remains white – the rest turns grey or black, depending upon the exposure duration.

Despite the simplicity of the procedure, some complex and sophisticated results can be produced. Interesting subject shapes are the first thing to look for – these should be reasonably flat to produce a clear image. Then refinement of their positioning, overlapping and exposure adds subtlety to the finished print. Translucent objects let unpredictable amounts of light through. Very small objects can even be placed in the negative carrier and the image projected on to paper.

COLORVIR

This unique toning process enables a wide variety of colour to be added selectively to black and white prints. Unlike other toners, Colorvir enables different densities to be produced in different colours. At relatively modest cost, a kit can simulate colour solarization or contour effects which are normally very complex to produce. The full kit contains a dozen separate liquids, including toners, additives, dyes and special effect chemicals. These are not used all at once, but a plentiful supply of dishes and storage bottles is needed all the same.

Pictures can be toned in normal room lighting, and you don't have to make your own prints; you can have ordinary resin-coated black and white (not colour) prints made, and treat them with Colorvir in daylight. The image should contain a full range of tones, and be of medium or slightly low contrast.

Protective clothing and gloves are essential, and as the chemicals include both acids and metallic salts, Colorvir should be used in a workshop or utility area rather than your kitchen. A detailed instruction book is supplied with the kit and is much needed. Never try the chemicals without reading up which ones to use.

LIQUID EMULSION

Rather than printing on paper, liquid emulsion allows pictures to be made on all kinds of surfaces, providing they are small enough to be transported into the darkroom. Try the emulsion on eggs, pieces of wood, pottery or plates. The surface you choose should be clean and may require a little preparation or 'subbing'. Certain metals, clay, wood and other porous materials require a coat of polyurethane varnish to seal the surface or prevent a reaction with the liquid emulsion. Non-porous materials such as ceramics or glass

MULTI-COLOURED PRINTS FROM MONOCHROME
This image started out as a normal black and white print. Treatment after regular processing in Colorvir toners and dyes makes different zones of grey take on different hues, with distinct lines between them. Colorvir can also be used for straightforward sepia, blue, and green toning or dyeing the print base a solid colour.

should be thoroughly cleaned with washing soda before immersion in a weak solution of gelatin.

Under safelight conditions, the liquid emulsion is melted in a container standing in a warm water bath. Only use enough to coat the surface you've chosen, as excess may become fogged and contaminate the remainder in the bottle. Once warm, the emulsion is poured or painted as evenly as possible onto the surface. A trial area is worth preparing first, to get the hang of the technique and to act as a test strip. The emulsion can be easily washed off once the correct exposure has been gleaned, and the surface recoated. Now the finished print can be made. The object must be handled carefully until the emulsion sets, but process normally allowing extra time in a hardening fixer. A further coating of polyurethane varnish protects the hardened emulsion.

MONTAGE

Of all special effects techniques, montage is perhaps the simplest but also one of the most effective. By snipping out parts of existing black and white prints and assembling them on another, the scope for creativity is immense. There are many ways to tackle montage, but two methods are most common. The first approach places pictures roughly together, so that the joins are obvious. The other procedure is to conceal the joins to give the impression there is only one image.

Selecting the background is often the first step, as this acts as a base for other material to be stuck upon. Rather than just laying cut-outs on this haphazardly, it pays to plan the appearance of the finished product. A sheet of tracing paper allows new elements to be accurately drawn in, and printed

to size if necessary. If an invisible join is desired, it pays to match lighting quality and direction of the subjects as well as paper characteristics. The piece to be layered on must be carefully cut out with a scalpel, and edges can be retouched when stuck on the background with pencil or photographic dyes.

Despite the absence of colour, a slickly produced monochrome montage can look highly realistic, or as bizarre as the creator wishes. Montages produced from colour prints, however, need extra care to be believable as differences in colour bias are readily apparent. If possible use cut-outs from the same type of paper rather than a mixture. Mixing colour and black and white prints can be employed to draw attention to particular subjects or areas.

Re-photographing the finished montage with a copying set-up

removes any visible edges and surface discrepancies.

Montages can also be made in-camera by using special effects filters such as the Cokin Double Mask. Two masks alternately shield specific areas of the picture to allow images to be overlaid.

TONE ELIMINATION

By borrowing a product widely used in the printing trade, high contrast images can be produced from any black and white negative. Lith film eliminates all the shades of grey in a conventional monochrome picture, rendering them as either black or white. By this method, extremely graphic results are possible *(right)*.

Lith emulsion is available in 35mm and sheet formats. The smaller version can be contact printed with a 35mm original under red safelighting, whereas the sheet sizes can be used on an enlarger baseboard and an original projected onto it as in regular darkroom printing. As this emulsion has little exposure latitude, a test strip is a must. Use the special developer, Kodalith, for processing. The resulting positive image should be contact printed to produce a negative, but there's no need to worry about loss of quality as the image is reduced to black and clear areas at the outset. The negative produced can then be printed normally, giving stark but highly effective pictures.

MULTIPLE PRINTING

This is a technique related to montage, but the effect is produced by exposing negatives onto a single sheet of printing paper. The simplest method involves sandwiching two negatives together in the carrier. Greater control is afforded when negatives are enlarged in turn; images can be produced to different sizes and placed in any position. Masking can also be used to refine the image.

As with montage it pays to work out the finished design on a sheet of tracing paper fixed to the easel or enlarger baseboard. Make a note of the enlarger height and settings that combine to give the image you want, and make test prints for each element. Multigrade paper and filters allow contrast to be controlled so that the pieces match. To avoid exposing areas of the paper you want to leave for other images, a series of opaque masks need to be made - shapes cut from black card are fine for this purpose. Hard edges can be avoided by raising the shading mask above the print surface and moving it slightly during exposure.

Multiple printing is a technique which demands a methodical approach and much practice to perfect, but the results can be well worth the effort. Refinements can be made by using two or more enlargers, with a negative set up to the correct magnification in each. Realism can be enhanced by creating shadows or reflections of added elements by inverting the negative and giving a shorter exposure.

MONTAGE PRINTING
A montage of four different black and white print elements produced by cut and paste methods, re-photographed on Ilford Pan F film and printed on Ilford Galerie paper. Techniques like this are popular with camera club and international competition judges.

GLOSSARY

ABERRATION
Optical fault in a lens which results in unsharpness or distortion at edge of the picture, or colour fringing. Corrected by compound lens constructions and by stopping down the lens aperture.

ANGLE OF VIEW
A measure in degrees of how much of a subject the lens includes. The longer the focal length, the narrower is the angle of view. Also dependent upon film format.

BETWEEN-THE-LENS-SHUTTER
Shutter mechanism sited within a lens. Composed of thin blades or leaves, which operate like an iris diaphragm. The blades spring open when the shutter button is pressed to expose film, then close again. One of the two main shutter types used in cameras. Provides flash synchronization at all speeds.

BOUNCE FLASH
Technique used to soften the harsh character and shadows of flash illumination by letting it fall on the subject indirectly. Pointing the flash towards a reflective surface, a suitable wall or ceiling, scatters and diffuses the light. Because light travels further to reach the subject, extra power or a wider aperture are needed.

BURNING-IN
Printing technique following the main exposure in which additional light is given to a localized part of the image. This improves the tone of a subject which would otherwise be too light, or can be used to darken an area. Achieved by creating a shape with the hands or cutting a hole in a piece of opaque card.

CONTACT PRINT
Print which is the same size as the negative. Produced by placing a sheet of paper in direct contact with one or more negatives, and exposing to light. A contact printer produces a set of positive images on a sheet of 10 x 8 inch paper, to permit assessment of a negative for later enlargement.

COLOUR TEMPERATURE
An expression of the relative redness or blueness of any light source, measured in Kelvin. As a theoretical black body is heated, it first glows red (2000 K), then orange, white and finally blue (6000 K and above).

DEPTH OF FIELD
Describes the zone of acceptable sharpness on either side of a point focused on. Extends roughly one-third in front and two-thirds behind this position. Increases with distance and by stopping down the aperture. Some cameras have a depth-of-field button, so depth of field can be previewed before exposure.

DIFFUSER
Any material which scatters transmitted light, effectively increasing the area of the light source, to produce softer illumination. Tracing paper is a typical low-cost example, while opal perspex is often used in studios.

DODGING
Printing technique which is the opposite of 'burning in'. Part of the picture is shaded during the enlarging exposure, to make this area lighter than it would have appeared normally. Can be done by hand or by using pieces of shaped card attached to thin wire.

EMULSION
In photography, the light sensitive layer in a film or printing paper. Consists mainly of silver halide crystals suspended in one or more gelatin layers.

EXPOSURE LATITUDE
Term used to describe the tolerance of film to under- and over-exposure, while still producing acceptable results. Slow slide films show the least margin for error, while faster negative materials exhibit the most leeway.

FILTER FACTOR
A figure which indicates how much an exposure must be increased to take into account the light absorption by a given filter. Exposure meter readings need to be increased by this factor for correct exposure when the filter is used. TTL meters automatically give the correct exposure when filters are fitted.

FOCAL PLANE SHUTTER
The second main type of shutter employed in cameras, mainly SLR designs. Employs a pair of shutter curtains made from cloth or metal. These create a slit which travels across film to expose it to light from the lens. The width of the slit is variable to control shutter speed.

GRADUATED FILTER
Filter which is half clear and half coloured or neutral density, with a graded area between the two. Used to reduce the light intensity in a bright sky, to bring the contrast within the range of film, or add colour to a featureless sky. Filter can be adjusted in position in a mount or holder, so that the bottom half of the picture remains unaffected.

GRAININESS
Subjective impression of how fine the grain texture is in a photographic image. The eye sees overlapping clumps of black metallic silver, not individual grains. Grain usually increases with higher emulsion speeds. In a colour picture, small areas of dye replace silver, but the effect is similar.

GUIDE NUMBER
Method of measuring the light output of a flash unit. Usually given in both feet and metres for a film of ISO 100, e.g. *GN120/ft at ISO 100*, or *GN28/m at ISO 100*. Dividing the guide number by the distance gives the aperture to use. So *(feet example)* a subject at 15 feet requires an *f*8 setting, or *(metric example)* at 10m, *f*2.8.

HIGH KEY
A photograph in which lighter, delicate tones predominate. The opposite of Low Key. Also refers to the lighting method which produces this effect.

HYPERFOCAL DISTANCE
For any given aperture, the nearest point to the camera which is acceptably sharp when the lens is set to infinity. Resetting the lens to this distance increases the zone of sharpness nearer the lens and retains sharpness to infinity, so depth of field is increased.

INCIDENT LIGHT READING
Accurate method of exposure calculation, achieved by measuring the light falling upon a subject, not reflected from it. Requires a separate meter fitted with an incident light diffuser. Often used for transparency film as this is least tolerant to exposure error.

ISO
The initials of the International Standards Organisation, which provides the universally accepted standard for rating film speeds. Uses the same numbering system as the previous ASA standard.

LATENT IMAGE
Exposing a film to light creates an invisible, or latent, image in the emulsion layer. This image is converted to a visible image by the action of a developer during processing.

LEAF SHUTTER
The same as a Between-The-Lens shutter – see reference.

LOW KEY
Picture in which dark or heavy tones are dominant, with few highlights. The opposite of the High Key. Also refers to the lighting method which produces this effect.

MACRO
Strictly speaking, reproduction of a subject on film at life-size (1:1)

or larger. Also refers to a lens specially designed to work optimally at close-focusing distances. The so-called macro focusing of some zooms should be termed 'close-focusing'.

MEMORY LOCK
Camera feature where an exposure reading is retained. Allows the picture to be recomposed before the shutter is released. Used when the meter is likely to be misled.

MICROPRISM
Focusing aid in the viewfinder of SLR cameras, in which part of the viewing screen is composed of a grid of minute prisms. When a subject is out of focus, its image is fragmented; when in focus, the grid disappears.

ND FILTER
ND stands for Neutral Density. Filters of this type are uniformly grey and are used on a lens to absorb light, thus reducing the amount of light transmitted. Colour content is unaffected, however. Often used with mirror lenses as they have no aperture diaphragm, or when a fast film is being exposed in bright light.

NEGATIVE
Developed photographic image which features reversed tones, so that a subjects' highlights appear as dense areas, and shadows are rendered as lighter parts. In colour negatives subject colours are represented as a complementary hue. Negatives are recorded on a transparent base, so that light can be passed through to form a positive image or print.

OVER-EXPOSURE
Results from allowing too much light to reach a film or print. This increases the density of negative materials, reduces contrast and makes printing more difficult. With transparencies colours are washed out and the appearance is too light. Prints are too dark when over-exposed.

PARALLAX ERROR
A discrepancy between the image as seen through a viewfinder and the actual image produced on film by a separate lens. Occurs in close ups taken on cameras with separate viewfinders, such as compacts.

POLARIZING FILTER
Colourless grey filter used on lenses to reduce specular reflections in glass, metal and water, boost colour saturation generally and intensify blue skies at right angles to the sun. Rotating the filter in its mount varies the effects possible.

POSITIVE
Image in which the tones or colours correspond to those in the original subject, therefore the opposite of a Negative.

RECIPROCITY FAILURE LAW
When exposures are very brief or very long, films exhibit a loss of sensitivity to light. To achieve a certain density on film with shutter speeds of one second or longer, for example, requires greater exposure duration. Also results in unpredictable film behaviour in colour response.

RECYCLE TIME
After a shot has been taken, the time taken for a battery- or domestic supply-powered flashgun to charge up the capacitor and ready itself for firing again.

REFLECTED LIGHT READING
An exposure measurement taken with light reflected from a subject towards the camera. Camera-integral meters use this method, plus some separate meters. See also Incident Light Reading.

SAFELIGHT
Special form of low intensity darkroom illumination. The light emitted is of a colour which doesn't affect the type of light sensitive material being used. Different lamps and covers are available for a variety of printing papers.

SINGLE LENS REFLEX
Often abbreviated to SLR. A popular camera design which permits the image focused on the film plane to be previewed by means of a pivoted mirror mechanism. Allows accurate composition and focusing, yet avoids close-up errors that cameras with separate viewfinders are prone to.

STOP BATH
Acidic solution used in processing to halt development. Simultaneously neutralises alkalinity of developer solution, so that acidity of subsequent fixing bath is not diminished.

STOPPING DOWN
Term used to describe the act of reducing the size of the lens aperture. Setting a higher f-number reduces image brightness and increases depth of field.

TEST STRIP
Thin strip of paper for trial exposures to determine the optimum printing duration or filtration settings. Economical on paper because several strips can be cut from a single sheet.

TRANSPARENCY
Positive image which is most frequently colour. Transparencies are usually placed in a card mount, and viewed by transmitted light on a lightbox or via a projector. Also known as slides.

TTL METERING
TTL is short for through-the-lens, and describes an exposure meter built into an SLR type camera. The meter is placed by the pivoted mirror mechanism and reads the light from any interchangeable lens attached to the camera body. In sophisticated models the metering area can be reduced for optimum accuracy.

UNDEREXPOSURE
When film receives insufficient light it is under-exposed. This produces darker than normal transparencies, or negatives of thinner density. Under-exposure can be deliberate, as the image can be overdeveloped to compensate.

VARIABLE CONTRAST PAPER
Printing paper with great versatility because a range of contrasts may be produced by placing special filters in the enlarger light path. This means one box replaces six conventional grades 0-5, or that a single image can contain areas of differing contrast when carefully printed.

VIEWFINDER
Camera feature which provides an optical method of framing the subject. In reflex versions such as the SLR design, also employed for focusing.

VIGNETTE
Technique of printing a picture so that the edges gradually fade to black or white. Also refers to the fall-off in edge illumination caused by a filter or lens hood too narrow for the focal length, and causing image cut-off.

WARM-UP FILTER
Filter which exhibits an amber or orange tint. Used to counteract the cold blue cast that often occurs in shadow areas or in early morning light.

WETTING AGENT
Solution employed to reduce the surface tension of wash water. Often used in the final rinse to aid draining of water, and ensure even drying of film without marks.

ZONE FOCUS
A method of focusing used in budget compact cameras where the lens can be set to one of a number of zones. These rely on lens depth of field to overlap and provide a sharp image from infinity to the closest focusing position. Also refers to a method of manual focusing when the precise position of a subject cannot be predicted.

INDEX

PHOTOGRAPHIC CREDITS

In alphabetical order of byline; page number of photograph/s followed by number of pictures used and/or position in brackets.

Alan Lines/Robert Scott Associates: *124/125.*
Andreas Vogt/Icon: *136.*
Angus Blackburn/Icon: *8; 8/9; 12 top; 13 (2); 14 (2); 15; 16 bottom; 17; 18/19; 23 (top); 25; 26 (top); 27 (top); 30; 34; 37 (3); 40 (bottom); 45 (2); 46 (3); 47 (top, bottom);*
Canon (UK) Limited: *10; 26 (centre); 47 (centre)*
Carroll Seghers/ACE: *126.*
Charles Green: *116.*
Christopher Lobina/Robert Scott Associates: *122.*
Dave Ellison: *168.*
David Kilpatrick: *12 bottom; 16 top; 20/21 (9); 24; 27 (upper strip); 28; 29; 31 (9); 32 (bottom pair); 33 (2); 36; 38; 39 (bottom right); 40 (top); 44; 48 (2); 49 (top); 52; 53 (2); 54 (bottom); 55 (top 3); 57 (3); 59 (top, centre); 60 (top); 63 (2); 66/67; 70; 72 (2); 73 (top 3); 74; 76; 78 (top); 79; 87; 91; 92 (2); 93 (3); 95 (6); 96 (6); 97; 100; 101 (bottom); 102; 103 (bottom); 104; 106; 107; 113; 114 (bottom); 117; 118 (2); 119 (2); 120 (top); 128; 130 (bottom); 131;132 (2); 134; 139 (bottom); 141; 142 (2); 143 (3); 149; 154 (bottom); 156 (2); 157 (bottom); 159; 161; 166 (bottom); 169 (3); 170; 171 (top).*
Derek Forrest: *68 (1); 69 (2).*
Duncan McEwan: *80 (top).*
Fotopic/ACE: *23 (bottom)*
Geoff Evans: *123; 163 (bottom).*
Geoff Redmayne: *155 (bottom).*
Geoff Stephenson: *41.*
Janet Walkinshaw: *60 (bottom 3).*
John Guidi: *152.*

John Tinsley: *27 (bottom strip); 61 (3).*
Kevin Wilson: *121.*
Lawson Wood: *148.*
Lee Frost: *22 (upper); 84; 89 (top); 140 (top); 153.*
Malcolm Birkitt: *6/7; 9 (four insets of photographers); 22 (lower); 32 (top pair); 35 (3); 50/51; 59 (bottom); 64; 65; 71; 73 (bottom); 75 (2); 80/81 (bottom); 81 (top); 82 (top); 85 (2); 86; 88; 89 (bottom); 90; 105; 109; 110/111; 114 (top); 129; 130 (top); 133; 140 (bottom); 146 (2); 154 (top); 157 (top 2); 158; 165 (3);*
Marie O'Hare: *112; 155 (top).*
Martin Lillicrap: *77; 135.*
Mike Taylor/Robert Scott Associates: *171 (bottom).*
P McDonald: *150 (2).*
Paul T Dooley: *58; 137; 138 (bottom); 139 (top).*
Polaroid (UK) Limited: *166 (top).*
Rex A Butcher: *82/83 (main); 147; 151 (2).*
Richard Bradbury/Icon: *138 (top).*
Richard Kilpatrick: *108 (3).*
Richard Walker/ACE: *127.*
Roger Lee: *39 (bottom left); 42; 43; 49 (bottom); 94.*
Roy Hampson/Robert Scott Associates: *167.*
Shirley Kilpatrick: *54 (top); 78 (bottom); 120 (bottom); 144; 145; 160 (2); 164.*
Tim Moat: *163 (top).*
Tom Hustler: *162.*

Portrait lighting sequence model, pages 95/96: *Paddy Bryant.*

ACKNOWLEDGMENTS

The author, editor and publishers wish to thank the following for technical assistance and facilities for photography:

A. V. Distributors (London) Limited
Agfa UK Limited: *portrait sequence pages 95/96, Optima 200 film*
Canon (UK) Limited
Canpro Limited
Camera Care Systems Ltd (CCS)
Clive Insley Associates
Elinca S. A. and The Flash Centre
Expressions Photolab, Berwick-upon-Tweed
Fuji Photo Film Co Ltd
Hasselblad (UK) Limited
Hector Innes ABIPP, Kelso
Johnsons Photopia Limited
Kaiser (UK) Limited
KJP Limited
Kodak Limited
Konica (UK) Limited
Kyocera Yashica (UK) Limited
Lastolite UK Limited
Leica Camera
Minolta (UK) Limited
Minolta Club of Great Britain
Morco Limited
Nikon (UK) Limited
Olympus (UK) Limited
Paterson Photax Group
Pentax (UK) Limited
Photo Studio Consultants
Polaroid (UK) Limited
Robert White Photographic
Spa Photo Ltd (Cromatek)

Colour graphics throughout: Oxford Illustrators Limited
Black and white diagrams and graphics: Icon Publications Limited